THE
ENCYCLOPEDIA
OF
MONSTERS

OTHER BOOKS BY DANIEL COHEN

THE GREAT AIRSHIP MYSTERY

THE FAR SIDE OF CONSCIOUSNESS

MASTERS OF THE OCCULT

MYSTERIOUS PLACES

A MODERN LOOK AT MONSTERS

VOODOO, DEVILS, AND THE NEW INVISIBLE WORLD

FOR YOUNG READERS

A CLOSE LOOK AT CLOSE ENCOUNTERS

DEALING WITH THE DEVIL

GHOSTLY TERRORS

THE GREATEST MONSTERS IN THE WORLD

MYSTERIOUS DISAPPEARANCES

SCIENCE FICTION'S GREATEST MONSTERS

SUPERMONSTERS

THE

ENCYCLOPEDIA

OF

MONSTERS

BY DANIEL COHEN

ILLUSTRATED

DODD, MEAD & COMPANY · NEW YORK

3   4   5   6   7   8   9   10

Library of Congress Cataloging in Publication Data

Cohen, Daniel.
   The encyclopedia of monsters.

   Bibliography: p.
   1. Monsters.   2. Animals, Mythical.
I. Title.
GR825.C6   1982   001.9′44   82-4574
ISBN 0-396-08102-9   AACR2
ISBN 0-396-09051-6 {PBK}

PICTURE CREDITS

The illustrations that appear in this book are courtesy of:

Dover Books for *Animals: A Pictorial Archive from Nineteenth-Century Sources*, by Jim Harter, pages 42, 93, 96, 120, 173, 226, 256, 267, 270, 278; *Curious Woodcuts of Fanciful and Real Beasts*, by Konrad Gesner, pages 59, 78, 229, 231, 253, 269; *North American Mammals*, by James Spero, pages 113, 186; *Treasury of Fantastic and Mythological Creatures*, by Richard Huber, pages 57, 179, 217, 232, 265.

United Press International, pages 5, 16.

The American Museum of Natural History, page 63.

Penticton Herald, page 137.

August Roberts, page 199.

The Flying Saucer News, page 201.

Illustrated London News, page 52.

The Age of Monsters, by Augusta and Burian, Courtesy Artia, page 89.

Illustration by Kathy Hirsh (after Metcalf) reproduced from *Searching for Hidden Animals* by Roy P. Mackal. Copyright © by Roy P. Mackal. By permission of Doubleday & Co., Inc., page 76.

CONTENTS

Contents

3. MONSTER BIRDS AND BATS

4. PHANTOMS

5. RIVER AND LAKE MONSTERS

6. SEA MONSTERS

7. VISITORS FROM STRANGE PLACES

8. WEIRD CREATURES IN FOLKLORE

INTRODUCTION

The subject of monsters lies somewhere in a misty realm between zoology and folklore. Much of this book concerns what has been called cryptozoology—that is, the study of animals that may, or may not, exist. Others would suggest that the subject is Fortean, a word coined from the name of the American writer Charles Hoy Fort (1874–1932), who collected odd information, bits and pieces that didn't seem to fit in with the orthodox scientific view of the world. Some of the creatures discussed in this book are pure folklore—we know that now—but a while ago we were not so sure. And there are some acknowledged hoaxes and frauds, but significant and influential ones.

All of this—cryptozoology, Fortean phenomena, folklore, and fraud—goes to make up the subject of monsters.

Monster is not a clearly defined word like *cat* or *frog*. One of the definitions in my old *Webster's Collegiate* is, "an animal of strange or terrifying shape," and that is a description which applies to most of the creatures in this book. But I've had to expand and bend that definition a bit.

Not all of the creatures in this book are truly terrifying. Even the Loch Ness monster is not really frightening, and the man who first applied the label *monster* to Nessie said he did so because he just didn't know what else to call it. In popular usage, practically any large unknown animal is called a "monster." In general, I have followed popular usage. I have also found it necessary to include information on several creatures that are neither unknown nor particularly monstrous in any way, but whose histories have had an influence on the general study of monsters.

Not all of the creatures discussed here are animals, at least not "lower animals." There is, for example, considerable debate as to whether Bigfoot and its kin are advanced apes or primitive humans. It matters little, for they are both monsters here.

Some of the space creatures are apparently not human, but they certainly are not animals. Generally, people refer to them as monsters, and that is why they have been included. At one time, persons with extreme physical deformities—Siamese twins, the Elephant Man— were labeled "monsters." It was a cruel definition, and you will find none of it in these pages. More appropriately labeled human "monsters"—Hitler, Gilles de Rais—are also excluded.

I have tried to stay away from ghosts, spirits, and other strictly non-material monsters, but the barrier admittedly becomes a bit fuzzy in spots, what with phantom lions and dogs. Even Bigfoot is sometimes invested with a somewhat supernatural or otherworldly aura.

Another criterion to be considered is that of belief. While there are a few clearly labeled exceptions to this rule, the vast majority of creatures in this book either command a considerable body of belief today or did so in the fairly recent past. Granted, few today believe in the reality of vampires or werewolves anymore, but there is still confusion about the existence of a "real" Dracula. Besides, how can you do an encyclopedia of monsters without covering vampires and werewolves?

Vampires and werewolves are genuine products of folklore, even though the original lore has been changed and expanded by books and films. Frankenstein's monster is a purely literary creation, the product of the imagination of Mary Shelley. Godzilla is the product of the Japanese film industry. Mummies are real enough, but "the mummy," the one that walks around strangling people who violate its tomb, is a Hollywood creation. The ancient Egyptians never thought their mummies were supposed to get up and go anywhere. Thus Frankenstein's monster, Godzilla, and the mummy will not be found in these pages. The zombie will, because some Haitians did and still do believe that corpses can be made to get up and walk around.

Even given these limits, the number of monsters that might be included in such a book is vast, and a book is finite. I have concentrated on monsters that are familiar to the English-speaking world, not that the Japanese, the people of Kenya, the Russians, and others in all other parts of the world do not have a rich lore of their own national monsters; it is simply that an investigation of that scope is way beyond the limits of a single volume. So too is an exploration of all the local examples of monsters even in the United States. There are scores of variations on the lake monster and Bigfoot theme. In each case, I have given separate listings to a few of the major variations, but if your favorite local monster is not mentioned, I'm sorry. No slight was intended.

What I am saying, in perhaps too many words, is that the selection of the items in this book is an entirely personal one. I tried to stick to certain general criteria, but in the end I relied on an instinct developed through a lifelong interest in monsters and nearly twenty years of professional involvement with them.

No writing and research project of this size (or of any size for that matter) is pure pleasure. But this one has afforded me, along with the usual headaches, a great deal of fun. It was a bit like meeting a lot of old friends and finding out what has happened to them in the past five or ten years. And I ran across a few new monsters—new to me at least.

I sincerely hope that as you dip into the following pages, you will find not only exotic and interesting information, but that you will also feel some of the mystery, excitement, and romantic joy of the quest for monsters, even if it is only an armchair quest.

1

HUMANOIDS

ABOMINABLE SNOWMAN   The Abominable Snowman, or yeti, is one of the truly great unknown animals of the twentieth century. It is a large hairy biped that lives in the Himalayan region of Asia. Interest in the Abominable Snowman in this century has rivaled the nineteenth-century interest in the great sea serpent, or eighteenth-century interest in the dragon.

The story of the Abominable Snowman is filled with mysteries great and small, and one of the most difficult of all is how it got that awful name. The creature is neither particularly abominable, nor does it necessarily live in the snows. *Yeti* is a Tibetan word which may apply either to a real, but unknown animal of the Himalayas, or to a mountain spirit or demon—no one is quite sure which. And after nearly half a century in which Westerners have tramped around looking for the yeti, and asking all sorts of questions, the original native traditions concerning the creature have become even more muddled and confused.

Early accounts of sightings of the Abominable Snowman are so vague, untrustworthy, or far removed from their original source as to be virtually worthless as evidence. The modern story of this creature must really begin in 1925 with the experience of N. A. Tombazi, a Greek photographer who was serving as a member of a British geographical expedition in the Himalayas. Tombazi was camping at an altitude of some fifteen thousand feet in the mountains of Sikkim, when his porters pointed to something odd moving across the lower slopes.

3

"The intense glare and brightness of the snow prevented me from seeing anything for the first few seconds," Tombazi recalled. "But I soon spotted the 'object' referred to, about two to three hundred yards away down the valley to the east of our camp. Unquestionably, the figure in outline was exactly like a human being, walking upright and stopping occasionally to uproot or pull at some dwarf rhododendron bushes. It showed up dark against the snow and, as far as I could make out, wore no clothes. Within the next minute or so it had moved into some thick scrub and was lost to view.

"Such a fleeting glimpse, unfortunately, did not allow me to set the telephoto-camera, or even to fix the object carefully with binoculars, but a couple of hours later, during the descent, I purposely made a detour so as to pass the place where the 'man' or 'beast' had been seen. I examined the footprints which were clearly visible on the surface of the snow. They were similar in shape to those of a man, but only six to seven inches long by four inches wide at the broadest part of the foot. The marks of five distinct toes and the instep were perfectly clear, but the trace of the heel was indistinct, and the little that could be seen of it appeared to narrow down to a point. I counted fifteen such footprints at regular intervals ranging from one-and-a-half to two feet. The prints were undoubtedly of a biped, the order of the spoor having no characteristics whatever of any imaginable quadruped. Dense rhododendron scrub prevented any further investigations as to the direction of the footprints. . . . From inquiries I made a few days later . . . I gathered that no man had gone in the direction [of the footprints] since the beginning of the year.

"When I asked the opinion of the Siddar and the coolies they naturally trotted out fantastic legends of 'Kanchenjunga demons.' Without in the least believing in these delicious fairy tales myself, notwithstanding the plausible yarns told by the natives, and the reference I have come across in many books, I am still at a loss to express any definite opinion. However, I can only reiterate with a sufficient degree of certainty that the silhouette of the mysterious being was unmistakably identical with the outline of a human figure. . . ."

Tombazi's account is quoted at length, for in the opinion of many

Abominable Snowman footprint

who have followed the Abominable Snowman phenomenon, it is simply the best firsthand sighting available. Tombazi's honesty has never been questioned; he was an experienced observer, and his "fleeting glimpse" was combined with a close-up examination of footprints. One can only be sorry that he did not decide to take photos of the footprints.

Tombazi himself did not forget the incident. In 1964 he wrote, "Although nearly forty years have passed, I still carry a vivid impression of the glimpse I caught at the time and I am convinced that the yeti in the form of a biped and not a quadruped is in existence."

There are, however, a number of points in this narrative which deserve additional comment. First, while forty years after the event Tombazi talks of the yeti, in his original account he speaks only of "demons" which he calls "delicious fairy tales." More important are the footprints. Traditionally, the Abominable Snowman makes huge footprints, much larger than those of a man, but those described by Tombazi are actually smaller than would normally be made by a human foot.

Then there is the general appearance of the creature—it was "exactly like a human being," not at all the lumbering, apelike monster that comes to mind when the word *yeti* is mentioned. Tombazi says the thing wasn't wearing any clothes, but he gives no indication if it was covered with hair, though admittedly he probably could not tell under the conditions.

So what did Tombazi see? Forty years after the event, he spoke of the yeti. But immediately after he made his sighting, he had another theory. "I conjecture then that this 'wild man' may either be a solitary or else a member of an isolated community of pious Buddhist ascetics, who have renounced the world and sought their God in the utter desolation of some high place, as yet undesecrated by the world. However, perhaps, I had better leave these conclusions to ethnological or other experts."

There are Buddhist and Hindu ascetics who seek out the desolation of high places. They can live at altitudes of fifteen thousand feet and can train themselves to endure cold and other hardships that would

kill the average person. They can and do walk about naked or nearly
so in the frigid mountain air. So Tombazi might really have seen a
wandering ascetic, as he first thought.

That is a disappointing beginning to the Abominable Snowman
story, but it is also quite typical, for the evidence that supports the
existence of this creature has frequently been less solid than it first
appears.

The best piece of material evidence are photographs of footprints
taken in 1951 by mountaineer Eric Shipton on the southwestern slopes
of the Menlug-tse in the Himalayas. Shipton believed the prints he
found to be those of the yeti, and he followed the trail for about a
mile until it disappeared on the hard ice. Unlike Tombazi, he took
photos of the footprints.

One of the pictures Shipton took shows a five-toed print compared
to the head of an ice ax. Another shows the print as being about the
same size as a climbing boot, and thus much larger than the ordinary
human foot.

The Shipton photographs have been reprinted many times, often
accompanied by another photo which shows a trail of prints. This was
always assumed to be the trail of yeti prints, but in 1973 primate
expert John Napier revealed that the photo showed the trail made by
a mountain goat. The picture has nothing to do with the yeti-footprint
photos. It was simply taken by Shipton earlier on the same day he
found the yeti prints. The negatives were presumably filed together,
and that is how the confusion began. For years, no one had bothered
to correct the mistaken impression.

The close-up footprint, the genuine yeti print photo, has been the
subject of a great deal of investigation and speculation. It certainly
does not look like the footprint of any known animal, but footprints
in the snow can be confusing. A print can melt, refreeze, and melt
again, so that the shape and size of the original print can be greatly
altered. Some have suggested that the prints were made by a group
of small animals moving in line through the snow. The leader breaks
the trail and the followers jump into the footprints of the lead animal,
enlarging the original indentation. Melting and refreezing would

make the numerous small prints look like a single big one. This theory is rejected by most monster enthusiasts, but it is not entirely implausible.

There were stories and even photographs of yeti "scalps" that were kept in Tibetan monasteries and treated as sacred objects. The scalps had an odd peaked appearance, and that led to the theory that the Abominable Snowman had a ridge running down the middle of its skull. It was often said that the lamas who had charge of these "scalps" would not allow them to be handled by outsiders, thus they could never be examined closely. This was not the case, and close examination proved to be the downfall of the "scalp."

In 1960 Sir Edmund Hillary, "the Conqueror of Everest," led a large expedition into the Himalayas. One of the announced purposes of the expedition was to search out information about the Abominable Snowman. Naturally, this sensational goal got a great deal of publicity.

Not only did Sir Edmund fail to find the yeti himself, his expedition destroyed what had up to then been one of the most intriguing bits of evidence, the "yeti scalps." Hillary was not only allowed to examine one of the yeti scalps, he was able to bring it back with him to be examined by Western scientists. It didn't take long for the scientists to decide that this "scalp" didn't come from an unknown anthropoid, but that it was a fur hat made from the pelt of a rare Himalayan goat, the serow. A close examination of the three "scalps" considered to be most genuine indicates that one appears to be a hat several hundred years old. Holes in it indicate where tassels or prayer flags were once attached. The other two "scalps" are of fairly recent vintage; they are either deliberate fakes or simply fur hats that have been the subject of a case of mistaken identity.

Sir Edmund Hillary, who is known for his outspokenness, roundly denounced the whole idea of the yeti as nonsense. Monster buffs fought back, saying that Hillary's investigations had been slipshod, that they had known the scalps were fake all the time, and that Hillary was just jealous he had not found the creature. But there is no doubt that Hillary's denunciation hurt the international reputation of the Abominable Snowman. After the 1960 expedition, interest shifted to other monsters, particularly Bigfoot in the United States and Canada. What made Hillary particularly difficult for monster enthusiasts to handle was that monster skeptics are generally scientists tied to laboratories or universities. Sir Edmund Hillary, the great mountain climber, could hardly be criticized as being an armchair critic.

Still, the case for the Abominable Snowman is not a negligible one. There are dozens of reported sightings by Westerners of the creature, and at least some seem quite credible. There are also many encounters reported by the natives of the Himalayan region, but these are difficult to evaluate, for the people of the Himalayas often do not make the same distinction between the material and spiritual worlds that is so important in the West today. On such matters, their thinking is far closer to that of a medieval European. A demon—even though it is not a material being—may be quite as "real" as an ape or a goat.

Mountaineers have from time to time come across puzzling footprints like those shown in the Shipton photographs.

Aside from the current yeti legends, there are a large variety of legends from mountainous regions throughout Asia of a hairy wild man. In China paleontologists have found the fossil remains of a giant ape, *Gigantopithecus*, possibly the largest ape that ever lived. Such a creature, if it survived into fairly recent times, could easily have given rise to Abominable Snowman stories.

And finally there are the Himalaya Mountains themselves. They are among the most inaccessible places on earth. If an unknown creature were to survive anywhere on land in the modern world, the Himalayas would be as good a hiding place as any.

See also: ALMA, BIGFOOT, CHINESE WILDMAN

ALMA   The alma is one name given to the Soviet version of the Abominable Snowman, or Bigfoot. Like their more famous counterparts, the almas are hairy bipeds that generally live in mountain areas, in this case the mountains of Soviet Asia. The bulk of the alma stories indicate that the creature is more human, more of a true wild man than either the Snowman or Bigfoot.

The most celebrated encounter with this Soviet wild man took place in August 1957, and the witness was a scientist, Alexander G. Pronin. Pronin was not looking for wild men; he was a hydrologist on an expedition to study the water resources of the Pamir Mountains.

"On August 12th at mid-day, I am following up a course of the valley of the river Balyandkiik, and I suddenly notice a strange sight. On the southward slope of the valley, at a distance of approximately 500 metres, up on the permanent snow, a being of unusual aspect is moving—reminiscent of a man's figure, but with a strongly hunched back. Against the white background it could be seen clearly that he was standing with his legs wide apart, and that his arms are longer than in the ordinary man. [In another account Pronin describes the creature as being covered with reddish gray hair.] I stood there not moving. And so five minutes elapse. The figure then vanished, hidden behind a rock."

Three days later Pronin saw the same figure again for a few minutes. A week later one of the expedition's rubber boats disappeared mysteriously, and just as mysteriously was found a few miles upstream. The local inhabitants spoke vaguely of a wild man, and of how common household utensils would sometime disappear from around their homes and be found in the mountains. "Are these facts not linked with the loss of our boat?" asked Pronin.

Stories of the alma or wild man extend from the Pamirs and Caucasus in the West all the way to China, and they have been recorded for at least a century. N. M. Pzewalski, discoverer of the Mongolian wild horse, collected stories of a wild man in his travels in Mongolia in 1881. In the early years of this century, a zoologist named Khaklov who had traveled widely in the regions of Dzungaria, between the Altai Mountains in the north and the Tien Shan range in the south, heard many wild-man stories from the Kazakh herdsmen. One man who claimed to have taken part in the capture of a wild man described the creature. This description has obviously been freely translated from the herdsman's original story:

"A male of less than average human height covered with brown to reddish hair, long arms reaching below his knees. Shoulders which are stooped with a narrow, hollow chest. His brow was sloped backwards from the bony crest projecting over his eyes. His lower jaw was massive, and he was chinless. The nose was small and the nostrils wide and flared. The skin on his forehead, forearms, and knees was horny and calloused. His legs bent and bowed at the knees. His feet resembled human feet and were one and a half times as broad. The toes were widely splayed and the big toe was shorter than in man and set apart from the others. The hands had long fingers and were similar to a man's hand."

While there have been a few reports of almas raiding farms and being shot by local inhabitants, in general the attitude toward these creatures seems to be one of tolerance—they are regarded as human, if a somewhat degraded and inferior form of human.

There is, for example, the Central Asian report which tells of two travelers who were being led into the mountains by a local herdsman. Early one morning the travelers saw a strange figure lurking near the horses. Thinking it was a horse thief, they took off after it and were able to capture it easily with their lassoes. But what they caught was not truly human.

The creature was about the height of an average man, but it was covered with hair, "just like a young camel." It had an apelike face, and the feet resembled those of a human being but were much larger.

The creature was not aggressive at all, and it squeaked miserably when caught. The herdsman didn't seem very surprised at the strange captive; he said it was a wild man, and that they were quite well known in the area and harmless. The travelers set the creature free, but followed it. They found the wild man lived in a sort of cave, a hollowed-out space beneath a cliff, which contained a bed made from straw and grass.

If the tribesmen of Soviet Asia take the wild man rather casually, more sophisticated Soviet citizens have an ambiguous attitude. There appears to be a general tendency to ridicule reports of the alma, and

Pronin complained bitterly of the ribbing that he took from his scientific colleagues after he described his sighting of the strange creature. On the other hand, a few Soviet scientists have taken a great interest in the subject and have expressed strong opinions about the existence of such creatures.

Professor Jeanne Josefovina Kofman has led expeditions into several areas which are supposed to be populated by almas, and while she has never come up with any tangible proof of the existence of such a creature, she has collected hundreds of reports about them and has lectured and read papers on the subject to gatherings of scientists.

The most outspoken supporter of the alma and the greatest expert on the subject has been Soviet historian Dr. Boris Proshnev. Proshnev headed a commission on the subject set up by the Soviet Academy of Science. Proshnev too has complained that he has faced a good deal of ridicule and indifference from his colleagues, but he has had enough support to publish some of his work on the alma, though in very limited quantities. His work may be better known in the West than in his homeland.

It is Proshnev's view that the almas are closer on the evolutionary scale to humans than to apes. He speculates that they may be some type of Neanderthaler.

In his works, mostly written in the 1940s and 1950s, Proshnev cites as evidence skeletons, mummified hands, and other alma remains that were supposed to exist but had not yet been examined by competent scientists. Today most of these relics have been examined, and they have without exception turned out to be something else. The "mummified hand," for example, was the preserved paw of a snow leopard.

What we are left with are the stories of recent encounters with the nearly human alma—but these are numerous enough to at least give one pause.

See also: ABOMINABLE SNOWMAN, BIGFOOT, CHINESE WILDMAN

BIGFOOT   Bigfoot is much more than a monster; it is an
extremely complex phenomenon, with no definite starting point and
few geographical limits.

But we must begin somewhere, so it may as well be with the tale
of Jacko, an apelike creature that was allegedly captured outside of
the town of Yale, in British Columbia, in 1884. The story is given in
great detail in the Victoria, British Columbia, newspaper the *Daily
British Colonist*. The hairy biped was not called Bigfoot, or Sasquatch, the Canadian name for Bigfoot; it was named Jacko and was
described as being "something of the gorilla type."

Among monster enthusiasts it has always been assumed that the
Jacko story is a description of the capture of a young Sasquatch. However, since the creature sounds so much like a chimpanzee, it is possible that it *was* a chimpanzee. Perhaps a chimp a sailor brought back
from Africa as a pet, which escaped or was turned out when it got
big and unfriendly. A better possibility is that the story was a complete hoax. Newspapers of the day regularly printed hoax stories that
were not considered dishonest; the hoax was practically a separate literary genre.

The name *Sasquatch* doesn't really become important in Canada
until the 1930s, when it appeared in the works of J. W. Burns, a British Columbian writer who used a great deal of Indian lore in his stories. Burns's Sasquatch was a giant Indian who lived in the wilderness.
He was hairy only in the sense that he had long hair on his head, and
while this Sasquatch lived a wild and primitive life, he was fully
human.

Burns's character proved to be quite popular. There was a Sasquatch Inn near the town of Harrison, British Columbia, and Harrison
even had a local celebration called "Sasquatch Days." The celebration
which had been dormant for years was revived as part of British
Columbia's centennial, and one of the events was to be a Sasquatch

hunt. The hunt never took place, perhaps it was never supposed to, but the publicity about it did bring out a number of people who said they had encountered a Sasquatch—not Burns's giant Indian, but the hairy apelike creature that we have all come to know.

One William Roe said he met the beast in October 1955, about eighty miles west of Jasper, Alberta.

"My first impression was of a huge man about six feet tall, almost three feet wide, and probably weighing somewhere near 300 pounds. It was covered from head to foot with dark brown silver-tipped hair . . . the hair that covered it, leaving bare only the parts of the face around the mouth, nose and ears, made it resemble an animal as much as a human. None of this hair, even on the back of its head, was longer than an inch."

Roe's account was more than matched by the story told by Albert Ostman, who said that in 1924 he had been kidnapped by a Sasquatch family and had spent several days living with them before he was able to make his escape. The creatures that Ostman described seemed human, but barely so. They lived extremely primitive lives. Their food consisted of roots and berries that they gathered. They did not know how to use fire, but did seem to possess a rudimentary language. To this day, monster enthusiasts are divided over whether Ostman accurately reported one of the most astonishing experiences in history or was pulling their leg. Ostman died sticking to the truth of his tale.

Interest in this creature south of the Canadian border, where it is commonly known as Bigfoot, really began in 1958, though there had been tales of such a being long before that. But 1958 was the year that bulldozer operator Jerry Crew found enormous footprints around the camp in which he was staying, while working in the mountain wilderness area of Humboldt County in northern California. Crew made a plaster cast of one of these prints and had his picture taken holding the cast. The footprint stretched from Crew's shoulder to his waist. The picture and story were picked up by a local newspaper, and then by newspapers all over the country. It was the picture of Jerry Crew holding that enormous cast of a footprint that really brought the creature to the attention of the people of the United States, and made the name Bigfoot stick.

Crew's story seemed to jog a lot of memories, because all over the Pacific Northwest, people stepped forward to say that not only had they seen Bigfoot's big footprints—they had encountered the beast itself in one way or another. There was one truly sensational account of an event that was supposed to have taken place in 1924, ironically, the same year as Albert Ostman's "capture" by the Sasquatch family.

Near Mount Saint Helens in the state of Washington there is a place known locally as "ape canyon." There, so the story goes, a group of miners was attacked by a party of seven-foot apes. Earlier in the day, a miner had shot one of the "giant apes," and in the evening a gang of them bombarded the miners' windowless cabin with rocks and boulders. The miners crouched inside the cabin for hours while rocks rained down on them. When the attack was over, the miners fled down the mountain and back to town. They returned to the canyon with a bunch of well-armed friends, but the apes had departed, leaving behind only their giant footprints and a badly battered cabin. The giant apes of Mount Saint Helens, if they were ever more than a tall tale, are doubtless extinct today because of the eruption of the Mount Saint Helens volcano. In 1982 a retired logger named Rant Mullens claimed he and a friend started the Mount Saint Helens story by rolling rocks down on the miner's cabin, as a joke.

But Bigfoot has been seen elsewhere in the region. According to a typical Bigfoot report in the *Oregon Journal,* "Three persons driving along a remote mountain road east of the Cascade wilderness area early Sunday say they saw a ten foot, white, hairy figure moving rapidly along the roadside. It was caught in the headlights as their car passed, but they were too frightened to turn around to investigate. Another Portland woman and her husband fishing on the Lewis River south of Mt. St. Helens saw a huge beige figure, 'bigger than any human,' along the bank of the river. As they watched, it moved into a thicket 'with a lumbering gait.'"

Interest in Bigfoot soared to new heights in October 1967, when Roger Patterson and Bob Gimlin, a couple of veteran monster buffs, rode out of a wilderness area northeast of Eureka, California, with the astonishing story that not only had they seen Bigfoot, but that they had filmed the creature in living color.

Here is the story as Patterson and Gimlin told it. At 3:30 P.M. on October 20 they saw "a sort of man-creature . . . about seven feet tall," walking through the woods about one hundred yards from where they were standing. "Gosh darn it. . . . And for pity's sakes she was a female!" Patterson exclaimed. The thing, whatever it was, had "big droopy breasts," and was covered with "short, shiny black hair."

Patterson and Gimlin had set out deliberately to find, and if possible photograph, Bigfoot, and therefore they had the camera equipment handy and were able to capture a short sequence of the thing before it disappeared into the dense woods.

The Patterson-Gimlin Bigfoot photograph

The films are not as clear as one might hope, but they are quite clear enough to rule out any chance of mistaken identity. The thing is not a bear or a cloud of dust or a strangely shaped rock. It is either America's Abominable Snowman or a man in a monkey suit; there are no other alternatives.

Unlike many who have claimed to have photographed this or that monster, Patterson and Gimlin did not become secretive about what they had. *Argosy* magazine, which published the monster hunters' story and photos from the film first, gathered a panel of scientists to view the film. The general attitude of the scientific panel was non-committal. "I couldn't see the zipper," quipped John Napier of the Smithsonian Institution, "and I still can't."

The walk bothered some viewers—the stride seemed too wide, almost as if a bad actor were trying to simulate a monster's walk. But no one could prove the film was faked, and so it has become an accepted classic in the field of Bigfoot lore.

There is a modest Bigfoot industry in the Pacific Northwest—there is at least one Bigfoot motel, and Bigfoot burgers have been served at some diners. There are regular Bigfoot expeditions for tourists:

"You *search* for Bigfoot with a scientist, naturalist and tracker in southwestern Oregon and Northwestern California. Unforgettable 22 day wilderness expeditions search. . . . You help solve a scientific mystery and keep safe an endangered species."

Bigfoot has been declared a protected endangered species by Siskiyou County, California. No one, however, has ever been prosecuted under that law.

The Humboldt State College Library at Arcata, California, in the heart of California's "Bigfoot country," collects material on the subject, and put on a special Bigfoot display in 1969. At Willow Creek, California, there is a "life-sized" Bigfoot statue lovingly carved out of redwood by a prominent monster buff.

Aside from the regular tourist runs, there have been reasonably serious Bigfoot expeditions, including one financed by Tom Slick, the late Texas oilman, who had also spent a lot of money pursuing the Abominable Snowman in the Himalayas. On the expedition, there were a few possible Bigfoot sightings, though perhaps what the expedition members had really seen was a bear. There were footprints, odd noises, and many, many tales of eerie feelings of "being watched," but no Bigfoot dead or alive was brought out of the wilderness by Slick's party. Lee Trippett, an electronics engineer from Eugene, Oregon, who claimed that he could capture Bigfoot by influencing the creature's mind through extrasensory perception, was no less successful, but no more successful, either.

There is a certain elegant logic behind a belief in Bigfoot. Tales of hairy bipeds can be traced from the mountains of Soviet Asia, across the mountains of Tibet, and almost to the Bering Strait, which narrowly separates Siberia from Alaska. The tales pick up again in western Canada and carry into the mountains of Washington, Oregon, and northern California. In theory, the creature could have evolved in Asia, then crossed over the Bering land bridge during the Ice Age, and taken up residence in similar high country in the Western Hemisphere. The ancestors of the American Indians came to the Western Hemisphere in just that way.

The major problem with this theory is that while many of the mountains of Asia in which Bigfootlike creatures are supposed to live are sparsely populated, Washington, Oregon, and northern California are not. The mountainous areas of the Pacific Northwest are indeed rugged, but they are regularly traversed by hunters, hikers, and forest rangers. Could such a large and singular-looking creature escape conclusive detection for so long? Why have no remains ever been found, where are the carcasses, where are the bones? Surely the creatures die. We have plenty of footprints, but footprints, as everbody knows, can easily be faked. Indeed, big plastic feet that you can strap to your boots and run around in the snow with, in order to fool your friends and neighbors, have been frequently sold as novelty items. The only evidence we have are the sightings—and the sightings alone.

Bigfoot, which was once believed to be limited to the Northwest, has become a nationwide phenomenon. Hardly a month goes by anymore without some wire service or newspaper syndicate coming up with a Bigfoot story from somewhere in the country. A November 1981 UPI dispatch from Yale, Michigan, is typical:

"Cindy Barone says it is not the torn down fences or the barn doors that have been ripped off the hinges, nor is it the high pitched screams her family often hears at night.

"'It's the unknown that scares us,' she said. 'If I knew what it was I could deal with it.'

"The rural St. Clair County woman is referring to a large hairy creature that she and her family is convinced is a Bigfoot, a creature that is said to walk on two legs and roam wooded areas from Maine to Washington."

The story goes on to describe how in the latest encounter the Barone's two daughters literally ran into the thing in the barn. The barn was dark, and Tina, a thirteen-year-old, reached for the light switch but instead felt something furry. Said the girl, "All I know is that its fur was about one inch thick and all matted and dirty."

Bigfoot encounters of one sort or another have been reported in virtually every state. Sometimes the reports have been persistent enough for the creature to rate its own local name, such as Mo-Mo, the Missouri monster; or the Fouke monster, from the state of Arkansas. This monster was also the subject of the motion picture *The Legend of Boggy Creek*. In Florida, Bigfoot is called the skunk ape, and in Texas, the Lake Worth monster. The stories about these creatures run from the fairly ordinary—a person driving along at night sees a strange apelike creature along the side of the road, but it disappears before he can get a good look at it—to the quite bizarre. A tale was told by two girls from Illinois about how the monster reached through the window of their parked car and battered the head of one of the girls against the inside of the windshield. In the vast majority of these cases, there is not a shred of material evidence, not even a footprint to back up the story. But such stories can start a "monster mania" that sends scores of armed men into the woods on a monster hunt.

What appears to have happened is that the idea of Bigfoot has merged with two older folkloric traditions in the United States—the monster animal, and the monster of lovers' lane. The monster-animal tradition is a very general one; it holds simply that there is some sort of monster animal living in the woods or some other deserted place outside of town. The animal was given a variety of descriptions, depending on where the stories originated. From time to time, these monster-animal tales would reach the newspapers. After about 1960 almost all of the monster-animal descriptions tended to make it sound like Bigfoot.

The monster of lovers' lane tradition holds that when couples go out and park at a deserted spot often used as a lovers' lane, they will be attacked by a "monster." It could be some sort of animal, or a "maniac." Today the monster of this tale, which is most frequently told among teenagers, is a Bigfoot type of animal.

Bigfoot has also become part of the newer lore of UFOs. A number of stories hint that Bigfoot and UFOs are connected in some unspecified way.

All of this, plus the fact that no material evidence of Bigfoot has been found, even in areas where it allegedly has been sighted frequently, has led some monster enthusiasts to the theory that Bigfoot is not a material creature but some sort of "psychic projection" or a visitor from "another dimension"—a real but not a material monster.

See also: ALMA, ABOMINABLE SNOWMAN, CHINESE WILDMAN, LAKE WORTH MONSTER, MINNESOTA ICEMAN, MO-MO, ORANGE EYES, SKUNK APE

CHINESE WILDMAN   Though China is a densely populated country, there are still some forested areas that remain relatively free of human habitation. From the thick forests of the Shennongija region of Hubei Province in central China come reports of a hairy apelike creature—generally referred to as a "wildman." It is sort of a Chinese version of the Abominable Snowman or Bigfoot. There are inevitably a large number of ancient legends and stories that refer to some sort of an anthropoidlike creature in China. But the most interesting evidence comes from modern times. Much of this evidence is presented

in a paper by Yuan Zhenxin and Huang Wampo, originally published
in the Chinese journal *Fossils*, and translated and printed in English
by the *Fortean Times*.

The Chinese authors report dozens of sightings and even closer
encounters with this hairy wild man. The most startling was the tale
of one Wang Zelin. Wang had been viewing a model of Peking man
in a museum when he astonished his companions by saying that he
had seen the "ape man." It happened in 1940: as Wang was traveling
along a road in the Shennongija region, he heard gunshots in the distance. He got to the place where the shots had been fired and found
a crowd surrounding the corpse of a wild man, or in this case a wild
woman. "The body was still supple and the stature very tall. . . . The
whole body was covered with a coat of thick greyish-red hair which

Chinese wildman

was very dense. . . . Since it was lying face down, the more inquisitive among the passengers turned the body over to have a better look. It turned out to be a mother with a large pair of breasts. . . . The face was narrow with deep-set eyes, while the cheek bones and lips jutted out. . . . The appearance was very similar to the plaster model of a female Peking Man. However, its hair seemed longer and thicker than that of the ape-man model. It was ugly because of the protruding lips."

The Chinese report goes on to state that an investigation team was set up to collect accounts of meetings with the wild man, and had found over a hundred of them, from people in all walks of life. The team also collected specimens of hair, droppings, and footprints that were all supposed to be from the wild man. An analysis of this evidence, however, proved inconclusive.

But the Chinese authors of the wild-man paper are convinced that the creature exists, and moreover that it is the descendant of the fossil giant ape of China, *Gigantopithecus:*

"Some people claim that *Gigantopithecus* has been extinct for a long time. Not necessarily so! It is known to all that the giant panda, who was sharing weal and woe with the *Gigantopithecus* for a few million years, is still very much in existence. [The giant panda was not discovered until 1869.] There is no reason why *Gigantopithecus* could not have overcome the environmental hazards and after having gone through the utmost sacrifices, left behind a generation to continue to accompany the giant panda."

Of the many tales of hairy bipeds, of unknown species that are reputed to inhabit the mountainous regions of the world, the Chinese wild man is the least known in the West.

See also: ABOMINABLE SNOWMAN, ALMA, BIGFOOT

GOATMAN   The tradition of the "monster of lovers' lane" is a persistent one in the United States. It is repeated, with local variations, all over the country. The basic theme runs like this: A teenaged couple drives out to some quiet dark spot that is often used as a "lovers' lane." They park the car and turn off the lights, but suddenly they are attacked by some sort of creature that bangs on the hood of the car, throws things at them, reaches through the open window with a hairy hand, and generally scares the hell out of them. They drive off in a panic, and others who are tempted to use that particular quiet dark spot for parking are warned off.

Usually the "monster of lovers' lane" is vaguely described as a Bigfoot type of creature. But in Prince George's County, Virginia, the monster of lovers' lane has very definite and unusual characteristics. It also has its own name; it's called Goatman.

Goatman is described as having the upper body of a human being and the legs of a goat, legs which end not in feet but in cloven hooves. Thus Goatman looks like the satyrs and the god Pan of Greek mythology, and bears a close resemblance to the traditional image of the Devil.

Opinions differ as to where Goatman came from. Some think he is some sort of primeval creature that has always lived in the area. A more popular idea is that he was once a scientist who worked at one of the many large government biological laboratories located in the region. The area is close to Washington, D.C., and is the home of many government-related research facilities. The scientist, so the story goes, was doing experiments on goats when something went seriously amiss, and he was turned into a half-goat, half-human monster. Horrified by his appearance, the unfortunate scientist fled into the woods near the laboratory. In his years of isolation, he has come to hate the human race that now scorns him. And so when a young couple parks on the lonely road near where he lives, he attacks their car. Some stories say that he hits the car with his bare fists, others contend that he beats on the car with an axe. Whatever he does, he usually scares people badly and drives them away.

Goatman is also blamed for killing dogs and other domestic animals. For a time, teenagers in the region would scrawl "Goatman was here" on sidewalks and walls.

Just exactly what road Goatman is supposed to frequent is never entirely clear. Several different locations have been given, and in general Goatman, in common with most of the other monsters of lovers' lane, seems to haunt whatever road it is that you plan to park on.

See also: ORANGE EYES

LAKE WORTH MONSTER   In July 1969, the sighting of a huge hairy "something" at Lake Worth, just outside of Fort Worth, Texas, set off what may have been the biggest monster hunt in Texas history. The creature was described as a biped, about seven feet tall, covered with short dirty white fur, and possessing a white goatlike beard.

Since Lake Worth is so accessible to the city of Fort Worth, the monster, whether it exists or not, became a menace. Hundreds of monster hunters, most of them gun-toting teenagers, turned out to look for the thing. One tall teenager, who happened to be wearing white coveralls, was actually shot in the shoulder by an enthusiast who thought he had the "monster" in his sights.

During the height of the 1969 excitement there were rumors of cattle and dogs killed and mutilated mysteriously, presumably by the monster. And there were stories that the monster was not a recent arrival, indeed, that in Indian times there had been legends of a monster in the Lake Worth region. The antiquity of the legends, however, has not been verified.

Sightings of the Lake Worth monster have continued on and off since the July 1969 flap. One very indistinct photo of what is supposed to be the monster exists—but it might be anything. A play called *The Lake Worth Monster*, written by a Fort Worth playwright, was successfully performed at a regional theatre. The play was very sympathetic to the monster.

See also: BIGFOOT

MINNESOTA ICEMAN   A thoroughly embarrassing but
rather humorous episode in the history of cryptozoology took place in
1968 when two of the world's leading authorities on unknown animals
were suckered into endorsing a carnival promoter's model as a genuine unknown animal.

Ivan Sanderson was the first to be told that a Bigfoot-like creature,
frozen in a block of ice, was being shown at carnivals throughout the
Midwest. The fee for getting a look at the thing was a mere thirty-
five cents. Sanderson traced the exhibit down to a Minnesota farm,
where its owner, Frank K. Hansen, a small-time carnival showman,
kept it stored during the winter months.

Sanderson asked Bernard Heuvelmans, the Belgian cryptozoologist,
who happened to be in America at the time, to travel to Minnesota
with him to examine the thing in the ice. The two men were not
allowed to get a close look at the animal. They had to examine it
through the foggy surface of the ice in which it was kept. But they
were so impressed with what they saw, or thought they saw, that both

Ivan Sanderson

men rushed into print with articles proclaiming the genuineness of the beast. The thing looked rather like a creature halfway between ape and human, and that is what both Sanderson and Heuvelmans proclaimed it to be. "Living Fossil" is how Sanderson's article in the magazine *Argosy* was titled.

Very suddenly, what had once been an obscure carnival exhibit was catapulted into worldwide fame. A lot of scientists were asked to comment on the "Minnesota Iceman," or "Bozo" as the creature came to be called. Most of them were reserved and cautious; they hesitated endorsing the genuineness of the thing in the ice, but they could not denounce it as a fake either, even if they thought it was.

John Napier, an expert on primates who worked at the Smithsonian Institution, almost persuaded the Smithsonian to conduct an examination of the Minnesota Iceman. But at that point, Frank Hansen began acting strangely. He insisted that he didn't own the thing, but that it belonged to a mysterious millionaire who for his own mysterious reasons did not want to have it examined closely. Hansen told different and contradictory stories about its origin. The Smithsonian, fearing it might be sucked into the position of appearing to endorse a hoax, or looking as though it had been fooled, withdrew the offer to examine the Iceman. Hansen would never have allowed that anyway. For once the ice was melted and the "body" examined, it would have been shown to be a rubber model. Several Hollywood model makers have claimed credit for the Iceman. The most likely candidate is the late Howard Ball, who made figures for Disneyland. Ball's son Kenneth, who helped construct the fake, said: "We modeled it after an artist's conception of Cro-Magnon man and gave it a broken skull with one eye popped out."

Hansen does not exactly deny the model story. From time to time, he will say that what people see is a "fabricated illusion," but that it is modeled on a real Iceman corpse that he, for varied and confusing reasons, has chosen to hide. Other times, he says that while he once used a model he no longer does so.

When Hansen began changing his story, and the claims of the California model makers surfaced, both Sanderson and Heuvelmans

backed off from their earlier support of the Iceman. Hansen withdrew
it from display for a while, but he has brought the exhibit back, and
as late as 1982 it was being displayed in shopping malls throughout
the eastern half of the United States.

See also: BIGFOOT

MO-MO   In the summer of 1971 two girls were driving from
Hannibal, Missouri, to St. Louis along Route 70. Just north of the town
of Louisiana, Missouri, they pulled off the road onto a quiet and
deserted spot to eat a picnic lunch.

As they started to eat, they became aware of a horrible smell, "like
a family of skunks," one of the girls said. But it was to be something
far worse than skunks. There was a noise in the bushes behind them,
"I turned around and this thing was standing there in the thicket. The
weeds were pretty high and I just saw the top part of the creature. It
was staring down at me."

The girls were terrified. They ran back to their car and locked
themselves in, determined to drive away as fast as possible. Too late,
they realized that they had left the keys to the car outside with their
lunch, and the monster had stepped out of the thicket, and was standing between the car and where the keys lay.

The girls described the monster as being, "ape-like, except that it
was also human. It was half-ape, half-man. . . . It walked upright on
two feet and its arms dangled way down. The arms were partially
covered with hair but the palms were hairless. We had plenty of time
to see this because the thing came right over to the car and looked at
it. . . . This ape-man actually tried to figure out how to open the
doors."

The girls were able to discourage the "ape-man" from examining
the car too closely by blowing the horn. It didn't like the horn, so it
wandered over to where they had left their lunch, ate a peanut butter
sandwich, and walked back into the woods. The girls retrieved the

keys and drove away as quickly as they could.

The two witnesses admitted that they couldn't prove that the story they told was true, "But all you have to do is go into those hills to realize that an army of those things could live there undetected."

This alleged encounter marked the most spectacular appearance of a Bigfoot type of creature that was to be dubbed the Missouri monster, or Mo-Mo.

By mid-1972, a genuine monster mania had broken out in the area of Louisiana. Reports, one wilder than the next, came in daily. A couple of boys said they met it in the woods and it growled at them. One witness said he had seen the monster crossing the road carrying a dead dog in its mouth, but another version of the same story held only that the creature was carrying a dead dog or sheep under its arm. There was even a story that the creature had tried to overturn a small car by picking up its rear end, though that story was later denied.

On July 19, 1972, twenty-five men went on a monster hunt near Louisiana. All day they tramped through the woods and hills where the monster was supposed to have been seen so frequently—but they found nothing, not even a footprint.

Historical monster hunters were more fortunate. Digging through old newspapers, they found stories of sightings of a creature "something like a gorilla" living in the swamps of southeast Missouri as early as the 1940s.

See also: BIGFOOT

NONDESCRIPT   Charles Waterton was one of those wealthy naturalist-travelers that Victorian England seemed to produce in such abundance. In his popular book *Wanderings in South America* Waterton says that during his final journey into the wilds of Guiana he procured an animal "which has caused not a little speculation and astonishment. In my opinion, his thick coat of hair, and great length of tail, put his species out of all question; but then his face and head

The Nondescript

cause the inspector to pause for a moment, before he ventures to pronounce his opinion of the classification. He was a large animal, and as
I was pressed for daylight, and moreover, felt no inclination to have
the whole weight of his body on my back, I contented myself with
his head and shoulders, which I cut off; and have brought them with
me to Europe."

In Waterton's book there is a drawing of this creature which its
owner called the Nondescript. It looks rather like an extremely hairy
man, or perhaps the Abominable Snowman. The head and shoulders
of this creature were put on display at Squire Waterton's home in
Walton Hall, and it was the most popular item among the squire's
unparalleled collection of stuffed birds and animals.

Almost from the start, people who knew Waterton suspected some
sort of trick, for the squire was known to be a master taxidermist, as
well as a diligent practical joker. It was the squire's friend the Reverend J. G. Wood who revealed that the Nondescript had been
formed from the head and shoulders of a red howler monkey. The
features had been so manipulated by the squire that they looked
remarkably human, and rather familiar. It seems that the squire had
made his creature look like an old enemy of his, a Mr. J. R. Lushing-

ton, a treasury official who had made Waterton pay a high duty on his collection. Waterton had often complained bitterly of the fee, and this was his revenge.

Peter Dance, zoologist and author of *Animal Fakes & Frauds*, calls the Nondescript "probably unique in the annals of taxidermy, politics and caricature."

See also: JENNY HANIVERS

ORANGE EYES   This creature is a central-Ohio variation of the ever popular monster of lovers' lane. As is traditional in stories of encounters with this type of monster, a young couple goes out to a dark and deserted road used as a lovers' lane. The parked and darkened car is then approached or attacked by a monster of some sort. In the orange-eyes variation, the creature is known mainly for its bright, shining orange eyes. Sometimes people report that the monster behind the eyes is a hairy Bigfoot type. Other times it is described as being even more exotic. Here is what one twenty-year-old Milan, Ohio, woman said about it:

"Orange Eyes is close to Ruggles Road. I think it is by a bridge that goes across the road called Blue Bridge. It is an eleven-foot, hairy, completely orange creature. And it is supposedly indestructible. People have tried to shoot it and kill it and it has no effect. . . ."

Some people say that Orange Eyes is really some crazy hermit who lives in the area, and that the monster illusion is created by a couple of automobile reflectors nailed on a stick. Others say there is no monster, and no hermit, but that the story is kept alive by local practical jokers, who use automobile reflectors, Christmas tree lights, or other sources of illumination to create the illusion of glowing orange eyes.

See also: BIGFOOT, GOATMAN

ORANG PENDEK   The people of the island of Sumatra have long told stories of the *orang pendek* or "little man." The *orang pendek*, according to the tales, is supposed to be a very shy biped that stands somewhere between two feet six inches and five feet in height. It is covered with short brown or black fur, and has a head of jet black hair which forms sort of a mane down its back. The *orang pendek* does not spend its time in trees like most monkeys and apes, but walks on the ground (though according to some stories its feet are reversed—with the heels in front and toes in back). Its arms are shorter than those of apes, and it is supposed to have a language of its own. It is more nearly human than ape.

There were relatively few who said they had ever actually observed the creature firsthand, but the wise traveler in the jungle left an offering of tobacco outside his camp at night. If he did not, the *orang pendek* would make life miserable for him by creating a continual racket at night and pulling down his hut.

In 1923 a Dutch settler named Van Herwaarden said that he actually saw one of the creatures and was about to shoot it but, "Many people may think me childish if I say that when I saw its flying hair in the sights I did not pull the trigger. I suddenly felt that I was going to commit murder. I lifted my gun to my shoulder again, but once again my courage failed me." Van Herwaarden dismissed the notion that the creature ran with its feet backward.

Others have not been so tenderhearted, and the dried bodies of what are called *orang pendeks* have occasionally been brought to Europe and America. The most recent case occurred in 1932 when, in response to a reward offer, four natives produced what they said was the body of an immature *orang pendek*. It turned out to be the shaved and altered body of a common form of langur monkey.

Apparently, the people of Sumatra had been given to this kind of trickery for centuries. Marco Polo was indignant over the sale of dried "pygmies" that he knew were nothing more than shaved monkeys which the natives "put into wooden boxes, and sell them to trading people who carry them to all parts of the world." On his way back from China, the great Venetian traveler had passed through Sumatra and had actually watched the manufacture of these "pygmies."

Could the belief in the *orang pendek* be based only on such fakes? Some think so.

The story of the *orang pendek* may have been strengthened by the discovery of the first known fossil man on the neighboring island of Java in 1894. *Orang pendek* stories became particularly popular after 1900. Java man was not a pygmy, but popular belief is not always logical in such matters.

It is certainly possible that the *orang pendek* tales have no basis in reality. No authentic tangible evidence of the existence of the creature has ever been produced. But as Bernard Heuvelmans wrote at the conclusion of his discussion of this creature, "Who knows?"

See also: WILD MAN

SKUNK APE   The skunk ape is one of the many local variations of the bigfoot phenomenon, this one from Florida. The creature became more than a local story in 1973, when a rash of reports brought it to national attention. The skunk ape was even covered by all three national TV network news shows, though Walter Cronkite looked as if he was having a hard time repressing a snicker as he narrated the account.

The report that made a celebrity out of the skunk ape was one in which a Florida man said that he had actually hit the creature while it was crossing the road. The monster was obviously hurt, the man said, but it managed to limp off the road and into the dense swamp, where it disappeared. Police examined the man's car and determined that he had indeed hit something—the fender was dented and there were traces of blood and fur on the car. The police thought he had hit a cow. The witness insisted differently, it was a large hairy biped with an evil smell, he said. It was the creature known as the skunk ape.

While a bad odor is a feature of many Bigfoot stories, the Florida variety appears to possess a particularly awful smell—hence the name skunk ape. When Ralph "Bud" Chambers reported spotting the thing near his Elfers, Florida, home in 1966, he says that he particularly remembers the creature's sickening odor. What Chambers saw was big, hairy, over seven feet tall, and four feet wide. The thing vanished into the swamp and when Chambers tried to track it with his dogs, the dogs seemed so disgusted by the strong odor that they would not follow the trail.

Chambers said that a year later the thing showed up in his back-yard. This time the dogs attacked it, but the creature barely noticed. According to Chambers, "The dogs kept biting at its ankles and feet." But the thing turned away slowly and started walking down the road that led back to the swamp.

A man named H. C. Osborn, an engineer and amateur archaeologist, said that he had been hearing skunk-ape stories for years, and he was told they had been circulated among trappers and fishermen since the 1920s. But Osborn insisted that he had never personally believed any of the stories until one day in the spring of 1970 he and four friends were digging up an Indian mound in the Big Cypress Swamp, Florida, and the creature popped up right in front of them. "It's made a believer out of me," said Osborn. He too said the creature was seven feet tall, and he estimated that it must have weighed seven hundred pounds.

The creature left footprints in the soft earth, and Osborn measured them at 17½ inches long, 11¼ inches across at the toes. "In later trips we found smaller tracks indicating that there are at least three of them in that section of the swamp."

One of the other members of Osborn's group, Frank Hudson, said, "We have talked to many old-timers in the area. They say they are afraid to talk openly about it. They thought people would laugh at them or think that they were crazy."

In June of 1977 a heavily advertised film called *Sasquatch* was being shown in Florida. Commercials for the film appeared regularly on television, and, as one might imagine, they seemed to stimulate a rash of skunk-ape sightings. Three youths told the Charlotte County Sheriff's Department that they saw the creature twice in one night. The first sighting took place at 9:00 P.M., the second around midnight. They said the creature was about seven feet tall, had reddish brown hair, and didn't seem friendly: it stood up and growled at them. Deputy Carl Williams drove around the area where the sightings were made. At a small pond he caught "something" in the beam of his spotlight. "It was a big animal. . . . It was hunched over and seemed to be drinking." It had long brown hair, and when hit with the spotlight the creature lumbered off into the woods.

The deputy's first thought was that the creature was a bear, for bears are fairly common in the region. "I couldn't say it wasn't a bear for sure, but it just seems logical that it must have been," Williams said. He did however, think it was a bit strange that the creature had reddish hair while most of the bears he had ever seen were black.

See also: BIGFOOT

WILD MAN   Throughout the Middle Ages, a familiar figure of European legend was the wild man or wodewose. The wild man was generally depicted as a human of enormous strength and size, covered with shaggy hair, and carrying a great club. This creature, it was believed, lived deep in the forests or in other wild and uninhabited regions, and rarely came into contact with human beings, which was a good thing because the wild man was reputed to be violent, and occasionally devoured humans that it captured, particularly children.

Richard Bernheimer, a scholar whose book *Wild Men in the Middle Ages* is the basic study of the European tradition, says of them:

"About the wild man's habitat and manner of life medieval authorities are articulate and communicative. It was agreed that he shunned human contact, settling, if possible, in the most remote and inaccessible parts of the forest, and making his bed in crevices, caves, the deep shadow of overhanging branches. In this remote and lonely sylvan home he eked out a living without benefit of metallurgy or even the simplest agricultural lore, reduced to the plain fare of berries and acorns or the raw flesh of animals. At times he had to be ready to defend his life, for the inner forests teemed with savage beasts real and imaginary, which were wont to attack him. If he was to survive, he had to be the physical equal if not the superior of creatures such as dragons, boars or primeval bulls. . . ."

Some wild men were fiercer than others. Those of the mountainous portions of central Europe and of the Alpine regions were the fiercest of all.

Writes Bernheimer: "As described by modern folklorists the Alpine wild man is a formidable creature, huge and hairy and mute and according to some so large that his legs alone have the size of trees. His temper when aroused is terrible, and his first impulse that of tearing trespassers to pieces."

Practically every medieval pagent had at least one figure in a wild-man costume. In 1392 Charles VI of France and five other nobles dressed as wild men for a court festival in suits covered in pitch and flax. The suits were highly flammable, and when a torch was inadvertently brought too close, they all caught fire. Four of the noblemen were killed, and although the king survived, he sustained painful burns as a result of his masquerade.

At first the wild man was shown as being truly wild, but later the image softened, until the onetime ferocious beast became almost a romantic figure, a symbol of the natural man, and of the lost freedoms of a theoretical primitive life. This change in attitude toward the wild man came only after belief in the reality of the wild man had disappeared.

What lay behind this popular and persistent myth? Some have suggested that the wild-man stories were inspired by individuals suffering from hypertrichosis, an exceedingly rare condition in which long hair grows all over a person's body, including his face. The condition, however, is so rare, appearing in about one in every billion births, that it is exceedingly doubtful that it would have inspired so widespread and persistent a legend. However, the appearance of an occasional hyper-trichotic individual certainly helped to spread and sustain the legend. In 1556 a hypertrichotic individual named Peter Gonzales was born in the Canary Islands. The child was sent to King Henry II of France, whose court was already home for a collection of dwarfs, giants, and other malformed individuals who have always seemed to have amused kings throughout history. Gonzales was apparently believed to be a genuine wild man, and the king had a cave specially con-structed for him so that he would not become homesick for his old "wild" life. Gonzales became quite a favorite of the king, and was permitted to marry. Several of his children showed the same hairy characteristics, and they too became attractions at different European courts. A number of pictures of the Gonzales family survive, and their appearance is striking, particularly when dressed in formal finery, as they were for the portraits.

A more popular explanation of the origin of the wild-man belief is that it was a survival from pagan times—a distant and distorted mem-ory of a former belief in forest gods like the Roman god Silvanus. Silvanus was a rather vaguely defined deity, who seems to have had power over all those lands which lay beyond the fringes of cultivation. He was not an evil god, but he was unpredictable and could be dan-gerous. Prudent farmers habitually made some sort of offering to Sil-vanus before felling trees to make a new field or otherwise making inroads in the wild god's domain.

A psychological theory holds that all of these creatures, Silvanus, the wild man, and the rest are really personifications of civilized man's yearning for freedom from the restraints of the society in which he lives.

Another theory about the origin of the wild-man legends is that they were inspired by contact with a real but unidentified hairy biped very like the Abominable Snowman, Bigfoot, etc. This creature may have once lived in Europe, or stories of it may have been brought to Europe by travelers from Asia. The thirteenth-century scholar Roger

Bacon wrote of the existence of a hairy wild man in the "high rocks" of Tibet and China. Bacon also described how the natives of Asia would capture these creatures by getting them drunk. This is reminiscent of an old Greek myth about capturing the hairy god Silenus by putting out a bowl of liquor for him. The god, a notorious drunkard, emptied the bowl, fell into a stupor, and was tied up before he was able to rouse himself.

A book of travel tales written in 1590 by the English adventurer Edward Webbe tells of seeing a hairy wild man in the East. This was a most ferocious creature that was chained to a post by its captors and could only be fed on human flesh, usually the corpses of executed criminals. Unfortunately, Webb said he saw this monster at the court of Prester John, an entirely mythical Christian king of the East.

European traditions concerning a wild woman are much more confused. She is described either as being very beautiful or very ugly, or both, because she possessed the magical ability to change her shape. The wild woman of European tradition is really more of a witch than anything else.

There is, however, one bit of wild-woman lore that connects up with more modern beliefs. In her ugly form, the wild woman was said to possess huge sagging breasts which she often slung over her shoulder for convenience while walking or running. This odd habit also comes up in connection with the behavior of the female Abominable Snowman.

See also: ABOMINABLE SNOWMAN, BIGFOOT, ALMA

2

LAND

MONSTERS

ACÁMBARO MONSTERS The pre-Columbian Indians of Central and South America were marvelous artists who depicted all manner of strange and wonderful creatures in their paintings, carvings, and particularly in their clay figurines and pottery. Most of the creatures represented are either fanciful representations of known animals or of creatures generally considered to be mythical. There is, however, one group of figures that has raised speculation that genuine unknown animals are being depicted.

A huge cache of clay figurines and pottery was found near Acámbaro, Mexico, in 1945. Among the thousands of items uncovered were many that appeared to be models of dinosaurlike creatures. There was nothing quite like them in other Indian art. The figures resemble in a rough way figures made by different pre-Columbian cultures, but they can not be assigned to any particular known culture.

Some claim that the Acámbaro monsters were made by an as yet unknown ancient civilization that had firsthand experience with dinosaurs. Most archaeologists have a quite different explanation. They say that the figures are fakes, of fairly recent vintage. Faking pre-Columbian pottery and figures is a major industry, and most of what unwary tourists buy as genuine pre-Columbian art are modern fakes.

Why the unknown faker—if that's who made these figures—chose so many dinosaurian shapes rather than more traditional Indian motifs can only be speculated on.

41

AMERICAN ELEPHANT   No one today seriously doubts that several species of elephant once roamed the Americas, and that elephants and human beings coexisted in the Western Hemisphere (though such ideas were highly controversial a century ago). And there is practically no monster buff no matter how enthusiastic and uncritical who believes that native American elephants are still roaming about today, with the possible exception of the woolly mammoth

Mammoth

in Alaska and the northern reaches of Canada. But between these two generally accepted conclusions there is a vast area of disagreement as to when the last American elephant gave up the ghost.

Conventional scientific opinion holds that both the mastodon and mammoth, which were once so common in America, died out in the great wave of extinctions that swept away the large mammals of the world at the end of the Pleistocene period or Ice Age. Unconventional scientific opinion suggests that the elephants survived until fairly recent times, probably becoming extinct sometime after the discovery of the New World by Europeans.

Evidence for later survival consists of a few Indian legends which might, or might not, relate to elephants, some travelers' tales recount the sighting of huge beasts with long noses, Indian mounds and their contents in North America, and Indian carvings in South America.

Throughout many parts of North America, Indians built ceremonial mounds, often in the shape of an animal or bird. One of these mounds in Wisconsin appears to resemble an elephant, yet the mound itself was built long after the Ice Age ended. Did the builders remember elephants from ages long past? Were they building a mound to resemble an animal they still knew? Or as many archaeologists believe, was this mound originally built in the shape of a bear, to which flooding or some other accident of nature added a trunklike extension on the front end?

Some artifacts in the shape of elephants have been found in Indian mounds, but it is widely suspected that these are faked. No piece of elephant ivory has ever been discovered in a mound.

In South America, a few Mayan drawings show what appear to be elephants, but the drawings of the Maya are too stylized to say with any degree of certainty that the animal depicted is an elephant. In one case, what looks like an elephant may in reality be a bird.

So, as far as the survival of the American elephant beyond the Ice Age, we have no tangible evidence. We have only rumors and shadows.

See also: WOOLLY MAMMOTH

BEAST OF LE GEVAUDAN   In mid-July, 1764, a young girl from the village of Saint Etienne de Lugdares in the rugged mountainous region of south-central France known as Le Gevaudan was found dead. Her heart had been torn out. This was the first recorded killing in a three-year reign of terror by a creature that came to be known as the Beast of Le Gevaudan. Within a few days there were several more killings of children reported.

As was customary in those days, the children had been left in charge of sheep and cattle grazing in isolated summer pastures high in the mountains. The killings spread panic among the peasants, who quickly gathered in their children and left their livestock to fend for itself.

A few weeks passed without any additional killings, and life began to quiet down and return to normal. Then, late in August, a peasant woman from the village of Langogne reported that she had seen a fantastic creature. It walked on two legs like a man, but it was covered with short reddish hair and had a piglike snout. It was big as a donkey and had rather short ears and a long tail. The woman said the creature had frightened off her dogs, but had itself been frightened by her cattle, which attacked it with lowered horns.

The description sounded so fantastic that even the most superstitious among the peasants laughed at it. They stopped laughing within a few days, however, when the monster was reported again. This time the witness was Jean-Pierre Pourcher, a man known for his courage and truthfulness. Pourcher fired at the creature with his musket, but either he missed or it was unaffected by the bullet.

And the murders of children began again. Many of the children who had been taken out of the isolated pastures after the first alarm had been allowed to return. Now some fell victim to a creature that killed and mutilated. Not surprisingly, rumors began to circulate that the region was afflicted by the *loup-garou*, the werewolf.

Even the king became alarmed by the events in Le Gevaudan, so he dispatched a company of soldiers to deal with the beast. The soldiers arrived in February of 1765, and almost immediately encountered the creature. They opened fire on it, but it ran off into the dense underbrush and could not be located. However, the killings ceased. The soldiers believed that they had mortally wounded the beast, and that it had hidden itself somewhere and died. They returned to the palace at Versailles and reported they had successfully accomplished their mission. But the terror wasn't over yet.

Beast of Le Gevaudan

As the weather warmed up and the children were again sent to the mountains to tend cattle and sheep, the murders began anew. Once again an appeal was sent to the King, but he seems to have lost interest in the problems of Le Gevaudan, and there was no response from the court until early the following year, 1766. A second military expedition set out, but this time instead of going directly to Le Gevaudan, the soldiers marched to a nearby area where another "great wolf" had been reported. They were successful in killing a large wolf, which they declared to be the "Beast of Le Gevaudan." They marched back to Versailles in triumph, and once again the king declared the emergency was over. And once again he was wrong.

The beast continued to stalk Le Gevaudan, and several villages were actually abandoned because of fear of the monster. Finally in June 1767, nearly three years after the depredations had begun, a local nobleman organized a huge party of hunters and declared that they would not rest until the monster really had been killed.

On June 19 the beast was surrounded in a patch of woods at Le Sogne d'Auvert. One of the hunters, Jean Chastel, had a gun loaded with silver bullets, and when he saw the beast he fired two shots—the second struck the monster in the heart and it fell dead.

The carcass was then carried from village to village as proof that the terrible monster finally was really dead. Unfortunately, the accounts are not clear as to just exactly what the thing looked like. Most descriptions make it sound like a very large but strange-looking wolf, with close-cropped ears and unusual hooflike feet.

In the warm June weather, the carcass began to putrefy, and it had to be buried. While no one seems to know where the remains of the monster were buried, tourists are still shown the spot where Jean Chastel is supposed to have felled it, and his gun can be seen at the church in Saint Martin-de-Bouchaux.

What was the Beast of Le Gevaudan? Today many believe that it really was just a large and exceptionally ferocious wolf, or perhaps several wolves whose killings were all attributed to a single creature by the panic-stricken peasants. The peasants are also thought to have exaggerated the extent and nature of the killings, attributing every death to the beast. One theory holds that there was an outbreak of rabies among the wolves of Le Gevaudan, and the disease is what caused them to behave in so vicious and uncharacteristic a manner. Others think the beast was a homicidal madman who never really was caught but died at about the same time Chastel shot the wolf. But there are those who contend that the Beast of Le Gevaudan was exactly what the peasants thought it to be, the *loup-garou*—the werewolf. In any event, this is among the most intriguing and well documented of all werewolf accounts.

See also: WEREWOLF

BEAST OF TRURO   In the fall of 1981, the people of Cape Cod, Massachusetts, began to suspect they might have a monster in their midst. The first evidence that there was some sort of unknown creature roaming the Cape came in September 1981, when several mangled cats were found in the vicinity of the town of Truro. Over the next few months, the mysterious killing or mauling of other domestic animals was reported.

At first the attacks were attributed to dogs or packs of dogs which run wild and are known to attack deer. But then people began seeing something that obviously was not a dog, and there were reports of strange noises heard during the night.

The most complete description of the Beast of Truro was given by William and Marsha Mendeiros of Truro, who said that they saw it on the beach, about fifty feet from where they stood.

"It had a very definite long ropelike tail like the letter J. It hit the ground and went up. We figured it was about as tall as up to our knees and weighed 60 or 80 pounds.

"We were frightened and froze. He was in the path and didn't see us at first. As we made some noise he turned and we saw his face with short ears."

The creature made no attempt to attack or run, but just sauntered easily into the nearby woods and was lost among the trees.

One theory is that the beast is an American mountain lion, also called a cougar or panther. There are no mountains on Cape Cod, much less mountain lions, for it is believed that the eastern mountain lion is extinct, and has been for a long time. But if one survived, somehow it might be able to hide itself in the undeveloped national seashore area near Truro. Others think that the beast is a mountain lion but not a wild one; rather it is someone's escaped pet—for mountain lions sometimes are sold and kept as pets. So are ocelots, a smaller wildcat, which has also been mentioned as a candidate for the beast.

And there are still others who believe that the beast of Truro is not a mountain lion, ocelot, wild dog, or any other known animal—that it is something else, something unknown.

See also: PHANTOM LIONS

BEHEMOTH   In the Book of Job (40:15–24) there is a description of a creature called behemoth:

"Behold now behemoth, which I am made with thee; he eateth grass as an ox.

"Lo now, his strength is in the loins, and his force is in the navel of his belly.

"He moveth his tail like a cedar; the sinews of his stones are wrapped together.

"His bones are as strong pieces of brass; his bones are like bars of iron. . . .

"Behold, he drinketh up a river, and hasteth not; he trusteth that he can draw up Jordan into his mouth."

Most scholars believe that the animal called behemoth in the Bible is a hippopotamus. However, in apocryphal literature and Jewish legend behemoth became a monster of formidable strength. Behemoth was often linked in legend with another unknown creature, which is described in the very next chapter of Job.

In the apocryphal Book of Enoch, the two creatures are described as follows: "And in that day will two monsters be separated, a female named Leviathan to dwell in the abyss over the fountains of waters. But the male is called Behemoth which occupies with his breasts an immeasurable desert named Dendain." In other legends the two are deadly enemies who battle at the beginning of time and must be destroyed by the Lord before they destroy his creation. In still other versions of these legends, the battle between the two monsters takes place on the Day of Judgment. In the Middle Ages, behemoth became the name for a demon.

Traditionally, however, any large, heavy, and otherwise unknown animal might be identified as behemoth. The notorious American fossil faker "Dr." Albert Koch put together an enormous skeleton, mainly out of mastodon bones, and sold it to Frederick William IV of Prussia as behemoth of the Bible. Other nineteenth-century showmen exhibited mammoth and mastodon skeletons (often outrageously reconstructed) as behemoth. Sometimes a traveling animal show would exhibit a hippopotomus as behemoth. That identification was probably a correct one, but the showmen didn't know it, or didn't care.

Frozen mammoths found in Siberia were often first identified as behemoth, simply because the Russians who found them had never seen a mammoth, or any other kind of elephant before. They didn't know what else to call the large, heavy, unknown thing in the ice.

See also: LEVIATHAN

BUNYIP   "Why search for the bunyip?"

That is an Australian expression which means roughly, Why try to do the impossible? Originally the word *bunyip* stood for some sort of god, spirit, or demon in the language of the Australian aborigines. The early white settlers in Australia took the word *bunyip* to mean something unseen, unknown, and inexplicable. Therefore whenever they ran across some animal that they could not classify, there was a tendency to call it a bunyip. There are a tremendous number of bunyip stories from Australia, some apparently refer to known animals, others to animals that are purely mythical. Most interesting are a large percentage of these stories that cluster about an animal of whose existence we are currently unsure.

In June 1801, a party of French explorers were traveling along the bank of the Swan River, above what is now the city of Perth. They heard a horrible roar coming from a bed of reeds in the river, and not knowing what they might find, they fled. That was the first story to connect the bunyip with an unknown lake or river animal.

Explorer Hamilton Hume actually saw something in Lake Bathurst. He said it looked like either a manatee or a hippopotamus. Other accounts of a similar-looking freshwater animal began to filter in from lakes and rivers in other parts of Australia. Yet a generous reward offered for the skin or skull of the unknown animal went uncollected. A supposed bunyip skull was determined by one naturalist to be that of a colt and by another to belong to a calf. What it really was we shall never know, for it has long since disappeared from the Australian museum where it was presumably taken for safekeeping. Reported native drawings of the bunyip have also vanished.

By the middle of the nineteenth century, searching for the bunyip had become a popular Australian pastime, though most of the searchers never really expected to find it and probably didn't even believe in it. The name continued to be troublesome, for as it meant "devil" or "spirit," every sort of strange and unexplained event or sighting was attributed to the bunyip, thus confusing the issue.

Yet at the core of all of this confusion there is a body of evidence which describes a quite ordinary, even mundane sort of animal. Australian scientist Gilbert P. Whitley concluded that "apart from the most extravagant fabrications, we must be struck with the comparative uniformity of bunyip descriptions over a long period." These descriptions are of a fur-covered animal, around the size of a large dog or a bit larger, with a doglike face and head. It has fins for swimming and lives in rivers, marshes, and inland lakes.

The known animal most closely fitting the bunyip descriptions is the seal, and the seal, perhaps of some unknown variety, is an excellent candidate for the origin of the bunyip legends. Seals have been known to make their way up rivers and fairly far inland. The sight of a seal in a lake would certainly startle anyone who was not expecting it.

But many of the bunyip stories come from places where access to the sea would be improbable. This brings up the suggestion that the bunyip is some kind of freshwater seal, not an impossibility, for there are freshwater seals in parts of Asia, and in Canada there are isolated colonies of the common seal in some freshwater lakes.

Seals abound in the waters off Australia, but inland the dominant animals are all marsupials, at least they were until the coming of man. This has led some to speculate that the bunyip is an otterlike or seallike marsupial.

Bunyip sightings began to decline by the end of the nineteenth century, and in the twentieth, reliable reports are almost nonexistent. This has led some to the sad conclusion that the bunyip, if it ever existed, is now extinct.

See also: WAITOREKE

B**URU**   Rumors of the existence of a lizardlike monster called the buru, in a "lost valley" somewhere in the Himalayas, first began to reach the West during the 1940s. One of the earliest reports came from Professor Christopher von Furer-Haimendorf, an anthopologist who had worked extensively among the tribes of the mountainous regions of northern India. In 1947 Professor von Furer-Haimendorf wrote of his visit to an isolated and virtually unknown valley inhabited by a people called the Apu Tanis. Although located on a high mountain plateau, the twenty-square-mile valley was swampy and thickly forested.

Von Furer-Haimendorf's original article on the "lost valley" contained only a sentence which referred to the possibility of an unknown monster: "The bottom of the valley—according to local tradition [was] once a marshy swamp inhabited by lizardlike monsters. . . ."

A somewhat later visitor to the valley of the Apu Tanis, one Charles Stonor, gave a fuller description of the "monsters." Stonor, who visited the valley in the company of an official of the Indian government, had also heard rumors of monsters. When he asked the people about the rumors, he was told that they were perfectly true, the valley had been inhabited by lizardlike monsters, but that the monsters had all been killed off in the fairly recent past.

According to the Apu Tanis, when their ancestors had first come to the valley much of it had been a great swampy lake. The lake was inhabited by large aquatic animals, the likes of which they had never seen before, and to which they gave the name buru. From the descriptions, the buru was clearly some sort of reptile, about fifteen

Buru

feet long, including its neck and tail. The body was rather broad. Stonor quoted his informants as saying, "A man could just put his arms
around [it]." The head was roughly triangular in shape, and the creature displayed a forked tongue much like that of a snake. Its teeth
were generally flat, except four sharp fanglike teeth, two in the upper
and two in the lower jaw. The stumpy legs ended in heavily clawed
feet. Perhaps the creature's most impressive feature was its long and
powerful tail. According to the Apu Tanis, the buru did "everything
with its tail." The skin was "fishlike," except for what appeared to be
a row of armored plates along the tail, and its color was a mottled
blue black above and whitish below. The creature did not lay eggs
like most reptiles: the young were born alive in the water.

The buru was a plant eater, and not considered dangerous to
human beings, despite its size and strength. There was, however, one
story about a hunter who had speared a young buru and then was

attacked by its mother, who coiled her tail around his legs and pulled him to his death in the water.

Generally the buru kept out of the way of human beings. Even those who lived by the lake rarely saw the creature, for it spent most of its time in the deeper water. During the summer months, burus occasionally crawled out of the lake to sun themselves on the shore. When they appeared on the surface, they occasionally let out a bellowing call, which may have accounted for their name. In the colder months, they disappeared into the mud on the lake bottom.

At first the buru and the new human inhabitants of the valley had little to do with one another. But as the human population grew, more and more land was needed for growing rice, so gradually the swampy lake was drained for planting, and the buru's habitat was reduced to some of the deeper pools in the lake. The creatures had become a nuisance, so the final burus in the valley were trapped in five of these pools, where they were destroyed by hurling stones and rocks onto them; the holes were then filled in, burying the remains.

Stonor's informants told him that the buru was now extinct, and they pointed out the exact spots at which the last of these creatures had been killed and where their remains presumably lay. All this had taken place many generations ago, but just exactly when the burus had become extinct was not entirely clear.

This then was the story told by Charles Stonor, and it is not an implausible one. A fifteen-foot lizard is no dinosaur in size, indeed, there is one nearly as large known to be alive today. It is the Komodo dragon. The Komodo dragon lives only on four tiny and remote islands in Indonesia. Though it is quite a spectacular and fierce creature, its existence was not definitely established until 1910, although rumors of the creature had been circulating for many years. If one great lizard could remain hidden on remote islands, why couldn't the buru have been hidden in a remote valley in the Himalayas? Further expeditions into the valley, however, have failed to turn up any concrete evidence of the existence of the buru. J. P. Mills, one of those who visited the area, was also shown the four sites at which the last of the burus were said to have been killed and buried. He noted that the Apu Tanis told him they never dug in any of these sites—so that the remains, if any, must still be there.

In 1948 a couple of London newspapermen led an expedition to find evidence of the buru. They were going to the valley of the Apu Tanis when they heard an even more intriguing rumor: that the buru, while extinct in that valley, still lived on in a nearby valley known as Rilo. Thus distracted, the expedition made for the second valley, but the end result was disappointment. No living buru was found, nor did the searchers come up with any concrete evidence that the buru had ever existed in the valley of the Rilo. The natives of the area continued to insist that burus lived in the swamp, but that the searchers had come at the wrong time of year, for this was the season when the creatures were inactive, and thus very hard to find. The members of the expedition, however, concluded that the creatures no longer lived in the valley, and perhaps never had. The failure of the expedition at the valley of the Rilo does not destroy the case for the existence or the recent extinction of the buru in the valley of the Apu Tanis, and possibly other nearby valleys as well.

American cryptozoologist Dr. Roy Mackal, who has examined the evidence, concludes, "Taken all together, the reports suggest that a large unidentified species of aquatic lizard lived or lives in the swampy lake regions of the outer Himalayas of Assam."

DE LOYS'S APE   While there are a great variety of monkeys throughout South America, it has been universally believed among zoologists that there were no apes of any sort in the Western Hemisphere. Therefore it was with considerable surprise, and not a small amount of skepticism, that scientists received the story told by a Swiss geologist François de Loys about an encounter that had taken place during an expedition into the forests on the borders of Colombia and Venezuela.

In 1920 de Loys and his little party had been in the jungle for nearly three years. They were ill with fever, exhausted, short of supplies, and anxious to get back to civilization, when they had an unforgettable experience. To their complete surprise, they came upon two apes walking through the jungle. The apes were angry and advanced in a threatening manner. De Loys and his companions shot one of the pair (the female) and the other fled. The dead animal's skull was taken, but unfortunately it disintegrated, and the pieces were lost during the expedition's return.

So far, a fairly typical story. Strange animal encountered in a remote jungle. Evidence unfortunately, or perhaps conveniently, lost before it can be examined by outside authorities, and so all rests on unsupported testimony. And so the controversy is never resolved.

But the story of de Loys's ape has a different twist. After shooting the creature, de Loys had it set up on a crate, its chin propped up by a forked stick, and he took a picture of it. Unlike so many similar stories, the camera was not washed overboard when the boat was swamped, the film was not fogged, the creature was not too far away—indeed, the picture is a remarkably good one. End of controversy? Unfortunately, no.

The story and the picture were given to Dr. George Montandon, who published a scientific paper on the creature in May of 1929. Dr. Montandon declared that a new species of ape had been found and named it *Ameranthropoides loysi*, "Loys's American anthropoid," after its discoverer. In Dr. Montandon's view, de Loys's evidence showed that, contrary to what everyone believed, anthropoid apes had developed in the Western Hemisphere, and at least one species still survived.

Most scientists are more cautious, however, than Dr. Montandon, and it takes more than a story and a single photograph to convince them of the existence of a new species, particularly one as remarkable as the American ape. In the very same publication in which Dr. Montandon endorses de Loys's ape, Professor L. Joleaud suggests that the creature looks extraordinarily like a heavyset spider monkey. The spider monkey is a common inhabitant of the jungles of South America. And about this point a controversy has, if not raged, at least bubbled ever since.

The most obvious difference between an ape and a spider monkey is that the spider monkey has an enormous prehensile tail, and an ape has no tail at all. Unfortunately, de Loys's ape in the photograph is placed in such a way that you couldn't see the tail even if it had one. If the creature was a spider monkey, de Loys was not guilty merely of making an error, but of attempting to commit a deliberate fraud, by hiding the tail.

Another difference would be size. A large spider monkey stood upright is just over three and a half feet tall. De Loys estimates that his creature was just under five feet. On this crucial point, the picture is not very helpful, for there is nothing in it against which one can accurately estimate size. Even the size of the crate upon which the creature is sitting is a matter of dispute.

And so there the case must rest. No further evidence has turned up since de Loys's photo. *Ameranthropoides loysi* is either the only unknown animal for which we possess a good photograph, or it is an exceptionally audacious fake.

DRAGON OF THE ISHTAR GATE   In 1902 a German professor, Robert Koldeway, was conducting excavations at the ancient city of Babylon, when he uncovered an enormous semicircular arch flanked by massive walls. It was the famous Ishtar Gate, known from legend but now seen for the first time in centuries. The reliefs on the gate were dominated by the representation of two types of animals. One, whose name was translated as Re'em, is a bull-like creature identified with a now extinct form of wild cattle, the urus. The model for the other creature, called the sirrush, has proved to be far more difficult to identify.

The sirrush is an odd-looking creature—long, scaly body and tail and long, graceful scaly neck with a small snakelike head, and a very prominent forked tongue. The head possesses a large horn and, most out of place, what appear to be ringlets or curls. But it is the feet of

Dragon of the Ishtar Gate

the creature that are really remarkable. The front feet resemble those of a cat, while the back feet are distinctly birdlike.

It would have been easy to dismiss the sirrush as another example of mythological imagination, like the sphinx or the winged bulls, but Koldeway didn't do that. At the time he made his discovery, there were other very important discoveries being made in another scientific field—paleontology—for it was a time of great discovery of dinosaur fossils. The world had really gone a little dinosaur crazy.

"If only the forelegs were not so emphatically and characteristically feline," Koldeway mused, "such an animal might actually have existed."

After some years of brooding over the subject, Koldeway decided that such an animal had existed, and he identified it with the iguanodon, at the time the best known of the dinosaurs. In fact, the sirrush does not look the least like the iguanodon, and Koldeway's identification appears to have been based on an early and incorrect reconstruction of the iguanodon as a four-legged creature. It actually walked about on large strong back legs like the tyrannosaurus.

About thirty years later, the story was picked up by Willy Ley, a

German-born science writer who became one of the most popular and influential writers on science of his day.

Ley traced the history of the sirrush, the creature he called the Dragon of the Ishtar Gate, in Babylonian art, and found it to be a common feature for thousands of years. He pointed out that the combination of a reptilelike body and birdlike feet did exist in dinosaurs; this, said Ley gave the sirrush "uncanny biological credibility."

Ley then went on to review the rumors of the possible survival of a dinosaurlike creature in central Africa, and speculates that it is possible that the Babylonians had heard of such a creature, and perhaps even seen one. Professor Koldeway had stressed that the Bible spoke of a dragonlike animal in Babylon that Daniel is said to have killed by giving it a pill made of bitumen and hair. Did the ancient Babylonians have in captivity one of the last living dinosaurs?

Paleontologists have been unimpressed by this argument, as they have been unimpressed by most arguments about dinosaurian survival, and Ley himself never claimed to have proof of the survival of dinosaurs, or of the existence of any creature that could have inspired the sirrush. But he does conclude, "It merely points to the existence of a zoological puzzle of fantastic dimensions; but as for conclusions we have to repeat that we do not know yet."

See also: DRAGON, MOKÉLE-MBÊMBE

GIANT ANACONDA   How large can a snake grow? Listen to this account.

"We were drifting easily along on the sluggish current not far below the confluence of the Rio Negro when almost under the bow of the [boat] there appeared a triangular head and several feet of undulating body. It was a giant anaconda. I sprang for my rifle as the creature began to make its way up the bank, and hardly waiting to aim smashed a .44 soft-nosed bullet into its spine, ten feet below the wicked head. At once there was a flurry of foam, and several heavy thumps against the boat's keel, shaking us as though we had run on a snag. . . .

"We stepped ashore and approached the reptile with caution. It was out of action, but shivers ran up and down the body like puffs of wind on a mountain tarn. As far as it was possible to measure, a length of forty-five feet lay out of the water, and seventeen feet in it, making a total length of sixty-two feet. Its body was not thick for such a colossal length—not more than twelve inches in diameter—but it probably had been without food. I tried to cut a piece of the skin, but the beast was by no means dead, the sudden upheavals rather scared us. A penetrating, foetid odour emanated from the snake, probably its breath, which is believed to have a stupefying effect, first attracting and later paralyzing its prey. Everything about this snake is repulsive.

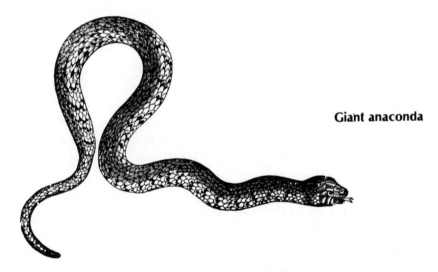

Giant anaconda

"Such large specimens as this may not be common, but the trails in the swamps reach a width of six feet and support the statements of Indians and rubber pickers that the anaconda sometimes reaches an incredible size, altogether dwarfing that shot by me. The Brazilian Boundary Commission told me of one exceeding *eighty* feet in length! In the Araguay and Tocantins basins there is a black variety known as the Dormidera, or 'Sleeper,' from the loud snoring noise it makes.

It is reputed to reach a huge size but I never saw one. These reptiles live principally in the swamps, for unlike the rivers, which often become mere ditches of mud in the dry season, the swamps always remain. To venture into the haunts of the anaconda is to flirt with death."

That account was written by Colonel Percy H. Fawcett, formerly of the Royal Artillery of the British Army. Colonel Fawcett was an experienced surveyor, and during the early years of the current century he spent nearly twenty years doing boundary survey work in South America, particularly in Bolivia and Brazil. Fawcett was more than a surveyor and explorer, he was a romantic and an adventurer. He disappeared in Brazil's Amazon Jungle in 1925 while searching for a "lost civilization" that he was convinced existed somewhere in that unmapped region. An aura of mystery still hangs over his disappearance.

So Colonel Fawcett was a romantic adventurer. Was he also a liar? When Fawcett's report was first published in England, a lot of people, particularly zoologists, thought he was. It is true that Fawcett occasionally reported seeing animals that no one else had ever seen, a large, toothless freshwater shark, for example. But then Fawcett had been places where few if any other Europeans had ever been. The zoologists had a point, however, for while the anaconda may be the longest snake in the world, the longest known anaconda is only 33 feet, and there is a reliable report that a 37½-foot specimen was killed in eastern Columbia, the longest snake ever, according to the *Guinness Book of World Records*. It is quite conceivable that an occasional anaconda might grow even larger, but not 62 feet, or 80 feet, as Fawcett thought possible. That was just too great a jump in size for zoologists to swallow without seeing the snake itself. Fawcett's 62-foot specimen can not be discounted as a mere observational error, for while he didn't actually measure the snake, he was close enough to get an accurate estimate of its length, something that, as a surveyor, he should have been able to do fairly well. Either the anaconda grows nearly twice as long as most zoologists think possible, or Colonel Fawcett was a liar.

However, Fawcett was not the only South American traveler to report the existence of a monstrous anaconda. Cryptozoologist Bernard Heuvelmans tells of his conversation with one Serge Bonacase, a Frenchman who had been in Brazil in 1947. Bonacase said that while he was traveling with a group of Frenchmen and Brazilians, the party spotted an anaconda asleep in the grass. They shot at it and killed it, but only after it was dead, and they were able to get close to it, did they have any idea of the size of the monster. "When we walked along the whole length of its body it seemed as if it would never end," said Bonacase.

The party didn't have any measuring equipment, but using a piece of string they roughly estimated the snake to be between seventy-two and seventy-five feet in length. The triangular head itself was some two feet long, and had an eighteen-inch base.

Unfortunately, no one in the group had a camera at the time, and no one thought to bring back the skull or skin of the monster to prove the veracity of the tale. Why not?

Said Bonacase, "The Brazilian officials who had spent much of their lives in this country did not seem particularly surprised. As for me, I had heard so many tales of giant snakes that I supposed the whole of the Amazon was crawling with monsters of this size."

A seventy-five-foot snake, it seems, was just too commonplace to bother with.

In his book *The Leviathans,* Tim Dinsdale reports seeing an article from a 1949 Brazilian newspaper which tells of the capture and killing of an anaconda that was at least 131 feet long and weighed five tons.

Dinsdale also examined two newspaper photographs of this giant anaconda, and while he believed the photographs are genuine, he admits that they are too poor in quality, and of too uncertain an origin, to constitute definitive proof of the existence of the fabled giant anaconda.

See also: GIANT BOA

GIANT SLOTH   Ramon Lista, explorer, geographer, adventurer, and for a time governor of Santa Cruz in Argentina (which turned out to be the most dangerous pursuit of all, for he was assassinated by political opponents), had a lot of strange experiences in his life. But none was stranger than his encounter with an unknown beast of gigantic proportions in the region of his country called Patagonia.

One night, Lista said, he and his companions saw at close range an animal that looked like a gigantic armadillo, covered with long hair. It lumbered off at considerable speed, while Lista and the others shot at it with their hunting rifles. Lista thought they had actually hit the beast several times, but that somehow it seemed impervious to their bullets. This encounter was supposed to have taken place sometime during the 1890s.

The story inevitably reached the ears of Professor Florentino Ameghino, a paleontologist and Argentina's greatest expert on fossils. Ameghino was known for his enthusiasm, and his imagination, but even he found it difficult to credit Lista's story. Lista had told some fairly wild tales in the past, and his word was not necessarily to be trusted. Yet Professor Ameghino could not discount the tale either, for it seemed to reinforce some other bits and pieces of information that he had been collecting about a gigantic unknown creature in Patagonia. There were, for example, Indian traditions about a nocturnal animal the size of an ox that lived in the pampas, sleeping during the day in burrows it dug with its large claws. The Indians considered the animal harmless, but when they tried to kill it they found that their arrows would not penetrate its skin.

The animal of the Indian tradition and the one Lista said he saw sounded identical, and both of them sounded very much like the giant sloth. The giant sloth, or rather a whole tribe of giant ground sloths ranging from the elephant-sized *Megatherium* to creatures just a few feet tall, had flourished in South America until about ten thousand years ago. Then, along with a majority of other large mammals throughout the world, they disappeared in the wave of extinctions that occurred at the end of the Pleistocene period or Ice Age. What caused these massive extinctions of large mammals is still a matter of dispute today, and it probably always will be. The only surviving descendants of these giant sloths are the tree sloths, small, sleepy creatures that spend much of their existence hanging upside down from the limb of a tree.

There was evidence that the ancestors of the modern Indians of South American had hunted ground sloths. Was it possible that the Indian legends really originated in memories of those ancient times, and that Lista was just making up whoppers based on what the Indians had told him? Possible, more than possible. But the stories might also be true, for Ameghino held in his hand a piece of hide that had come from a medium-sized sloth known as a *Mylodon* and the hide seemed remarkably fresh. The hide of the sloth was studded with small, hard calcium nodules, which made it extremely tough and difficult to penetrate. This, in addition to the creature's long hair, would have rendered it nearly impervious to the fangs and claws of Pleistocene predators, or to Indian arrows or Ramon Lista's bullets. Ameghino named the creature *Neomylodon listai* ("Lista's new *Mylodon*") in honor of the man who had been ridiculed for his story about seeing the unknown animal.

Giant sloth

The "fresh" piece of hide had come from a ranch in far southern Argentina near a place called Last Hope Inlet. The rancher, a German immigrant named Eberhardt, had discovered the skin in a cave on his property in 1895.

Repeated expeditions to Eberhardt's cave brought forth some fairly spectacular finds, including another "fresh" piece of hide that had been cut and rolled up. There was other evidence that man, as well as *Mylodon*, had lived in the cave. Indeed, one scientist thought the remains in the cave showed that *Mylodons* had been stabled there, like domestic animals. He pointed to the remains of a wall he thought was used to keep the sloths in the cave. He even gave the animal a new scientific name, *Grypotherium domesticum* ("domesticated griffin animal"). However, others have disagreed with this interpretation. *Mylodon* and man, they said, may have lived in the same cave, but at different times.

Several other presumably fresh pieces of hide were found in other caves in southern Argentina. At the time there was no way of determining the age of the hide. After the Carbon-14 dating process was developed, the *Mylodon* dung in Eberhardt's cave was tested—all of it turned out to be ten thousand years old, or older, well within the conventional date set for the extinction of the giant sloth. What about the fresh pieces of *Mylodon* hide? The conditions within the caves may have allowed them to retain their fresh appearance for thousands of years. Or possibly they were brought from a place where the sloth survived to a later date. According to one estimate the hide was 5,000 years old.

In any event, no further evidence of a surviving giant sloth has been found in this century, and so what once appeared to be one of the most promising cases of an "extinct" animal turning up alive may end with the conclusion that the creature really is extinct after all.

See also: IEMISCH, SU

I EMISCH   Professor Florentino Ameghino was a great promoter of the theory that the giant sloth survives or did survive into fairly recent times in the southern part of his native Argentina. So when he heard of the iemisch, a monster much feared by the Tehuelche Indians, he unhesitatingly identified it as a giant sloth—which only shows how far astray one can be led by enthusiasm.

Here is a description of the iemisch (or *hymché* as it is spelled in this account) written in 1900 by a French traveler named André Tournouer who was on an expedition in Argentina:

"Lying in wait one evening on the bank of a river in the interior, beside which I had pitched my camp, I saw emerge in the middle of the stream the head of an animal the size of a large puma. I fired, the animal dived and did not reappear.

"As far as I could see in the dusk, its round head had dark brown fur, its eyes were encircled with light yellow hair, stretched in a thin line to the ear hole. There was no external ear.

"I described it to the Indian who acted as my guide; he seemed very frightened and assured me I had seen the mysterious hymché."

In other accounts, the iemisch is described as attacking people and carrying its victims off into the water. Its fierceness earned it the title "water tiger." This sort of activity is unlikely to be found in a slow-moving, plant-eating ground dweller like the giant sloth. But such was Ameghino's stature, that for years his identification has confused the issue of what the iemisch might really be.

Others have more plausibly suggested that the iemisch is some sort of unknown feline. Dr. Robert Lehmann-Nitsche, an anthropologist from the Natural History Museum of La Plata, studied the iemisch tradition and concluded that there really was no such animal, but that the stories arose as the result of a confusion between a jaguar, which can be quite ferocious and is also unafraid of water, and the otter, which is not ferocious but is fully aquatic.

Bernard Heuvelmans sees much merit in Lehmann-Nitsche's theory, but also suggests the possibility that there might exist some sort of unknown giant otter. Dr. Roy Mackal is even more enthusiastic about the giant-otter theory.

"Now my suggestion as to the nature of the iemisch is that it is a rare large, ferocious species or subspecies of otter. . . . Its range is restricted and may still be shrinking."

See also: GIANT SLOTH

MINHOCAO   During the late nineteenth century, scientific journals in Europe printed a number of reports about the Minhocao, or gigantic earthworm, that was supposed to live in some of the highlands of South America.

An article in the February 21, 1878, issue of the prestigious British publication *Nature* stated: "The stories told of this supposed animal, says Fritz Muller [a German who lived in Brazil and supplied the information], sound for the most part so incredible that one is tempted to consider them as fabulous. Who could repress a smile at hearing men speak of a worm some fifty yards in length and five in breadth, covered with bones as with a coat of armour, uprooting mighty pine trees as if they were blades of grass, diverting the courses of streams into fresh channels, and turning the dry land into a bottomless morass?"

Yet the correspondent for *Nature* was not entirely skeptical of these tales. " . . . After carefully considering the different accounts given of the 'Minhocao' one can hardly refuse to believe that some such animal does really exist, although not quite so large as the country folk would have us believe."

Most of those who believed in the existence of the Minhocao had never actually seen it; they drew their belief from what they took to be the underground burrowings of the creature.

"About fourteen years ago," said the *Nature* article, "in the month of January, Antonio Jose Branco, having been absent with his family eight days from his house . . . on returning home found the road undermined, heaps of earth being thrown up, and large trenches made. These trenches commenced at the source of a brook, and followed its windings; terminating ultimately after a course of from 700 to 1,000 metres. The breadth of the trenches was said to be about three metres. Since that period the brook has flowed in the trench made by the Minhocao. Paths of the animal lay generally beneath the surface of the stream; several pine trees had been rooted up by its passage. One of the trees from which the Minhocao in passing had torn off the bark and part of the wood, was said to be still standing and visible last year. Hundreds of people from Curtibanos and other places had come to see the devastation caused by the Minhocao, and supposed the animal to be still living in the marshy pool, the waters of which appeared at times to be suddenly and strangely troubled. Indeed on still nights a rumbling sound like distant thunder and a slight movement of the earth was sensible in the neighboring dwellings."

While tradition held that the Minhocao was a gigantic worm or some kind of snake, the anonymous author of the *Nature* article had an intriguing alternate suggestion. He thought that the creature might in reality be some kind of gigantic armadillo. The author pointed out that at least one known species of armadillo was almost entirely subterranean, and that armadillos of enormous size were once common in South America. He even went so far as to ask, "if the suggestion be not too bold, even a last descendant of the Glyptodonts?" The glyptodont was an elaborately armored giant armadillo that was once common in South America but died at the end of the Pleistocene era, along with many other large mammals throughout the world.

See also: GIANT SLOTH

MNGWA   The most feared and mysterious animal in central Africa may be the *mngwa*, a name which translates roughly as "the strange one." Stories about the beast are vague. It is supposed to have a rather catlike appearance and the ability and desire to tear to pieces any human being unlucky enough to meet it in the jungle. *Mngwa* figures in a number of Swahili songs and tales, usually about a fearless warrior who sallys forth to slay one of the monsters.

Europeans who heard *mngwa* stories tended to regard the creature as sort of an African dragon—an entirely mythical animal. But in the 1920s there were a series of killings in some of the fishing villages on the coast of Tanganyika which led some to wonder if the *mngwa* was more than a legend.

The victims in the killings were usually horribly mutilated, and they were often found clutching grayish hairs that had been pulled from some unidentified animal—clearly the animal that had killed them. The beast's *modus operandi* was quite unlike that of known carnivores, and local natives insisted that the culprit was *mngwa*. All attempts to capture the killer animal were in vain.

See also: NANDI BEAR

MOKÉLE-MBÊMBE   The idea that there is some sort of dinosaur surviving in the swamps of central Africa has been around for over a century. Nineteenth-century travelers in Africa brought back a confusing collection of stories of unknown reptilelike creatures of enormous size. There were a variety of descriptions and a tongue-twisting proliferation of names. But as Africa was explored, and no tangible evidence of this creature (or creatures) was produced, interest began to fade. However, due primarily to the efforts of crypto-zoologist Dr. Roy Mackal, there has been a rebirth of interest in the central African dinosaur during the 1980s, making it one of the most eagerly sought and well-publicized monsters of the era.

An early and popular account of a dinosaurlike creature came from the tales of Alfred Aloysius Horn, or "Trader Horn," a late Victorian traveler, adventurer, and storyteller:

"Aye, and behind the Cameroons there's things living we know nothing about. I could 'a made books about many things. The Jago-

Nini they say is still in the swamps and rivers. Giant diver it means. Comes out of the water and devours people. Old men'll tell you what their grandfathers saw, but they still believe it's there."

Horn had never seen the thing himself, but he thought it must be the same as the creature called the Amali. He had never seen that either, but he had seen its footprint, "about the size of a good frying-pan in circumference and three claws instead o' five."

Trader Horn not only repeated legends, he exaggerated them in order to make a better story; but still at least come of his tales had a bit of truth behind them.

C. W. Hobley, an early twentieth-century crytozoologist, collected stories of an African creature called the *dingonek*. At first he thought them to be mere travelers' tales, but then he met a man that he considered to be a reliable witness: "He emphatically asserts that he saw this beast. He was at the time about where the Mara River crosses the frontier, and the river was in high flood. The beast came floating down the river on a big log, and he estimated its length at about sixteen feet but would not be certain of the length as its tail was in the water. He describes it as spotted like a leopard, covered with scales, and having a head like an otter. . . ." Hobley found that Masai tribesmen in the region knew of the beast, but they called it *Ol-umaina*.

Hobley suggested the thing might be a dinosaur and added: "A survival of some extinct race of saurians is a thing to thrill the imagination of the scientific world."

Carl Hagenbeck, a well-known collector of African animals, also collected tales of a beast called the *chipekwe*, though he didn't see it himself:

"From what I have heard of the animal, it seems to me that it can only be some kind of dinosaur, seemingly akin to the brontosaurus. As the stories come from so many different sources, and all tend to substantiate each other, I am convinced that some such reptile must be still in existence."

Hagenbeck even financed an expedition to find the *chipekwe*, but the expedition was a failure. "In the part of Africa where the animal is said to exist, there are enormous swamps, hundreds of square miles in extent, and my travellers were laid with very severe attacks of fever."

Another traveler, John G. Millais, reported an experience attributed the late King Lewanika of the Barotse Empire. The king "frequently heard from his people of some great aquatic reptile, possessing a body larger than that of an elephant, and which lived in the great swamps near his town." The king gave orders that the next time the monster was seen he should be informed at once so that he could go and see for himself.

About a year later the king was told that the monster had crawled out of the water of a nearby lake. "The beast was said to be of colossal size, with legs like a gigantic lizard, and possessing a long neck. It was also said to be taller than a man, and had a head like a snake."

The king immediately rode to the spot, but the monster was already gone; however, as it had dragged itself through the reeds, it had flattened a path about four and a half feet wide.

In 1932 a Swiss zoologist named A. Monard tried to track down rumors of a huge reptilian monster in Angola. He didn't find what he was looking for, but he was still convinced that "the existence of a large saurian descended from the reptiles of the Mesozoic era is by no means theoretically impossible."

That same year the British-born cryptozoologist Ivan Sanderson was also traveling in Africa. He had come across "vast hippo-like tracks" in a region where there were no hippos, for they were said to have been driven out by a creature whose name he gives as *mbulu-eM'bembe*. A few months later he was paddling down a river when he heard terrific noises coming from the caves on the river's bank, "and *something* (and it was the top of a head [I] feel sure) much larger than a hippo rose up out of the water for a moment, set up a large wave and then gurgled under."

Of all the available accounts of a central-African dinosaur, the one that Dr. Roy Mackal found most impressive was one written by Captain Freiheer von Stein zu Lausnitz, leader of a German expedition to the Congo just prior to World War I. Von Stein had only heard of the creatures:

"The animal is said to be brownish gray with a smooth skin, its size approximately that of an elephant, at least that of a hippopotamus. It is said to have a long and very flexible neck and only one tooth, but a very long one—some say it is a horn. A few spoke about a long muscular tail like that of an alligator. . . . It lives in the caves that have been washed out by the river in the clay of its shores sharp bends. It is said to climb the shore even in the daytime in search of food; its diet is . . . entirely vegetable. . . ."

Von Stein called the creature *mokéle-mbêmbe*, and it lived in the region which Mackal later chose to investigate.

But between the early traveler's tales and the modern investigation, there were a number of notable hoaxes, which tended to bring ridicule on the whole subject of a central-African dinosaur. The most elaborate hoax was one which began in 1919. It started with stories appearing in London newspapers about an "extraordinary monster" raging through the swamps and villages of central Africa. For some reason the thing was called a brontosaurus, though the descriptions of the monster with horns, tusks, and cloven hoofs did not sound the least bit brontosauruslike. There was a story that the Smithsonian Institution had sent an expedition to capture the beast, but several members of the expedition had been killed in a train crash. Therefore, the rumor ran, the Smithsonian had offered a huge reward to anyone who would go to Africa and kill or capture the thing.

That promise brought them out of the woodwork. A Captain Leicester Stevens announced that he was heading for Africa on Christmas eve in order to hunt the brontosaurus. His only companion was to be his faithful dog Laddie, his only weapon a relatively small Manchester rifle. He said that the monster would fall dead immediately when the bullet struck its "vital spot," but he declined to say where the "vital spot" was.

The excitement over the brontosaurus had grown so great that by February, 1902, the members of the Smithsonian expedition had to write to the *Times* of London to explain that the whole story was a practical joke. Just who was responsible for the joke, and how it was allowed to get so far, was not explained.

A dozen years later there was another hoax, this time concerning a monstrous lizardlike creature called the "Chepeke" or "water lion." A picture of this monster was even produced, but it was so clearly fraudulent that it could not be taken seriously for a moment.

Given the rather checkered history of the search for the central African dinosaur, it took an act of almost foolhardy courage for Dr. Mackal to make a genuine attempt to find it. But Mackal, a veteran of the search for the Loch Ness monster, as well as a professor of biology at the University of Chicago, had become convinced that there just might be something in all the old stories. At least he thought it was worth a look.

Along with associate James Powell, a Texas herpetologist and monster enthusiast, he went to central Africa in February, 1980. The pair trekked to the remote and swampy Likouala region of the Republic of the Congo. While they didn't see *mokéle-mbêmbe* themselves, they talked to many who said they had.

The best evidence they found was a report that one of these creatures had been killed in 1959 because it disturbed the fishermen on Lake Tele. The animal was killed with a spear and then cut up, a tedious job because of the creature's extremely long neck and tail. A rather fantastic end to the story was that everyone who ate the creature's meat died. Mackal said that there appeared to be a superstitious dread attached to even talking about the beast, though people did talk.

One witness, Nicholas Mondongo, who came from a village on the fringe of the Likouala swamp region, told how his father had often seen *mokéle-mbêmbe*. Nicholas Mondongo himself saw the creature up close one day while on a hunting trip along the Likouala-aux-herbes River. Says Mackal, "He [Nicholas Mondongo] said that the reddish brown animal stood upright on its short legs, which he thought had been collapsed when it was submerged. He saw its back and part of its tail. On the head was a frill resembling a chicken's comb. After about three minutes the animal submerged."

The witness estimated the creature to be about thirty-two feet long, ten feet of which were head and neck, the rest body and tapering tail.

The head was somewhat larger than the neck. The descriptions collected by Mackal and Powell led them to suspect that *mokéle-mbêmbe* is a dinosaur, most probably a pygmy version of one of the great sauropods like the brontosaurus. The long neck and tail, plus semiaquatic habits, make it sound very much like the brontosaurus, as most scientists imagine it to have been.

Dr. Mackal has found few enthusiastic supporters for his theories among his scientific colleagues, but his efforts have not met with the scientific scorn usually accorded monster hunters.

Science 80, a publication of the American Association for the Advancement of Science, stated, "Paleontologists like the Smithsonian's George Zug do not scoff at the efforts to document the existence of such 'cryptozoological' specimens. But they certainly withhold judgement until there is some direct physical evidence. . . ."

Mackal has offered a $2,000 reward for such evidence, a piece of hide, a bone, anything that could have only come from this unknown central-African animal. So far the reward has gone uncollected.

A second Mackal expedition in 1981 also failed to turn up any physical evidence, nor did Mackal see the animal itself; but he photographed some large and puzzling footprints, and of course collected more stories of *mokéle-mbêmbe.*

A few weeks after Mackal returned, the newspapers were full of accounts of an expedition that had been undertaken in the same area by a group from California led by Herman and Kia Regusters. They said that they had seen and possibly photographed the creature in the Lake Tele area.

The animal was described as being dark brown in color, with a slick skin and a long neck and snakelike head. It was supposedly seen by a number of people on the expedition on several different occasions. The photographs, which were said to have been taken under very difficult conditions, did not show very much.

See also: DRAGON OF THE ISHTAR GATE

N ANDI BEAR   Throughout Kenya there are rumors of a large and terrifyingly ferocious creature called by many names, among them the Nandi bear. Nandi, because it is from the land of the Nandi people that most of the rumors originate; bear, because the creature is said to look like a bear—though no native species of bear is known to exist on the African continent anymore. The natives have a number of names for this creature, among which *chemosit* is perhaps the most common.

The traditions and tales concerning the Nandi bear are confusing; they run from the very ordinary to the almost supernatural. Geoffrey Williams, who had taken part in an expedition into Nandi territory in 1912, described his sighting of the strange beast:

"Looking in the direction to which he [my guide] pointed I saw a large animal sitting up on its haunches not more than 30 yards away. Its attitude was just that of a bear at the 'Zoo' asking for buns, and I should say it must have been nearly 5 feet high. . . . Before we had time to do anything it dropped forward and shambled away. . . ."

A number of other equally moderate reports led some zoologists to conclude that there might indeed be some yet unclassified species of bear or bearlike animal in Africa. As they began to question the natives about the creature, they were told, yes indeed there is a bear-like animal living in the jungle, but it is no ordinary animal; it is the most ferocious and bloodthirsty animal in all Africa. One of its nick-names is "brain eater," meaning that when it kills it eats only the brain of its prey. According to one report:

"Men told me it came down to the villages at night and murdered the inhabitants in their huts. It made its entrance through the roof, killed the occupants, and ate their brains. That was one of the beast's pecularities; it ate only the brains of its victims. Women gathering firewood in the forest would be missed, and later their bodies would be discovered, always minus the tops of their skulls."

According to the stories, the Nandi bear would crouch on a low-lying branch above a path. When a potential victim ambled by, the beast would rip off the top of its skull with a single swipe of its great claws. Then it would eat the unfortunate victim's brain. In his book *On the Track of Unknown Animals*, cryptozoologist Bernard Heuvelmans makes a heroic effort to sort out the various traditions attached to the Nandi bear. He found that many of the stories apparently relate to known animals like the hyena, the ratel, even the baboon, that have simply been misidentified. But he also cites the "daring theory" of Dr. Charles Williams of the British Museum of Natural History, who suggested that the Nandi bear might be a survivor of a unique mammalian group, the *Chalicotheridae*. These strange-looking beasts had short hind legs, sloping backs, heavy heads, short tails, and enormous claws. They were, however, vegetarians who used the claws for tearing down leaves and branches. No one knows exactly when these creatures became extinct, but it appears to be in fairly recent times.

Writes Heuvelmans: "There is no doubt that if a Chalicotherium were clad in a furry coat—which is pure supposition —it would agree perfectly with most witness' descriptions [of the Nandi bear]. And that is all that one can say for the moment."

See also: MNGWA

OKAPI   The okapi is not an unknown animal. Though they are exceedingly rare in the wild, you may well have seen an okapi in the zoo, for they have adapted very well to captivity, and they are displayed in many large zoos throughout the world. The okapi is a shy animal, and not at all monstrous in appearance. It looks somewhere halfway between a zebra and a giraffe. In fact, it is the closest living relative of the giraffe.

Yet the okapi must be mentioned in a book of monsters and unknown animals, for it is the last large and singular-looking land animal to be discovered by science. The discovery took place at the turn of the century, at a time when most scientists believed that all the important animal discoveries had already been made.

Explorers in Africa had long heard rumors of the unknown animal, and its first appearance in print dates back to about 1890, when Sir Henry Stanley's book *In Darkest Africa* appeared. It was another ten years before Sir Harry Johnston sent back from the forests of the Congo a complete okapi skin and two skulls. During the 1920s some living okapis were sent to European zoos, and the first American okapi arrived in the Bronx Zoo in 1937.

Okapi

The okapi had escaped scientific detection for so long because it made its home in the depths of inhospitable Congo (now Zaire) jungle, where few Europeans cared to linger. Being a secretive creature, the okapi was simply overlooked, and the Europeans brushed aside as untrustworthy the stories of the native pygmies, who knew the animal well.

Other land animals, the pygmy hippopotamus, the mountain gorilla, and the pygmy chimpanzee, for example, were discovered even more recently, but they closely resemble known species and could easily be confused with them. The okapi does not really look like any other animal and it represents a type of creature thought to be long extinct. The okapi is now being considered as the symbol of the International Society of Cryptozoology.

Su   In the mid sixteenth century, the humanist Konrad Gesner published the first major naturalistic treatise on the animal life of the world since before the triumph of Christianity. Gesner's four-volume *Historia animalium* is a complete collection of what was known and believed about the animals of that time. The work contains descriptions and marvelous drawings of many known, and some mythological, animals. And there are a few entries where one is not quite sure if the creature is mythological, or if a fanciful description of a real animal is being given, or if possibly the people of Gesner's day knew of the existence of an animal that is unknown to us today.

One of the most puzzling creatures in Gesner's book is the Su, an animal said to live in Patagonia, in the southern part of what is now Argentina.

"The Most Obnoxious Animal that might be seen, called Su in the New Lands. There is a place in the newly found land where lives a people calling itself in its language Patagones, and since the land is not very warm they cover themselves with fur from an animal they call Su, which means Water, by reason of its dwelling mainly near water. It is very dreadful and obnoxious, as may be seen. [The picture shows an animal with a feathery tail and a distinctly human head, which was probably the artist's fancy.] When hunted by hunters it takes its young upon its back, covers them with its long tail and flees; will be caught in pits and killed with arrows."

Gesner's information was based on an earlier (1558) work by Father André Thevet, a French priest who had traveled widely throughout the New World collecting observations and tales of "prodigies of nature." The Su was one of them.

The animal was also mentioned by the Portuguese historian Lozano in 1740. Lozano agreed that the creature was hunted to make cloaks

Su

or capes of its hide, and that is was called *succarath* or Su. Argentinian paleontologist Professor Florentino Ameghino suggested that the Su was a species of giant ground sloth which had somehow survived the extinctions of large mammals that swept the world, and particularly the Western Hemisphere, at the end of the Pleistocene or Ice Age. Others have suggested that cloaks or capes made from the thick, studded hide of a giant sloth would have served as armor.

See also: GIANT SLOTH, IEMISCH

TASMANIAN TIGER   The Tasmanian tiger, or thylacine, most certainly did exist, and there is some evidence to suggest that it still does. It was or is the largest of the carnivorous marsupials, being about five feet in length overall. It looks more like a wolf than a tiger, indeed, it is also known as the Tasmanian wolf. The tiger title comes from the distinct stripes on the lower part of its body. In fact, it is more closely related to the kangaroo, and has been known to hop like one.

The Tasmanian tiger was once thought to be numerous on the Australian mainland, but the arrival of the dingo presumably caused their extinction. However, the creatures remained common on the small island of Tasmania until fairly recent times. Since the arrival of white settlers, the Tasmanian tiger has become increasingly rare, and the species seems to be extinct.

There has been no positively confirmed sighting of a living Tasmanian tiger for many years, but in August 1961 it was reported that one of the rare creatures had been trapped, but then escaped, on the west coast of Tasmania. It left behind blood and hair which were later identified as belonging to the tiger.

More recently there have been other reports of sightings of a living Tasmanian tiger, but these have not been verified. Footprints of the creature have also been reported, but again the reports are unconfirmed. The Tasmanian tiger was a solitary and nocturnal animal, and so it is quite possible that a few of these creatures may survive undetected in inaccessible mountain regions.

Monster enthusiasts ask, Why, if this unique-looking animal can escape detection for so long, is it not possible for others to have done so?

TAZELWURM   The tazelwurm is not large or fearsome enough to be truly monstrous. But it does carry with it an air of mystery and uncertainty that qualifies it for inclusion in this work.

The tazelwurm, or "worm with feet," is a thick-bodied lizardlike creature two to three feet in length that lives in the valleys of the Swiss, Bavarian, and Austrian alps. Descriptions vary somewhat, and there are a variety of different local names, but all apparently refer to the same unknown creature. Among its many names are bergstutzen ("mountain stump"), springewurm ("jumping worm"), and stollenwurm ("tunnel worm").

Descriptions and accounts of the creature and its habits are found in a number of nineteenth-century almanacs and natural-history guides to the Alpine regions. Compilers of these works seem unsure as to whether the tazelwurm really exists or is simply a product of Alpine folklore. But all agree that belief in the tazelwurm was widespread.

There is no known physical evidence of the existence of such an animal, but a work on animals of the Alpine region published in 1841 states:

"In 1828 a peasant in the Solothurn canton found one in a dried-up marsh and put it aside intending to take it to Professor Hugi. But in the meantime the crows ate half of it. The skeleton was taken to the town of Solothurn, where they could not decide what it was, and sent it to Heidelberg—where it was lost."

In 1934 a Swiss photographer produced a photograph of a tazel-wurm that he said he had taken by accident. He was photographing a tree stump when a large and angry lizard poked its head out just as he snapped the shutter. The picture shows what appears to be the blunt head and forepart of a rather lizardlike body. The picture also looks very much as if what has been photographed is a crudely made model rather than a living creature.

There is, however, plenty of anecdotal evidence. The tale of an Austrian schoolmaster who was exploring a cave in 1929 is fairly representative:

"Suddenly I saw a snakelike animal sprawled on the damp rotting foliage that covered the ground. Its skin was almost white, not covered with scales but smooth. Its head was flat, and two very short feet on the fore-part of the body were visible. It did not move but kept staring at me with its remarkably large eyes. I know every one of our animals at first glance and knew that I faced the one that is unknown to science, the tazelwurm. Excited, joyful, but at the same time somewhat fearful, I tried to grab the animal but I was too late. With the agility of a lizard the animal disappeared in a hole and all my efforts to find it were in vain. I am certain that it was not my imagination that let me see the animal but that I observed it with a clear head."

Others have reported somewhat more alarming encounters with the beast. It is said by some to be very aggressive, and a Swiss hunter who told of having to defend himself from an attack by an angry tazelwurm said that his knife would barely penetrate its skin. There is also a persistent rumor that the bite of the tazelwurm is poisonous.

Neither the virtually impenetrable skin nor the poisonous bite are biologically improbable. Belgian cryptozoologist Bernard Heuvelmans points out that the Gila monster of the American Southwest and its close relative, the Mexican beaded lizard, both have venomous bites. These large heavy-bodied lizards also have protectively studded skins which are extremely hard to penetrate.

A source of confusion is the number of legs possessed by the tazelwurm. Many accounts give it four legs, but there are a significant number that say it only has two short front legs. This too is not a biological impossibility, for there is a variety of Mexican lizard that has only two short front legs, and the glass snake, which is really a lizard, has no legs at all. It is also possible that the creature's legs are so short that the rear ones are often overlooked.

Heuvelmans also notes that there is a species of American salamander known as the greater siren that has only two front legs. This creature may reach a length of three feet, making it a giant among salamanders. During periods of dry weather, the siren burrows into the mud and appears only after the rain. Many accounts say that the rare and elusive tazelwurm is most commonly seen after the first rain which breaks a long drought. Heuvelmans thus raises the possibility that the tazelwurm might be an amphibian of some sort, rather than a reptile, as most commonly believed.

WAITOREKE   In the middle of the nineteenth century, several settlers in New Zealand's remote Canterbury Province reported the existence of an otherwise unknown otterlike creature called the waitoreke. Ferdinand von Hochstetter, writing about New Zealand in 1863, said that the waitoreke was one of those "few sporadic mammalia which have thus far escaped the searching eye." If the waitoreke really exists, it has still escaped the searching eye.

When Bernard Heuvelmans reviewed the evidence, he suggested that the waitoreke might be some sort of unknown otter, or even a type of large platypus. Naturalist S. J. Watson was more pessimistic, concluding that there was "very little ground" for believing in the animal at all. But even he said that "it would be unwise to ignore the possibility [of the existence of the waitoreke] however remote it may be."

Monster enthusiast Peter Costello unearthed a privately published 1964 pamphlet that contains many recent sightings of an unknown otterlike animal, mainly from an area of South Island in New Zealand, in the mountain country around Lake Ellesmere. Costello rejects the otter theory and points out that placental mammals like the otter are recent arrivals in New Zealand and Australia. There is one exception—the seal; several varieties of seal are found along the New Zealand coast. Costello believes that the identification of waitoreke with an otter was established on very little evidence and has never been properly examined. He concludes it is far more likely that the waitoreke is some sort of seal, perhaps of an unknown variety.

See also: BUNYIP

WOOLLY MAMMOTH   The woolly mammoth, a thickly coated, elaborately tusked relative of the modern elephant, once roamed the northern portions of the globe in enormous numbers. Its remains, bones and tusks, were found in such abundance in parts of Siberia that fossil ivory from mammoth tusks was a major item of trade. But the mammoth, along with the majority of other large mammals, died out at the end of the Pleistocene era or Ice Age. At least that is the orthodox scientific belief. The extinction of the mammoth, however, and a number of other Pleistocene giants, has been disrupted by cryptozoologists who contend that a few may yet survive in remote corners of the earth.

Of all the Pleistocene animals, the possibility of the survival of the mammoth has received the most attention. One of the reasons that the mammoth has been the object of so much speculation is that its remains have been so abundant, and in some cases so remarkably well preserved. Specimens of frozen mammoths have been found in the ice and permafrost of northern regions, particularly Siberia. While these finds have been neither as frequent, nor have the specimens been as perfectly preserved, as popular belief holds, they have been nonetheless quite remarkable. In 1980 the Soviet Academy of Science reported an attempt to "create" a living mammoth from the cells of a frozen specimen. The plan was to thaw some of the frozen mammoth cells and then implant the nucleus into the fertilized egg of a modern elephant. The egg would then be placed in an elephant's womb. If all went well, the elephant would then give birth to a woolly mammoth. However, the project went awry from the start, as scientists were unable to revive any of the frozen mammoth cells.

But according to some, there is no need to revive frozen cells, for the mammoth still lives. The ancestors of the modern-day Indians hunted the woolly mammoth and its relative the mastodon during the Ice Age. But there are Indian legends, apparently of more recent origin, about large, shaggy elephantlike creatures. A few traveler's tales from the early days of European exploration of the New World also mention elephantlike monsters.

Yet no storytelling tradition is pure, and what sounds like an encounter with a real mammoth may, in fact, be something quite different. Here is an example of how a misleading story can take hold: During the 1890s, large quantities of fossil mammoth ivory was being found in Alaska. The Eskimos had no idea of what sort of a beast this ivory had come from, so a friendly naturalist showed them a picture of a reconstruction of a woolly mammoth. The Eskimos were fascinated by the odd-looking creature and made sketches of the drawing to show to their friends, who also made copies.

Pretty soon there were a lot of Eskimo mammoth drawings circulating, and the origin of the drawings had been all but forgotten. It seemed as though the Eskimos were drawing pictures of an animal that should have been extinct, but how, asked some people, could the Eskimos possibly know what a mammoth looked like unless they had actually seen one—Eskimos, they pointed out, did not have access to books on paleontology. So it was assumed that the drawings had been made from firsthand observation. Thus the rumors of surviving mammoths grew more numerous than ever, and they were brought south from Alaska and Canada to the United States by fur trappers and traders. Around the turn of the century, there was a vigorous belief that the woolly mammoth lived.

In 1899 a popular American magazine printed an account of the killing of "the last woolly mammoth in Alaska." The report told of how the beast's hide was sent to the Smithsonian Institution for display. The story was fiction, but it was not labeled as such in the magazine. "Hoax" stories of this type were common in the journalism of that era. A lot of people believed the account of the mammoth killing and went to the Smithsonian to see the beast's remains. When they were told there was no such exhibit, many became angry and insisted that the Smithsonian was trying to hide something from them.

The best stories of surviving mammoths come not from Alaska but Siberia, where the mammoth was more common. In 1918 an old Russian hunter is reported to have told the French consul at Vladivostok that he had tracked a "huge elephant with big white tusks, very curved; it was a dark chestnut color as far as I could see. It had fairly long hair on the hind quarters but it seemed shorter on the front."

Another tale concerns the Don Cossack Yermak Timofeyvitch, who in 1580 saw "a large hairy elephant" in Siberia. These elephants were supposed to be well known by the natives in the remoter parts of Siberia, where they were referred to as "the mountain of meat."

It has been suggested that some of these stories were inspired by the sight of frozen and preserved mammoths rather than the living thing.

One major objection to the idea of surviving mammoths is that they would be unable to escape detection on the open and treeless tundra. But the habits of the woolly mammoths are not really known, and it has been suggested that rather than being a creature of the tundra, the mammoth really lived and lives in the taiga, the vast belt of forest that stretches across Soviet Asia. The taiga may represent the least explored land area in the entire world, and if a mammoth, or herd of mammoths, was going to hide anywhere on earth, the taiga would be the place.

See also: AMERICAN ELEPHANT, BEHEMOTH

3

MONSTER

BIRDS

AND

BATS

ATHOL   From the island of Java come stories of a large flying creature known as the Athol. The name is derived from its call *Ah-OOoool*. It is described as having a body about the size of a one-year-old child, and a wingspread that may reach twelve feet. It has a flat monkeylike face and is covered by short gray fur. What most astonishes those who first see it is that the creature's feet appear to be turned backwards. It lives in caves by the side of the rivers and feeds on fish which it scoops up with the long claws that top each of its wings.

According to most reports, the Athol is a rare creature and one that avoids contact with human beings whenever possible. But there is one published account of a native of the area who was attacked and badly wounded on both arms by one of these creatures.

Dr. Ernest Bartels, a European-educated resident of Java, is responsible for preserving and transmitting most of the Athol accounts to the West. Dr. Bartels, who himself encountered the creature, believed it to be some sort of giant bat. Cryptozoologist Ivan Sanderson agrees. The bat is the only fur-covered flying animal. Its feet, which are adapted for hanging upside down, do point backwards, and many bats do have pushed-in faces that might be described as resembling that of a monkey. There is even a variety of fish-eating bat which scoops up its prey with its long claws while flying low over the water.

The difference between the Athol and known bats is size. The largest known bats are the fruit-eating bats, or flying foxes. They have a wingspread which may reach five feet. However, the fruit eaters, as the name flying fox implies, have elongated snouts and could not possibly be described as having monkeylike faces. The bats with pushed-in faces are primarily insect eaters, but they are much smaller, usually having a wingspan of under a foot.

Sanderson, however, believed that the Athol was an as yet unknown giant variety of these micro, or small, bats.

MOA   The moa is a popular name for a group of large, ostrichlike birds that once lived in great numbers on the two islands that make up New Zealand. Moas ranged in size from a modest five feet in height, to real giants which stood twelve feet.

There are a number of intriguing mysteries connected with the moa, the most important being the time that it became extinct, if indeed these giant flightless birds really are extinct.

When Europeans first came to New Zealand in the seventeenth century, the native Maoris appeared to know nothing of moas, though they did tell the explorers all about a number of other perfectly wonderful and entirely imaginary creatures.

The first written mention of moas comes in a book on New Zealand by J. S. Polack, a trader who had lived there from 1831 to 1837. Polack said that on North Island, where he lived, "there once existed a bird of the struthious [ostrichlike] order equal in size to the emu," and he said that he had seen the bones of that bird and believed that it was still alive on South Island. Once Polack's book appeared, others claimed that they too had seen the remains of moas, and had seen them even earlier than Polack did. More significantly, a number of Maoris stepped forward with tales of how they had participated in moa hunts in their youth. Other tales spoke of how the survivors of these monstrous birds lived high in the mountains, fed on air, and were guarded by giant lizards while they slept. One explorer found it impossible to hire Maoris who would guide him to Mount Whakapunake, the supposed home of these monster birds.

At first many European scientists doubted the existence of the moa at all, or at least doubted that the giant birds could have lived in New Zealand at the same time as the Maoris, who had only been on New Zealand for a few hundred years. Both of these doubts were swept away, first by the discovery of moa bones, and then by the discovery of the remains of moas in ovens that had once been used by the Maoris.

Some of the moa remains looked amazingly fresh, as if they had been part of a living bird only a few weeks earlier. But unusual conditions can preserve remains for hundreds, even thousands of years in a remarkably fresh-looking state. In the nineteenth century, when most of these complete remains were discovered, there was no method of accurately dating them. Since the development of radiocarbon dating, the remains of one bird have been dated at A.D. 1300, about the time that large numbers of Maoris came to New Zealand. So it is possible that the Maoris hunted the great birds to extinction.

Moa

They may have been fairly easy prey. However, the freshest-looking moa remains have long since been contaminated, and thus can not be accurately dated by radiocarbon, so the time of moa extinction can not be fixed with any certainty. And there are still all those detailed personal accounts in the nineteenth century of moa hunts by some New Zealand natives.

T. Lindsay Buck, a student of the moa, says that there are no good European accounts of meeting a moa, but he does cite the 1823 story of a man named George Pauley, who said that he had seen a moa about twenty feet tall, much taller than any known moa. "No sooner had the man and the bird sighted each other than, as Pauley says, 'I ran from it, and it ran from me,' so that, by mutual consent, the crisis was soon over, and our information is tantalizingly brief and amazingly inaccurate."

In 1878, a New Zealand newspaper ran an account of the sighting of what it labeled "the last moa." The tracks had been seen repeatedly by the (unnamed) European farmer. "On a recent occasion his shepherd—an intelligent man—started the bird itself out of a patch of manuka scrub, with his sheep dog. The bird ran from the dog till it reached the brow of a terrace above him, some thirty or forty yards off, when it turned on the dog which immediately ran into the shepherd's heel. The moa stood for fully ten minutes on the brow of the terrace, bending its long neck up and down exactly as the black swan does when disturbed. It is described as being very much higher than any emu ever seen in Australia, and standing very much more erect on its legs. The color is described as a sort of silver grey with greenish streaks through it."

While there is no way of checking the story, since no names are given, it is not an entirely improbable account. Was that the "last moa," perhaps, or one of the last, for even if the moa survived as late as 1878, it would have been very rare. It is highly improbable that such a large and singular-looking bird could have survived much longer on increasingly populous New Zealand without being conclusively detected. Improbable, but not entirely impossible.

See also: ROC

ROC   We are most familiar with the roc from the tales of Es-Sinbad, or Sinbad the Sailor, as related in *A Thousand and One Nights*, a collection of ancient tales from the Middle East.

The size of the roc is expressed in nothing but superlatives. When Sinbad first saw the roc's eggs, he thought it was the dome of a great building. The sky darkened and Sinbad saw "a bird of enormous size, bulky body, and wide wings, flying in the air; and it was this that concealed the body of the sun and veiled it from view." The roc, says the story, fed elephants to its young. When Sinbad angered one of the monster birds, it took its revenge by dropping stones on his ships and sinking one.

A Thousand and One Nights is originally based on tradititional tales of the Middle East and India, some of which may date back to the third or fourth millennium B.C. And the roc is really the rukh, a huge bird that figured prominently in the mythology of the time and region. The roc-rukh probably began in stories about the eagle or some other large bird of prey, for these birds seem to have played an important part in Middle Eastern mythology from the earliest histor-ical times. Eaglelike figures appear in the art of the Sumerians, the first known civilization. After centuries of retelling, one branch of the legendary cycles surrounding the eagle must have grown into the leg-ends of the huge rukh, or roc.

So far this is quite straightforward legend building, but what makes the story interesting is that in later centuries travelers began bringing back roc feathers and eggs. Marco Polo mentions the roc and says that the Great Khan of Cathay wanted something that would prove the creature's existence. An envoy presented the khan with a gigantic feather from the island of Madagascar off the east coast of Africa that was supposed to have been the roc's home. Marco reports that the khan was impressed.

Madagascar once was the home of a really gigantic bird, *Aepyornis maximus*, or the elephant bird. It looked like a big ostrich and was

among the biggest birds that ever lived. But more impressive than the
size of the bird itself was the size of its eggs. One elephant-bird egg
was equal in size to 6 ostrich eggs or 148 chicken eggs.

The elephant bird is now extinct, but the time of its extinction is
uncertain. It may well have survived into the sixteenth century, and
its end was probably brought about by hunters who preyed both on
the huge birds and on their eggs. The trip from Madagascar to Bagh-
dad, the city of A *Thousand and One Nights*, is a long one, but medieval Arabs were great sailors and traders. They conducted thriving
trade along the east coast of Africa, before the trade was disrupted by
the Portuguese in the fifteenth and sixteenth centuries. Arab traders
undoubtedly visited Madagascar and might have seen living specimens of *Aepyornis maximus*. Large numbers of broken eggshells of
the giant bird have been found along the coast, and this has given rise
to the theory that the Arab sailors themselves helped kill off the birds
by stealing eggs for food. The eggshells could have been used for cups.
Such monstrous eggshells would also have been valuable trade items
and intriguing souvenirs to bring back to show family and friends at
home.

These same Arab merchants traveled as far as China and carried
the tale of the roc with them to the court of the Great Khan. The
"feather" shown at the khan's court could have been the frond of
Sagus ruffia, a palm tree that grows on Madagascar. This particular
tree has enormous fronds. The general similarity between the shape
of the palm frond and the feather would not have escaped the notice
of canny merchants anxious to impress a rich ruler with the wonders
of the Africa trade. A dried palm frond, if not examined too closely,
could be passed off as a giant feather.

See also: MOA, THUNDERBIRD

THUNDERBIRD   The thunderbird is a gigantic bird drawn
from the mythology of the American Indian. Most scholars believe
that the thunderbird myth was based on the condor, or possibly the

California condor

eagle. But there are a few who believe that the Indian story of the thunderbird started with the observations of a truly gigantic, yet unknown, bird. And there have been suggestions that the unknown giant bird has survived into fairly recent times, and may even be alive today.

According to one of the most persistent of the modern thunderbird stories, in 1886 a group of ranchers living in the vicinity of Tombstone, Arizona, shot and killed a monster bird. They nailed it up, wings outstretched on the side of a barn, and took a picture of it. In order to give a size comparison, six men stood in front of the bird with their arms outstretched, fingertips just touching. Six average-sized men with outstretched arms would cover a distance of between thirty to thirty-six feet, meaning that the bird nailed to the barn would have had a wingspread of about that size.

The figure is an astonishing one, for the California condor, one of the largest of living birds, has a wingspread of a paltry six to eight feet. Ostriches and other birds of that type are much larger than the condor, but since they don't fly, they don't count in this discussion.

The thunderbird photograph was supposed to have been printed in the newspaper the *Tombstone Epitaph*. But a search of the files of the newspaper reveal no trace of such a picture. Crytozoologists Ivan Sanderson said that he once had a copy of that particular photo in his files, but it had disappeared. No one else seems to be able to find a copy, though a number of people (including this author) vaguely recall having seen it at one time. Such a photo could easily have been faked, and only an examination of the original, if such a thing exists, would be able to determine its worth as evidence.

Another version of the Tombstone thunderbird story holds that the creature that was shot was not a bird at all, but a smooth-skinned featherless monster with enormous jaws and razor-sharp teeth. Most astonishing in this tale were the monster's wings that were supposed to be thin membranes of skin which measured up to 160 feet from tip to tip!

The whole idea could be dismissed as just a wilder version of an already wild legend, except for one thing. This creature sounds a lot like one of the ancient flying reptiles called pterosaurs. The existence of pterodactyls, or pterosaurs, was known before this story began to circulate. However, in 1972, long after the tale of the reptilelike thunderbird had been discussed, the fragmentary remains of an unknown but truly gigantic species of pterosaur were discovered in Big Bend National Park, in southwestern Texas. This ancient creature may have had a wingspread of up to 50 feet, twice as large as any previously known pterosaur, and so large that conventional scientific wisdom holds that the thing couldn't become airborne at all. Yet there it was, and conventional scientific wisdom has been revised to fit the new discovery. These remains were found in the heartland of the thunderbird legend, and while the wingspan of this creature does not match the 160 feet of the second thunderbird story, it matches and surpasses the wingspan of the creature in the original story attributed (incorrectly) to the *Tombstone Epitaph*.

There are a couple of giant-bird stories from the East as well. There is the case of a private-plane pilot who was flying along the Hudson Valley in May 1961 when he sighted what appeared to be another and slightly larger plane in the vicinity. This other "plane" seemed to be trying to chase him. In an attempt to get a closer look at the hostile "plane," the pilot circled back. Then he noticed that the other "plane" began flapping its wings, and that it wasn't a plane at all but an enormous bird. The pilot departed the area in great haste.

Another case involves the crash of a United Airlines plane in a wooded area of Maryland near Washington, D.C., in November 1962. There were no survivors of the crash, but on the wreckage were found traces of blood and feathers. Investigators for the government said that the plane had collided with a flock of geese, a few of which were sucked into the plane's engine, causing it to crash. Predictably, there are those who snort at such suggestions. They point to gouges and slashes on the plane's tail assembly and insist that it had been attacked and brought down by an angry thunderbird.

See also: ROC

VAMPIRE BAT   The image of a caped Bela Lugosi being transformed into a bat is stuck in almost everyone's mind, so that it is difficult to believe that the association of bats and vampires is not particularly ancient. Vampires, that is, the undead, were thought to change themselves into wolves. Bats, being creatures of the night, have always possessed some unpleasant and supernatural associations. However, there are no vampires, that is, blood-drinking bats, in Europe.

It was only after the discovery of true blood-drinking bats in South and Central America that the European idea of the vampire and the bat were fully merged. The real blood-drinking bats were naturally named vampire bats.

There are three species of vampire bat, and they live on the blood of larger mammals, and possibly large birds. To feed, the vampire bat alights gently on or near a sleeping animal. The bat's teeth are adapted to make a small and painless incision through which blood flows. The bat feeds not by sucking blood, but by lapping it up with its narrow tongue. Coagulation of blood in the wound is prevented by a special chemical in the bat's saliva.

The bite of a vampire bat is so carefully inflicted that it rarely wakens a sleeping victim. One bat cannot take enough blood from an animal the size of a goat to do it any harm from loss of blood. The bite

Vampire bat

of a single vampire bat is of no danger to a human being. However, the bats can present a danger to livestock in areas where they are numerous and attack frequently. A more serious problem is rabies and other diseases which vampire bats are known to transmit.

Vampire bats are tiny and rarely, if ever, are shown in vampire movies. The bat most often used in the movies is the flying fox, the largest of bats, but a harmless vegetarian.

See also: VAMPIRE

4

PHANTOMS

BERKELEY SQUARE HORROR   The beliefs surrounding the events at 50 Berkeley Square represent a blending of ghost and monster traditions.

For over a century, the house in the fashionable London square has been the focus of tales of terror. It was said that anyone who spent a night in the "top room" would either be dead or totally insane in the morning. Because of its sinister reputation, the house was often unoccupied.

One of the most celebrated stories connected with it concerns three sailors who broke into the empty house one night looking for a place to sleep. During the night they were awakened by strange and horrible noises. One of the sailors was so frightened that he rushed out of the house without ever seeing what was making the noise. The other two stayed behind to confront "the horror."

The sailor who got out located a policeman and persuaded him to come back to the house. When they returned they found the other two sailors were already dead. No exact cause of death was ever determined, but both died with a look of utter terror frozen on their faces.

There are many theories and tales regarding the origin and nature of "the horror." According to one account, a madman was kept in the "top room" until he died. Another tells of a former owner with some terrible secret in his past who lived a melancholy and hermitlike existence in the house until his death. The madman and/or the hermit are supposed to be haunting the place. These are fairly traditional ghost stories.

There are, however, other accounts which assert that "the horror" is not a ghost at all, but a shapeless and slimy thing, too grotesque to describe accurately, that had crawled up out of the sewers and was hiding somewhere in the house. It was said that the noises that so terrified people were the gruesome slopping noises the thing made as it slithered up and down the stairs.

For many years now, 50 Berkeley Square has been the headquarters for a very respectable firm of London booksellers, and they have reported no unusual occurrences. "The horror" seems to have disappeared.

Black Dogs

"Footprints?"

"Footprints."

"A man's or a woman's?"

Dr. Mortimer looked strangely at us for an instant, and his voice sank almost to a whisper as he answered:

"Mr. Holmes, they were the footprints of a gigantic hound!"

And thus we are introduced to *The Hound of the Baskervilles*, the most celebrated fictional treatment of a very real belief, a belief in a monster or phantom dog, often called the black dog.

In Sir Arthur Conan Doyle's novel, Sherlock Holmes finds a perfectly natural explanation for the apparently supernatural hound. But it really isn't the explanation that sticks in our minds after reading the book, it is the idea of the hound itself.

"The moon was shining bright upon the clearing, and there in the centre lay the unhappy maid where she had fallen, dead of fear and fatigue. But it was not the sight of her body, nor was it that of the body of Hugo Baskerville lying near her, which raised the hair upon the heads of those three dare-devil roysterers, but it was that, standing over Hugo, and plucking at his throat, there stood a foul thing, a great black beast, shaped like a hound, yet larger than any hound that ever mortal eye has rested upon. And even as they looked the thing tore the throat out of Hugo Baskerville, on which, as it turned its blazing eyes and dripping jaws upon them, the three shrieked with fear and rode for dear life, still screaming across the moor. One, it is said, died that very night of what he had seen, and the other twain were but broken men for the rest of their days."

Conan Doyle may well have drawn his inspiration for the Hound of the Baskervilles from the legends attached to a creature called the Black Dog of Dartmoor, which was sort of a demon in the shape of a dog. But black-dog or phantom-dog stories occur in all parts of the British Isles, and some have been imported to the United States as well. And the dog of the accounts is not always as terrible as the Hound of the Baskervilles either.

Here is a story told by a Mrs. Jewell of her firsthand meeting with a creature called the Black Dog of Torrington. The event was said to have taken place in the 1870s when the narrator was only about ten years old.

Late at night she was walking down the road with her father. "It was a moonlight night," she said, "and suddenly a sound of something panting came from behind us, and a great black dog, big as a calf, with great shining eyes, came along side us. I caught my father's hand and cried out. Father said, 'Tis the Black Dog! Hold my hand, don't speak, walk along quietly, and don't cry out.'"

The dog trotted alongside them for about a quarter of a mile. Then father and daughter turned to go into their cottage. The dog showed no further interest in them and continued on down the road. The girl's father said that he had seen the black dog many times but had never known it to harm anyone.

Mrs. Jewell added that later in life she also saw the dog several times, but never again at close range. She insisted that many other people in her district had seen the dog, but would not talk about it with outsiders because they feared being ridiculed.

The woman who collected old Mrs. Jewell's account, Barbara Carbonell, said she believed the story because her own daughter had reported an encounter with the animal. This incident took place in 1932, when her daughter and son-in-law were driving down a road in the Torrington region at night. Suddenly an enormous black dog appeared in the middle of the road, illuminated by the car's head-lights. The driver slammed on the brakes, but was sure that it was too late and that there was no way to avoid hitting the beast. They waited for the impact. It didn't come. When the car stopped, the couple got out to investigate; they could find no trace of the animal that both had seen so clearly.

A more typical black-dog story comes from a place called Tring in Hartford, England, at a spot where legend had it that a woman had been hanged for witchcraft and a demon dog appeared from time to time. This account comes from the early nineteenth century.

A man and his companion were riding home in a cart late one night when they passed the accursed spot. There was a sudden flash of light.

"What was that?" the man cried out.

"Hush," said his companion, and he pulled the horses to a stop.

"I then saw an immense black dog just in front of our horse. It was the strangest-looking creature I ever saw. He was as big as a New-foundland dog, but very thin and shaggy. He had long ears, a long tail, and eyes like balls of fire. When he opened his mouth we could see long teeth. He seemed to grin at us. In a few minutes the dog disappeared, seeming to vanish like a shadow, or to sink into the earth."

Black dogs, or spectral dogs of one color or another, have often been regarded as harbingers of evil news. Several old English families are supposed to be cursed with a black dog, and whenever the dog appears someone in the family is supposed to die. A small white dog was reputed to appear before every execution at the notorious Newgate prison in London.

Throughout the British Isles there is a tradition that graveyards were guarded by a spirit in the form of a black dog. Though the black dog was supposed to protect those recently buried in the graveyard from the Devil, it was considered to be extremely bad luck for any living person to see the dog. In fact, anyone who saw one of these graveyard black dogs was fated to die within a year.

The tradition of the graveyard dog was carried over to the United States. The author encountered it while growing up in Chicago in the

1940s. A cemetery near the house was supposed to be haunted by a white dog, and anyone who saw the dog would die within a year.

One of the favorite pastimes was to take a new kid in the neighborhood through the cemetery and tell him the story. After a few minutes of walking, you would point and shout, "There it is. My God. Don't look!"

See also: PHANTOM LIONS

DEVIL'S FOOTPRINTS   On the night of February 7, 1855, there was an unusually heavy snowfall in the county of Devonshire, England. When the people awoke the next morning they found that the fresh snow had been broken by footprints, of a very mysterious sort.

The prints were U-shaped and about 4 inches long by 2¾ inches across. At first glance they looked as if they had been made by a small pony. But closer examination showed that the prints were in line, one in front of the other. They had apparently been made by a two-legged rather than a four-legged animal.

That wasn't the oddest thing about the tracks either. In one place a line of tracks led right up to a twelve-foot-high stone wall. The gates of the wall were securely locked and had not been tampered with. The snow lay undisturbed on top of the wall. Yet the line of tracks continued on the other side, just as if a stone wall had been no obstacle at all to the creature.

At another place the prints marched to the edge of the Exe River near where it met the sea. The river there is two miles wide and was not frozen, yet the trail continued on the opposite shore just as if the creature had swum or walked across the water.

The line of prints was found to zigzag its way from the town of Topsham southward to the town of Totnes, a distance of approximately ninety-seven miles along the south Devon coast. The prints didn't make an unbroken line; sometimes they followed an irregular course, and at others they disappeared for a distance of several miles.

The strange tracks seemed to be anywhere and everywhere. Practically every town and village in the area, as well as isolated farms, were marked by the horseshoe-shaped tracks. They were found in town squares and lonely beaches; cemeteries and public roads; woodlands; and even on the tops of houses.

The snow had stopped falling in Devonshire at about midnight. The tracks had been made between that hour and about 6:00 A.M., when people arose and first began to notice them. Yet not a single person reported seeing or hearing anything unusual during the night, and certainly no one reported seeing whatever it was that made the tracks.

When people first saw the prints, they had a good deal of fun speculating what they might be, but as the day wore on, and the extent of the trail of strange prints became known, the fun went out of the speculation. The rumor spread that the prints were not horseshoe-shaped at all, but were the prints of a cloven hoof! It was said that the Devil had been abroad that night in Devonshire.

The following night poeple in the district locked themselves indoors, for fear of meeting the Prince of Darkness walking about that night. But in the morning there were no fresh footprints. Nor were there any the next morning, or the next, and gradually the hysteria died down.

What made the "Devil's footprints"? A local clergymen suggested that they really had been made by the Devil and that they were a warning against the swearing, drunkenness, and generally poor morals of the district. But another local clergyman said this was a "gross and incredible superstition." He had heard that a couple of kangaroos had escaped from a nearby zoo, and they might be responsible for the prints, since they would presumably be capable of jumping over walls. The prints in no way resemble those of a kangaroo.

Sir Richard Owen, one of the most distinguished biologists of the day, had a more reasonable explanation. He suggested that the prints had been made by a group of badgers that had been driven out of

I HAVE read with great interest the paragraph in your last publication giving an account of the most extraordinary prints in the snow, which have occasioned such excitement and fomented so melancholy a mass of superstitious folly in the villages lying southward of Exeter, on either side of the river Exe. Permit me, however, to state that the outline accompanying your intelligent Correspondent's recital of the circumstances hardly conveys a correct idea of the prints in question. As an amateur accustomed to make most accurate drawings from nature, I set to work soon after these marks appeared and completed the accompanying exact fac-simile of those that were visible on the lawn of our clergyman's garden in this parish. He and I traced them through a low privet hedge, by a circular opening of one foot diameter. On applying a rule, the interval between each impression was found to be undeviatingly eight inches and a half. On the same day a mutual acquaintance, familiar with natural history, and not long since returned from the Pacific Ocean, measured the intervals between similar prints in his garden, above a mile and a half distant from the Rectory, and found it to be exactly eight inches and a half. This, in my opinion, is one of the most remarkable and confounding circumstances we have to deal with. In the course of a few days a report was circulated that a couple of kangaroos had got loose from a private menagerie (Mr. Fische's, I believe) at Sidmouth.

Few of us had had opportunities of seeing the impression made on sand or loam by the hinder feet, or hocks rather, on which this animal sits; and we were not unwilling to give credence to the suggestion that the exotic quadruped (walking, when it does walk, as a biped; but bounding over vast lengths of space more like a chamois) might have been loose and vagrant in the neighbourhood, and left the strange impress here referred to. Still, it was quite inexplicable that the animal, considering the scale of the foot, should leave, in single file, one print only, and, as has been already observed, with intervals as exactly preserved as if the prints had been made by a drill, or any other mechanical frame. A scientific acquaintance informed me of his having traced the same prints across a field up to a hay-stack. The surface of the stack was wholly free from marks of any kind, but on the opposite side of the stack, in a direction exactly corresponding with the track thus traced, the prints began again! The same fact has been ascertained in respect of a wall intervening.

count of the Devil's footprints

hibernation by hunger and were scurrying about the countryside in search of food. The badger's characteristic print, he said, had been distorted by the melting and refreezing of the snow.

Other animals, such as otters, racoons, skunks, jumping rats, and of course ponies, were put forth as the possible source of the prints. So were a variety of birds, including swans and cranes. Someone even suggested a swarm of frogs. None of these explanations even gained general acceptance.

To this day no one really knows whether the strange prints were made by an animal or if they have some other origin. Perhaps they were made by something that fell from the sky, or by a change in weather. The phenomenon of "Devil's footprints" however, has been observed in a few other places and is generally connected, at least in the popular mind, with the appearance of some sort of devil or monster.

See also: JERSEY DEVIL

GEF—THE TALKING MONGOOSE   In the annals of strange phenomena, the case of Gef is quite unique. What was it, monster, ghost, poltergeist, or what he called himself, "a little clever, extraclever mongoose"? Readers may classify this creature however they wish.

Gef first made his presence known in September 1931 in a lonely farmhouse on the Isle of Man, a small island in the Irish Sea. The house was occupied by James T. Irving, a piano salesman turned farmer, his wife, and their youngest daughter, a girl of about thirteen.

The family began hearing strange noises in the attic, and as time went on the noises grew stranger and stranger. There were barkings, growlings, hissing, and spitting. It was almost as if some creature were trying to imitate the noises made by other animals in the house. Then it began making noises like a gurgling baby!

Irving would make noises, and the thing would repeat them. Said

Irving, "I was carried away with wonder. An animal was taking lessons from me in human speech! . . ." And within a few weeks it was speaking very well.

Gef, for that is what the creature called itself, remained hidden behind the paneling on the walls, in the tall grass around the house, in the dark attic, and any other place where it could be heard but not seen. Only the girl ever claimed to have seen Gef, and then none too clearly. She said it looked like a weasel or other small animal of that type.

Whatever it was, Gef proved to be a troublesome guest. It often threw things around the house, and once pretended to have been poisoned, which alarmed the Irvings greatly. It was often so noisy it was hard for the Irving family to sleep, and more than once they threatened to move out of the house. The threat upset Gef, who complained, "Would you go away and leave me?"

Some twenty years before Gef's appearance, a neighboring farmer had released some mongooses in his fields to kill rabbits. Gef, however, insisted that it was not a local product, but that it had been born on June 7, 1852, in Delhi, India. It never explained how or why it had come to the distant Isle of Man. There is a tradition in India that the mongoose is capable of learning human speech.

Gef wandered about the neighborhood listening in on the conversations of others and reporting them to the Irvings. Several neighbors also claimed to have heard the creature talking, or at least making strange noises.

The stories of Gef's exploits came to the attention of psychical researchers in Britain and the United States. Several of them visited the Irvings in the hope of seeing or hearing the remarkable mongoose. They saw and heard nothing, but came away convinced that the Irvings were honest people who were reporting what they really believed to be happening.

The Irvings continued to describe Gef's activities for several years. Then in 1937 they abruptly sold their farm and disappeared. The new owner never reported any dealings with Gef or any other strange phenomena. In 1947 the new owner claimed that he shot a strange-look-

ing mongooselike animal. Some people said it was Gef, but most think
it more likely the "extraclever mongoose" disappeared with its friends
the Irvings.

HAIRY HANDS

In the Dartmoor region of England there is
a stretch of road between the villages of Postbridge and Two Bridges.
It's a rather ordinary piece of road, running through slightly rolling
moors, on a generally straight path. Yet during the early years of the
twentieth century an unusually large number of accidents were
reported on this road.

First it was horses that would suddenly panic and throw their
riders. Ponies pulling carts would veer off the road for no apparent
reason, dumping their driver into the ditch. With the advent of the
bicycle, cyclists reported they felt as if the handlebars were suddenly
torn out of their control, and they plunged into a ditch or crashed into
a wall. Motorcycles, cars, and buses had more serious accidents, and
there were a number of fatalities.

Everyone figured there was something wrong with the road, but no
one knew what. Then in 1921 a young army officer was seriously
injured when his motorcycle crashed along that stretch of road. He
seemed to have suddenly turned off and hit a wall. Later, he recalled
what happened just before the crash. He said that he distinctly saw a
pair of large hairy hands clamp down over his own and twist the
motorcycle's handlebars, forcing him off the road.

The story caught the attention of a London newspaper, and when
reporters came out to interview people in the area, they found quite
a number who said that they felt the presence of "something" when
they went down that road.

Engineers were called in and they agreed that the hairy-hands tale
was nonsense. According to the engineers, the whole problem was the
way the road was constructed—too many little ups and downs. So
they had the road resurfaced.

But the story didn't end with road repairs. Three years later a woman and her husband parked their trailer near the spot where the hairy hands had first been reported. That night the woman was awakened by a scratching noise on the window. She said she saw a large hairy hand clawing at the glass. She sensed something very evil. The woman slipped out of her bunk and fell to her knees to pray. After she made the sign of the cross the hand disappeared, but the feeling of an evil presence remained. She said she and her husband never again went into that part of the country.

PHANTOM KANGAROO   A persistent and truly puzzling figure in American monster lore is the phantom kangaroo, a large kangaroo which appears where no kangaroo should or could be. These kangaroos are sometimes reputed to be aggressive, even dangerous. Yet after they are sighted, no material trace of them can be found.

An early phantom-kangaroo story comes from the community of South Pittsburg, Tennessee. In January of 1934, according to a newspaper report, the beast was spotted by the Reverend W. J. Handcock, among others. According to the Reverend Handcock, "It was fast as lightning and looked like a giant kangaroo running and leaping across the field."

The same newspaper story tells of a large dog in the area being killed and eaten. The phantom kangaroo was blamed for the killing, and also for the destruction of a large number of chickens. Direct evidence linking the phantom kangaroo to the killing of domestic animals is not reported, but the kangaroo was blamed anyway. A report of unknown origin speaks of someone having seen the kangaroo carrying a dead sheep or dog under each arm.

A search for the mysterious animal was carried out, but there were no results.

In January 1949, Louis Staub was driving at night outside of Grove City, Ohio, when he saw something strange hop into the beam of his headlights. "It was about 5½ feet high, hairy and brownish. It had a pointed head. It looked like a kangaroo but it appeared to jump on all fours. I'm certain it wasn't a deer."

Then there was the Minnesota "big-bunny" flap. For several years children in the area of Coon Rapids, Minnesota, reported seeing something that they described as "a very big bunny," a "bunny" that was as tall as they were. One adult, a woman named Barbara Battmer, said that she got a clear view of two of these "bunnies" hopping through the woods, but she knew they weren't bunnies, they were kangaroos. As is usual in such cases, a search was made but no trace of the kangaroos could be found. There were also the usual inquiries to nearby zoos to see if any of their kangaroos were missing. All zoo kangaroos were present and accounted for.

Probably the most astonishing of all of the phantom-kangaroo stories of recent years was the one that came out of Chicago in 1974. According to the newspapers, early in the morning of October 18, the police on the northwest side of the city received a call from a man who said that there was a kangaroo jumping around on his front porch. While the police didn't take the call too seriously, a couple of patrolmen were nevertheless sent out to investigate.

Much to their surprise, they found the kangaroo and chased it, finally cornering the beast in a dark dead-end alley. The kangaroo didn't like being chased, and apparently didn't want to be captured either, so it began kicking with its big powerful hind legs as kangaroos do when they are on the defensive. The police, who were more puzzled than anything else, didn't want to shoot, so they backed off. Then the kangaroo hopped over a fence and disappeared down the street.

During the next few days, a lot of people on the northwest side of Chicago reported that they had seen a kangaroo in the neighborhood. A newsboy selling papers on the street corner turned around and saw the kangaroo standing just a few feet away from him. "He looked at me, I looked at him, and then away he hopped," the boy said.

The Chicago police got a lot of calls from people who insisted that there was a kangaroo in their backyards rummaging through their garbage cans. Most of the calls were probably the result of mistaken identity—people heard something in the back yard, probably a dog or a cat or a raccoon knocking over the garbage can—but with all of the kangaroo excitement, they assumed, or perhaps hoped, that it was the phantom kangaroo they heard. There were undoubtedly a fair number of out-and-out kangaroo hoaxes as well. The newspapers had a lot of fun with such headlines as: KANGAROO STAYS A JUMP AHEAD OF THE POLICE.

Kangaroo sightings then began to spread to towns to the west of Chicago. On November 2, just outside of the town of Plano, Illinois, about fifty miles from Chicago, three young men were driving along when:

"We almost ran over it. It jumped onto the road about twenty feet ahead of us . . . it landed on the road near the intersection with the main road, and there was no traffic. It sat up on its haunches . . . and then jumped over a fence about five feet high and disappeared into the woods."

Ten days later in Rensselaer, Indiana, it hopped out of a cornfield and up to a drugstore. It was early in the morning and the only observer around was an employee opening up the drugstore:

"I hope some farmer or somebody else sees it or everybody'll think I'm a nut. But it was the kangaroo. . . . I know it was." No one else saw it that morning. The mystery beast just hopped down the street and vanished into another cornfield. But other people did report seeing it around the same area later.

By the end of November 1974 the Great Midwestern Kangaroo Flap had died down, but there was another rash of sightings in Illinois the following year and again in 1976. Other waves of phantom-kangaroo sightings have broken out in Wisconsin, Colorado, and Ohio.

When the kangaroo was sighted in Ohio in 1967, reporters talked to the director of the Cincinnati Zoo. He said, "We had a kangaroo story about two years ago. I doubt if there's a kangaroo around here on the loose. We never found one. Down the years we've chased after reported black leopards, panthers, and even a polar bear. Anyone seeing the kangaroo, which I doubt exists, should try to keep it in sight and call the zoo."

See also: PHANTOM LIONS

PHANTOM LIONS   In the district of Surrey in England there is the Surrey puma. In Nottingham it is the Nottingham lion and in the Midwestern part of the United States it's Nellie the Lion. These are but three local examples of the widespread phenomenon of the phantom lions—a lion or some other large cat, which appears in a place where no lion or large cat should be, is seen by many people, but seems to disappear before anyone can locate any physical traces of it.

Of the many phantom lions, the Surrey puma is probably the best known, for it has been seen on a fairly regular basis since the early 1960s. The sightings have been so numerous that they are almost commonplace, and a local newspaper complained about the annual "summer ritual of puma spotting."

What is a typical puma spotting like? On July 19, 1977, London newspapers carried an account of sighting a "large, grey and lean animal with a small head and 3 ft. tail," seen on the grounds of a nursing home at Patchem, near Brighton. One man got within forty feet of the lion before it disappeared, but a police search of the grounds turned up no material evidence of the creature's existence.

In October that same year near Reigate, Surrey, several workmen claimed to have seen the creature, one even said he had taken a picture of it. The police were unimpressed. The image on the photo was too tiny to identify conclusively, though it definitely looked catlike. Police were of the opinion that the animal in the photo was simply a large house cat.

Often the Surrey puma has been described as a large, growling, and rather menacing creature. But there is one odd report in which the creature is said to have behaved like—well, a real pussycat. On September 1, 1966, a woman walking through a thistle patch in Hampshire, near Surrey, stepped on the tail of a puma. The animal reared up on its hind legs and struck out at her with both its paws, but the woman displayed either extraordinary courage or extreme foolishness.

Puma

Instead of running she picked up a stick and hit the beast on the nose. The blow so frightened the poor animal that it clambered up a tree. The woman went for help, but when she returned with others the animal was gone.

The Nottingham lion was first spotted on the morning of July 29, 1976, by two milkmen who were making their rounds near the entrance to the Nottingham airport. They both saw what they were sure was a lion, " . . . its head down and its long tail had a bushy end. It was walking slowly away from us."

They watched the beast disappear around the edge of the field and then they called the police. The story made the newspapers and suddenly everybody in Notingham seemed to be seeing "the lion." There were over sixty sightings reported to the police in the following weeks.

The police checked with all the zoos and private animal collections within a hundred miles, but no one reported a missing lion. A massive search was carried out using dogs and even a helicopter. At first the police had been quite sympathetic to the lion reports, but as time went on and no evidence turned up, they became more skeptical, and finally official police sources indicated that the whole thing had probably started as a mistake, and the story was being kept alive by sensationalistic journalism and deliberate hoaxes. There is no doubt that the British press, some of which leans heavily toward sensationalism, had a field day with the Nottingham lion.

Phantom lions were spotted in other parts of the British Isles, and today they seem as common as the phantom black dogs once were. While the black dog inspired Sir Arthur Conan Doyle's novel *The Hound of the Baskervilles*, the phantom cats inspired two less famous pieces of fiction—*Man-eater* by Ted Willis, and *The Surrey Cat* by Andrew Sinclair.

In the United States similar phantom-cat sightings go back over a century. In 1853 a huge "tiger" was supposed to have been seen around Russelville, Kentucky. While the people of Kentucky have long been famed for their marksmanship, not one of them seemed able to shoot this beast, though several "tiger" hunts were organized.

In December 1877 a large cat of unknown origin attacked a young woman named Mary Crane near the village of Sun, Indiana. There had been rumors of a lion in the vicinity, and one evening she and a young man were walking through the woods when they heard a terrible shriek behind them. Turning, they saw a pair of glowing eyes approaching rapidly. Behind the eyes was something "big as a good sized calf, with a tail as long as a door." That was enough; the couple broke into a run, the young man proving to be the fastest of the pair. The big cat caught up with Mary Crane and tore at her dress with its claws.

She fainted, and when she awoke she found the thing licking her face, so she just shut her eyes and prayed. After an agony of waiting, she heard voices coming from the direction of the village. The approach of other humans seemed to frighten the animal, for it ran away without hurting Mary Crane, and she was left with nothing worse than a torn dress and some scary memories.

In 1917 people in central Illinois reported seeing something that looked like "an African lion." According to one report, the lion jumped out of the grass onto a car, then slid off and ran away. The central Illinois beast was nicknamed "Nellie the Lion," but despite several searches, no trace of Nellie was ever found, nor was there ever a clue to where she might have come from or where she went to.

A mysterious giant black cat was reported near Cairo, Illinois, in April 1970. The press called it a panther, but once again no trace of a real panther could be found.

The mountain lion, or puma, is native to the United States, and though it has generally been considered to be extinct in those areas in which phantom lions have been sighted, it is still possible that a rare individual puma survived, to terrify and perplex the local residents. But it is far more likely that Nellie the Lion and all of her elusive companions are really part of modern folklore.

See also: BEAST OF TRURO, BLACK DOGS, PHANTOM KANGAROO

5

RIVER

AND

LAKE

MONSTERS

BEAST OF 'BUSCO   A large pond on a farm near the city of Churubusco, Indiana, is reputed to be the home of a monster turtle, sometimes known as Oscar, and more ominously as the Beast of 'Busco.

In 1948 the owner of the pond noticed that there were fewer fish than usual, and that ducks resting on the pond sometimes disappeared mysteriously. The cause of these disappearances was a gigantic snapping turtle. The largest of the snapping turtles, the alligator snapper, has been known to weigh up to two hundred pounds, and is strong enough to break a broomstick with its horny jaws, or snap off a finger. But this snapping turtle was much bigger, though accounts differ as to its size. Some say it was only as big as a dining-room table while others insist it was as big as a pickup truck.

Turtle hunts were organized, and the men went at the pond with baited hooks, traps, and guns, but were unsuccessful in their efforts. The farmer who owned the pond, however, studied the monster turtle's habits, and one day while it was sleeping he slipped a rope or chain around its middle, attached the other end to four strong horses, and tried to pull Oscar out of the pond.

The horses pulled and the turtle dug its claws into the mud. The contest finally ended in a draw when the rope (or chain) broke. Oscar slipped back into the murky waters of the pond and was never seen again. Some say he died from the exertion, and others insist that he is just hiding and waiting, for turtles live a long time and can be very patient.

119

Alligator snapping turtle

Every year the people of Churubusco celebrate their local monster with a festival called Turtle Days, where visitors are encouraged to buy turtle models, turtle T-shirts, eat a variety of dishes that are in one way or another named after turtles, and in general spend money.

ⅭHAMP　　　The event that put the Lake Champlain monster, Champ as it is affectionately known, on the map took place on July 5, 1977. Sandra Mansi was standing at the edge of Lake Champlain when she saw a disturbance in the water. At first she thought it was just a school of fish, but then a long neck broke the surface.

"I was scared to death," Mrs. Mansi said. "I had the feeling I shouldn't be there."

Just another unsupported sighting of a lake monster? Not quite, for not only was there another witness, Mrs. Mansi's future husband, she also had her camera with her. It was a Kodak Instamatic and, scared or not, Mrs. Mansi had the presence of mind to snap a picture. When she had the picture developed, it showed what looked like a long-necked creature emerging from the water. But Mrs. Mansi decided not to say anything about her picture, because people might think she was crazy or a faker. As more people reported seeing Champ, however, she decided to go public.

Scientists who have looked at the photograph are equivocal. Dr. B. Roy Friedan, professor of optical sciences at Arizona State University, examined the photo and found it to be a high-quality print that "does not appear to be a montage or a superimposition of any kind" and that "the object appears to belong in the picture."

"We don't see any evidence of tampering with the photo," Dr. Friedan concluded.

Of course, someone could have hauled a monsterlike object out into the lake and had it photographed. Mrs. Mansi insists the thing couldn't be a hoax, because she saw the object move. However, she says she is unable to remember exactly where she took the photo, and the negative of the picture has been lost. This makes more intensive investigation of the photo impossible. The result is that the photograph, while interesting, is inconclusive.

But the publicity generated by the Mansi photo was just enough to move Champ into the monster-star category.

In many respects, Lake Champlain is an excellent place for an unknown animal, because it is extremely large, over one hundred miles long, and thirteen miles wide at its widest point. It is also fairly deep, four hundred feet at its greatest depth. Most of the lake is in New York State, although the northernmost tip, which drains into the Saint Lawrence, is in Canada. Most of the best freshwater-monster reports come from deep, cold-water lakes like Lake Champlain.

The first recorded observation of Champ was made by the lake's European discoverer, the French explorer Samuel de Champlain, in 1609. Champlain said he observed a twenty-foot-long snakelike creature with a horselike head in the lake. Back in the nineteenth century the Lake Champlain monster was well known enough for the showman P. T. Barnum to offer a $50,000 reward for the carcass of the creature. Barnum never had to pay a penny.

Sightings have multiplied over the last few years as the Champ publicity has increased. Most of those who report seeing the creature speak of humps in the water or occasionally a snakelike neck and small head. All in all, the sightings tend to follow the pattern set at Loch Ness or other lakes which are supposed to contain monsters.

Despite all the publicity to date, there has been only limited scientific investigation of the area. A scientific conference on Champ was held at Port Henry, New York, in 1981, and among the participants was Dr. Roy Mackal of the University of Chicago, who once again pressed his zeuglodon, or primitive-whale, theory as the possible source of this and other freshwater monster sightings.

In the meantime Port Henry, New York, and other towns that border the lake have been prospering from the excitement by selling "Port Henry, Home of Champ" T-shirts, and other monster souvenirs to tourists.

On both the New York and Vermont sides of the lake there have been moves to have the animal declared an endangered species to protect it from would-be "sportsmen." And Port Henry has passed an ordinance protecting the creature, if creature there be.

See also: CHESSIE, ZEUGLODON

C HESSIE The first recorded sighting of the Chesapeake Bay monster, or Chessie, came in the summer of 1978. The creature was described as "grayish . . . about 25 feet long . . . swimming with an undulating motion." It was reported in the bay near the mouth of the Potomac River.

From time to time there have been other reports of the monster, though it has never become a major water monster like the Loch Ness monster, Ogopogo, or Champ. Some insist that the sightings are probably a misidentified seal, a porpoise, a floating log, a sea otter, or just plain hoax or hallucination. A three-minute videotape shot by Robert Frew created some excitement during the summer of 1982. But the pictures were unclear and hard to interpret.

But at least one "sportsman" took off after what he thought was Chessie with a rifle, though he missed his target and whatever it was that he was shooting at disappeared. This attack prompted Fortean writer George W. Earley to propose in a Baltimore newspaper that Chessie be protected by law, just as Bigfoot and Champ already are. Wrote Earley:

"So how about it Marylanders—why not follow the lead of the good people of Port Henry [New York] and Skamainia County [Washington] and get some protection for your monster? After all, why shouldn't they be afforded the same consideration we give the snail darter, bald eagle, California condor and other officially endangered species?"

See also: CHAMP

FLATHEAD LAKE MONSTER   Visitors to Flathead Lake, Montana, have occasionally spotted something "huge and black" in the water. In 1963 Ronald Nixon, who lives near the lake, saw "something at least 25 feet long and with enough substance that as it moved near the surface, it threw up a two foot head wave. It was perfectly black, and it didn't have any sign of a fin on back. It couldn't have been a fish, and I'm sure it wasn't man made."

Some local opinion holds that the Flathead Lake monster is a fish, some kind of giant sturgeon perhaps. Peter Costello, author of *In Search of Lake Monsters*, does not believe that available evidence supports the fish theory, but some residents of the Flathead Lake area have formed a company called Big Fish Unlimited, and a number of attempts have been made to catch the monster. Once giant hooks baited with whole chickens were used, but without any success. A skin diver searched the lake for four days without finding anything, and a reward for the first good photograph of the monster has gone uncollected. So has a $1,000 reward for the capture of the monster or any fish over fourteen feet long that might account for the sightings.

GIANT BOA   Reymonod Zima, a Portuguese merchant living in Brazil, said that one night in 1930 he was going up to Jamundá River when he saw a light on the river. At first he thought it was the light from the house on the far shore that he was looking for, so he switched on his searchlight.

"But suddenly we noticed the light was charging towards us at an incredible speed. A huge wave lifted the bow of the boat and almost made it capsize. My wife screamed in terror. At the same moment we made out the shape of a giant snake rising out of the water and performing a St. Vitus dance round the boat. After which, the monster crossed this tributary of the Amazon about a mile and a half wide, at fabulous speed leaving a huge wake, larger than any of the steamboats make at full speed.... Owing to the understandable excitement at the time it was not possible for me to reckon the monster's length. I presume that as a result of a wound the animal lost one eye, since I saw only one light. I think the giant snake must have mistaken our searchlight for the eye of one of his fellow monsters."

The giant anaconda of Brazil is a monster that has received a good deal of publicity. However, mixed in with the reports of this huge snake are others which indicate the possibility of the existence of an even larger giant water snake, or giant boa, *sucuriju gigante*, from approximately the same region. Zima's story is one such account. Various individuals who have collected reports of the giant boa conclude that it may be 130 or even an incredible 200 feet in length, and since it is basically aquatic in nature, it has been described as an "inland sea serpent."

Descriptions of this creature tend to vary a great deal, but practically every story contains some mention of its eyes, which in the words of one witness "were as large as plates." The eyes are also luminous or phosphorescent, as mentioned in Zima'a narrative. A priest who encountered the monster while sailing down the river first thought that its eyes were navigation lights on the bridge of a river boat. Later, when he got a closer look at the giant snake (too close for comfort he thought), "We were able to appreciate clearly the difference between the light of the lamp and the phosphorescent light of the monster's eyes."

See also: GIANT ANACONDA

LOCH NESS MONSTER   The Loch Ness monster, or Nessie, is quite justifiably the most celebrated of all the modern monsters or unknown animals. The subject of Nessie has been investigated with unusual care, and while the evidence produced has not convinced everybody that there is a large unknown creature (or herd of creatures) living in Loch Ness, even skeptics have been impressed by the quality of some of the evidence.

Loch Ness is the largest freshwater lake in the British Isles. It is approximately twenty-four miles long and a mile and a half wide at its widest point. In most places the loch is about 450 feet deep, but there are spots where the depth plunges to 900 feet. The shores of the loch are quite steep. Though it is far to the north, Loch Ness never freezes, but it never gets very warm either, the temperature hovering around forty-two degrees Fahrenheit year round. The water itself is very murky, and there are dangerous currents, making any underwater search an uncertain and risky business. Loch Ness is very like many of the other cold northern lakes in which monsters have been reported over the years.

The loch forms a portion of what is called the Great Glen, a split in the earth which cuts completely across the Scottish Highlands. The Great Glen contains a chain of lochs, rivers, and canals which connect the Atlantic Ocean with the North Sea. Loch Ness itself was once an arm of the sea and is still connected to the North Sea by the river Ness.

Like all of the other highland lochs, Loch Ness had its share of ancient legends about water kelpies and other monstrous creatures living in its depths. Unlike most other Scottish monster tales, which were conveyed only by word of mouth, the story of a monster in Loch Ness was written down in A.D. 565. The monster, it seems, ran afoul of Saint Columba, the great Christian missionary to Scotland. According to Adamnan, the saint's biographer, the saint saved a swimmer from the rampaging monster by saying, "Think not to go further, touch not thou that man. Quick! Go back! Then the beast upon hearing the voice of the saint was terrified and fled backwards more rapidly than he came." This, by the way, is the only aggressive act ever attributed to the Loch Ness monster.

It is probable that the monster story predates Saint Columba, for it was traditional in pagan societies for heroes to slay dragons and monsters, and it was also traditional when these pagans became Christians to alter the old story to accommodate the new faith.

In the centuries that followed there were vague stories of "something" in the loch, but there was nothing to distinguish these accounts from all of the other myths and legends of the Highlands. The modern story of the Loch Ness monster begins in 1933.

At that time a road was built around the once isolated loch. The construction brought a large number of outsiders to Loch Ness, and clearing the shore of the loch for the road gave observers a much better view of the water.

The first recorded modern monster sighting was on April 14, 1933. Mr. and Mrs. John Mackay were driving home from the city of Inverness along the new road when they saw an "enormous animal" in the water, and watched while the beast "disported itself, rolling and plunging for fully a minute." The Mackays happened to own the inn at Drumnadrochit, which is still a center for monster hunters and more casual tourists. This fact has not been overlooked by skeptics who tend to set the whole Loch Ness phenomena down as a tourist-grabbing hoax.

The Mackays told their friend Alex Campbell, the water bailie on Loch Ness, that is, the man in charge of regulating salmon fishing in

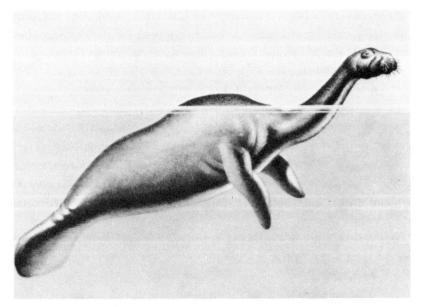

Theoretical Loch Ness monster

the loch. Campbell, who lived on the shores of the loch and spent a lot of time looking at the water, said that he had seen the monster many times since he was first told of it by the Mackays.

Campbell was also a correspondent for the *Inverness Courier*, and he wrote up the story on the Mackay sighting for the May 3, 1933, edition of the paper. Campbell says that he is the man who first called the thing a monster, not because there was anything particularly horrible about it, but because of its great size. Campbell's description of the monster has become the standard:

"It had a long, tapering neck, about 6 feet long, and a smallish head with a serpentine look about it, and a huge hump behind which I reckoned was about 30 feet long. It was turning its head constantly."

The Loch Ness monster story has been told many, many times, and it is appropriate here only to touch upon the high points.

While there have been a number of alleged sightings of the Loch Ness monster on land, the most famous came early in the monster's modern history. That was the night of January 5, 1934. Arthur Grant, a young veterinary student, was riding home on his motorcycle when he practically ran over the Loch Ness monster, which was crossing the road in front of him.

It was a bright moonlit night, so Grant got a good view of the thing. He described it as having a long neck, smallish head with large oval eyes, a thick body, and a large round tapering tail. Grant saw that it had front flippers, but could not be sure about flippers in back. Overall, he estimated the length to be about fifteen or twenty feet, much smaller than the beast reported by Campbell and Mackay. Grant said he tried to chase the thing, but it plunged into the loch and disappeared.

When he got home, Arthur Grant made a quick sketch of what he had seen, and the drawing looked remarkably like everybody's idea of a *Plesiosaurus*.

The first known photos of "something" in the loch were taken in November of 1933, but they were too vague and fuzzy to show anything. The next picture, taken in April 1934, was critical in the growth of the Loch Ness story. This is the photograph taken by "the London surgeon," a man named Kenneth Wilson who was on vacation at Loch Ness when he saw something in the water. Wilson snapped two pictures, the first showing what appears to be a long neck and small head sticking up above the water's surface. It is to this day the clearest photo of the Loch Ness monster ever taken. Yet the photo has always been controversial, partly because Wilson was very publicity shy and simply didn't want to talk about how he had taken the photo. In fact, his name was not used in connection with the photo until after his death.

The problem with the photo is that it shows water and the object and that's all. There is no identifying landmark to show that it actually was shot at Loch Ness, though few doubt that it was. More significantly, there is nothing by which the size of the object in the water can be judged. The object itself is completely in silhouette and no features are visible. While many who look at it say it must be the neck and head of the monster, others think it is a piece of a log, the head and neck of a diving bird, or the tail of an otter. The London surgeon's photo aroused interest in the monster but did not settle the problem.

Interest in Nessie declined sharply during the war years, and there was even an absurd rumor that the monster had been killed by a German bomb. Nothing of importance really happened until 1960, when the first good motion pictures of the monster were taken.

In April 1960, Tim Dinsdale, an aeronautical engineer and monster buff, took what he believed to be a very brief film of the monster swimming rapidly on the far side of the loch. To the untrained eye, the film showed little more than a dot moving across the water. It could have been a powerboat, and that's what some said it was. However, in 1965 the Dinsdale film was examined by photographic experts of the Royal Air Force. The RAF study concluded that the object in Dinsdale's film was "probably" animate, and might be as much as ninety feet long. While everyone recognizes that photo analysis is not an exact science, the RAF report was impressive and stimulated a burst of serious Loch Ness monster investigation.

In 1970 a team from the American Academy of Applied Science,

The London surgeon's photograph of the Loch Ness monster

headed by Dr. Robert Rines, came to the loch with a variety of new equipment and approaches. Not much happened that year, or the next, but in 1972 one of the team's automatic underwater cameras shot four frames of what appeared to be a diamond-shaped flipper that might have been from six to eight feet long. It was a highly impressive series of photographs because there was no suspicion of a hoax. Scientists could not agree what sort of animal the flipper might be attached to, but further investigation was very clearly warranted.

It wasn't until 1975 that the next good evidence turned up. Again it was underwater photos. The pictures themselves were very far from clear, but one of them shows a close-up of a wrinkled, knobby object that could be the face of the Loch Ness monster. Another photo may show about three-quarters of a long-necked creature swimming away. The pictures had to be computer enhanced, and even so, they are quite vague and fuzzy. Interesting evidence, fascinating even—but not conclusive. However, it seemed that the scientists were really moving in on the monster.

A really big expedition sponsored jointly by the Academy of Applied Science and the *New York Times* went to the Loch in 1978. No monster-spotting expedition has ever been as well financed and elaborately equipped. But this expedition added nothing to our total knowledge of the Loch Ness phenomenon and must be counted a failure. Since that time interest in the Loch Ness monster has dropped off considerably, though serious monster buffs and casual tourists still come to the loch every summer in the hopes of seeing the thing. Very few of the hopeful visitors ever see anything out of the ordinary. Indeed, many longtime residents of the Loch Ness area have never seen the creature, and some of the Scots who live around the loch are hardened monster skeptics, who are alternately amused and irritated by the many monster enthusiasts from around the world.

Most Loch Ness monster sightings are not of the impressive head-and-neck type as seen in the London surgeon's photograph. What people most frequently report seeing is a hump or humps in the water.

If the Loch Ness monster is a real animal, and not some sort of

Searching for the Loch Ness monster

mythical beast, then there simply has to be more than one monster. The thought that the loch is inhabited by a single immortal monster that has lived in its depths, undetected at least from Saint Columba's day to our own, is absurd. Cryptozoologists speak of a viable breeding herd of the creatures—perhaps as many as a hundred. There have been some sightings and a few photos and films which seem to show more than one of the creatures at one time.

Speculating over what the Loch Ness monster might be has always been one of the most popular sports at the loch. Everyone's favorite candidate is the ancient marine reptile plesiosaur—it looks like the London surgeon's photo and the drawing by Arthur Grant. It might have fins like those shown in the underwater photo, and since no one knows what a plesiosaur's face looked like, there is no reason why it could not have a face like that seen in the 1975 photo.

The most persistent objection raised to the plesiosaur identification (aside from the fact that plesiosaurs are assumed to have been extinct for 70 million years) is that it is a reptile, hence it is cold blooded and could not survive in the very cold waters of the loch. The answer to that objection is that we do not know whether ancient reptiles like plesiosaur really were cold blooded. There is some evidence that the dinosaurs, which were contemporaries of plesiosaur, may have had internal temperature controls.

Dr. Roy Mackal, who first entered the world of cryptozoology through an interest in the Loch Ness monster, suggested at one time that it might be a variety of giant sea slug that had adapted to fresh water. What made this suggestion attractive was that the giant slug would not have had to spend much time on the surface, and that when it died its remains would sink to the bottom and decompose completely. A telling objection to the case for the monster is that no bones or other remains have ever been found. A number of other possible invertebrate candidates have also been put forth, but none has ever gained wide support.

Mackal discarded the sea-slug theory and suggested the possibility that the monster might be a giant amphibian. Others have suggested gigantic eels or other types of elongated fish. But neither amphibian nor fish has ever been popular.

Next to plesiosaur, the most popular candidate for the Loch Ness monster has been some sort of mammal. An unknown variety of giant otter or a long-necked seal have been suggested. Mackal for a while toyed with a theoretical long-necked sirenian, a type of manatee or sea cow. Most recently he has supported the primitive whale, zeuglodon. The principal objection to all mammals is that they are air breathers and should spend more time on the surface than the Loch

Ness creature appears to.

Another problem is food. It is generally assumed that the monster is a fish eater, and there are enough salmon in the loch to support comfortably a small herd of fish eaters. But if the monsters are fish eaters, they should leave their mark—some of the fish should get away and later be caught by human fishermen who would notice strange wounds on them. While there have been a few reports of wounded salmon, there has been nothing conclusive.

Since the Loch Ness monster seems so elusive, many have wondered if the creature (or creatures) are only part-time residents of the loch, for Loch Ness is connected with the sea. But this would mean the creatures had to migrate up the river Ness, which runs right through the middle of the city of Inverness. It is impossible to imagine any large creature going up that river unobserved. At the other end the monsters would have to navigate the locks of the Caledonian Canal, an even more absurd idea. There have been theories about an underground tunnel connecting the loch to the sea, but no evidence of such a connection has ever been found. If the Loch Ness monster exists, it is a full-time resident of Loch Ness.

Since about 1969, attention has also been focused on Loch Morar, about seventy miles from Loch Ness. A creature dubbed Morag has been reported in this smaller but deeper body of water. On August 18, 1969, a couple of fishermen said that their boat had actually rammed a large, unknown animal in Loch Morar. The fishermen took a couple of shots at it, but the creature submerged, apparently unhurt. There have been other sightings since, but Morag has never captured the public imagination as has Nessie.

Short of draining the loch and sifting the silt on the bottom, it is probably impossible to disprove the existence of the Loch Ness monster. Proving its existence, however, should be relatively easy. A bone, a piece of hide, an unambiguous close-up photo—any of these would prove the reality of the creature. Since intensive investigation has been going on since the 1930s, it is not unreasonable to wonder how the creature has escaped detection for so long. Loch Ness is large, deep, and dark, but how many years can it hold its secret before we begin to wonder if there really is any secret after all?

But still there are the photographs, and thousands upon thousands of sightings, many from reliable and experienced observers.

News of the final proof of the existence of the monster may be in tomorrow's newspaper, or the next day's. Until then the Loch Ness monster remains what it has always been, the most tantalizing and best of all the modern world's cryptozoological mysteries.

See also: CHAMP, CHESSIE, MANIPOGO, OGOPOGO, STORSJÖN ANIMAL, ZEUGLODON

MANIPOGO   Ogopogo, the popular name for the monster of Okanagan Lake in British Columbia, has proved infectious throughout Canada. A monster reputed to live in Lake Manitoba has been dubbed Manipogo.

The story of Manipogo is a familiar one. There are the usual Indian legends, a few sightings by early settlers of "something" in the water, and then a stream of more modern sightings with their attendant newspaper publicity. Most of the reports made Manipogo sound like a large snake.

The Manipogo reports were numerous enough to attract the attention of Professor James A. McLeod, head of the Department of Zoology at the University of Manitoba. Dr. McLeod organized two summer expeditions at the lake, the first in 1960. That was an excellent year for monster sightings. Unfortunately, though a lot of people at the lake reported seeing the monster while McLeod was there, he never was at the right place at the right time. Once, he arrived on the scene less than an hour after the creature had been sighted and disappeared.

In 1962 a couple of Canadian cameramen said they had better luck. "We first spotted the object to the left of our boat about three hundred yards away. After swinging into the direction in which it was heading, we saw what we believed to be either a huge black snake or an eel. The back was at least a foot across and about twelve feet of the monster was well above the water. At no time were we able to see the head or tail. We were about fifty to seventy-five yards away when the photograph was taken."

The photograph, which to the untrained eye looks a bit like a giant inchworm in the water, is too indistinct to be conclusive proof of anything. Still, McLeod was impressed. "If this isn't a photo of the monster, then I'd like to know just exactly what in the world it really is. In certain respects it very closely resembles photographs taken of the monster in Loch Ness."

Professor McLeod took a somewhat different approach than most modern lake-monster hunters. He wasn't only looking for a sighting or a contemporary photograph, he was looking for remains of the creature. If Manipogo or any of the other modern monsters exist, they must be real animals that breed and die. There should be bones or other remains.

One of the district residents, Oscar Frederickson, reported that he had discovered an unusual bone on the north shore of another Manitoba lake, Winnipegosis. The monster that allegedly lives in Winnipegosis is predictably called Winnipogo. Winnipegosis is a shallow lake and seems a highly unlikely place for an unknown creature to hide. But Professor McLeod followed Frederickson to the lake to search for more pieces of bone. The search was unsuccessful.

The original bone Frederickson found is supposed to have been destroyed in a fire, and only a wooden model remains. The model, which is six inches by three inches, apparently represents a spinal vertebra. Cryptozoologist Dr. Roy Mackal comments, "Even if there were no fraud involved, the model was of no evidential value. One cannot, for example, determine from the model whether the original was fossilized or 'green.' In spite of the inadequacy of such evidence, this report, coupled with the 'monster' sighting reports from the area was sufficiently intriguing to move Professor McLeod to investigate further."   .

One final descendant of Ogopogo is Igopogo. Back in the 1950s a cartoon strip about a possum named Pogo was extremely popular. "I go Pogo" was a slogan used in the comic strip, and that gives you an idea of how seriously this particular monster is taken. Igopogo is supposed to live in Lake Simcoe, Ontario. The problem is that the lake is a bare forty miles from Toronto, and is a crowded summer resort area. The appearance of a monster amid the bathers and boaters of Lake Simcoe should create more of an impression than it has. Evidence for the existence of this creature is little more than a handful of newspaper clippings about vague sightings by unnamed individuals.

See also: OGOPOGO

⬤GOPOGO The most euphonious name in the monster world comes from a really silly little English ditty of the 1920s:

> I'm looking for the Ogopogo. The funny little Ogopogo.
> His mother was an earwig, his father was a snail.
> I'm going to put a little bit of salt on his tail.
> I want to find the Ogopogo while he's playing on his old banjo.

For some unknown reason the song crossed the ocean and wound up in a service-club review in the town of Kelowna, British Columbia, on the shores of Okanagan Lake. Rotarian W. H. Brimblecombe decided the song might be given a local twist when he sang it. "At the time," he wrote, "there was considerable talk about the mysterious creature in Okanagan Lake, and the possibilities of making a little fun were recognized." So Brimblecombe wrote a parody of the original which he sang at a club luncheon in 1926.

> I'm looking for the Ogopogo,
> The bunny-hugging Ogopogo.
> His mother was a mutton, his father was a whale.
> I'm going to put a little bit of salt on his tail.
> I'm looking for the Ogopogo.

The reference to mutton is an allusion to the statement of several witnesses that the "mysterious creature" has a head like a sheep.

The day after the luncheon, the *Vancouver Daily Province* declared Ogopogo to be the official name of the "Famous Okanagan Sea Serpent." It is a foolish and meaningless name, but it has stuck.

Long before Brimblecombe's song, there had been tales of a creature in the lake, and it was known under a variety of difficult to pronounce Indian names, the most popular of which was Natiaka, which may be translated as "snake of the water," though the creature was regarded not only as a snake but as a water god and a lake demon.

Visitors to the Okanagan Valley will find the monster's supposed image all over the place. In the town of Kelowna there is an "Ogopogo corner," which contains a snakelike statue painted green with a forked red tongue, pointed ears, and horns. A sign next to the statue reads:

"The story of Ogopogo is centuries old, going back before the days of the white man in the Okanagan. Originally called by the Indians 'Natiaka' or 'N'ha-a-atik' meaning 'The Lake Monster' or 'Lake Demon.' Since seen and described by scores of reliable witnesses.

Hoax photograph of Ogopogo

"Descriptions vary but the length is said to be from thirty to seventy feet. The body is long and serpentlike, one to two feet in diameter, and the head is shaped like a horse's head. [The statue, however, has a dragon's head.] Ogopogo is able to move very rapidly. Protected by law. Watch for Ogopogo!"

Yet for all the foolishness, boosterism, and tourist trapping, Okanagan Lake is, next to Loch Ness itself, the site of the most promising of freshwater monsters. Indeed, the comparisons between the British Columbian lake and Loch Ness are often striking. Both are long, deep, cold-water lakes formed by glaciers. Okanagan is seventy-nine miles long and about two and a half miles wide and 800 feet deep at its deepest point. That makes it longer, wider, and nearly as deep as Loch Ness. Lake Okanagan never freezes, but it never gets very warm either. The water temperature hovers around thirty-four degrees Fahrenheit, just a few degrees colder than Loch Ness, where the water temperature is forty-two degrees Fahrenheit.

There had been Indian water-demon legends attached to the lake, as there had been to most large lakes in Canada and elsewhere. And there were a fair number of rather vague stories of sightings by early white settlers in the area. But the Ogopogo story really got going during the 1920s, with a long string of impressive sightings.

One of the best took place on July 19, 1926. John L. Logie, his wife, and their two grandchildren were driving along the west shore of the lake. It was about seven in the morning:

"The lake was perfectly calm at this time, and this brought our attention to the fact that something must be causing the undulations that we saw. My wife, Isabella, called my attention to it first.

" . . . what appeared to be causing the swell, we discovered was a rather strange looking animal. It created quite a trough in the water, was about twenty feet long with a head rising some eighteen inches above the body.

"We had to go faster to overtake the creature. Travelling alongside it, we had every opportunity of observing the creature. What was our surprise to see that it resembled very much the descriptions of the strange sea serpent (so-called) that we heard so much about. We couldn't tell whether it was covered with scales or hair. The back of its head looked like that of a bulldog without ears. The face resembled that of a sheep, with the pointed nose."

A little later the same year some local pranksters fashioned a monster model out of old automobile tires and other scrap material. They had the thing towed out at the start of the annual regatta at Kelowna. On the second day of the regatta some canoeists saw what they took to be the model—until the thing dived, and they realized that they had been gazing not at the model, but at the monster itself.

Throughout the rest of the summer and well into the fall, Ogopogo continued to be seen by visitors to the lake. A most unusual sighting took place in November 1926 when some fifty or sixty people attending a baptism on the lake shores were treated to a sight of the monster cavorting in the water.

The December 27, 1926, edition of the *Vancouver Star* headlined a story that Ogopogo had been found dead in the ice on the lake. In response the *Kelowna Daily Courier* wired the *Star*, "No ice on lake. Ogopogo invisible. Somebody should sober up—Christmas is over." The whole story it seems had been concocted as a joke on the Vancouver paper, and the paper swallowed it and was forced to print a retraction headlined LAKE SERPENT STILL LIVING. Investigation fails to support theory of·death."

Ogopogo sightings dropped off rather dramatically during the thirties and forties, but picked up again after World War II, and now hardly a year goes by without one or more good sightings discussed in the area newspaper. In mid-December 1969 the publisher of the *Kelowna Daily Courier* himself saw the creature from the picture window of his living room, which faces the lake.

"The humps were silhouetted against the light and the body seemed to be as big around as a new automobile tire, twelve to fourteen inches across, but no scales were visible. . . .

"Suddenly, the north end of the humps, which were parallel to the shore, seemed to rise out of the water again. I didn't see a head."

Though local interest in Ogopogo has always been keen, the people of the Okanagan Lake region appear to take a fairly lighthearted view of their most famous resident. Unlike Loch Ness, which has been the object of repeated serious investigations, attempts to organize a thorough scientific search for Ogopogo have often been discussed but never successfully carried out. Photographs and films of the monster have also been disappointing. In August 1968, Arthur Folden, a sawmill worker from Case, British Columbia, took about one minute of motion-picture film of something that he thought was Ogopogo. For about a year and a half he showed the film only to friends because he feared ridicule. By the time he was persuaded to give a public showing, the film was in pretty bad shape. At best, the object in the film was indistinct. While some of those who saw it thought that it definitely showed the monster, others were openly skeptical. Folden, apparently stung by the disbelief, simply disappeared with the film and could not be contacted again according to Mary Moon, author of *Ogopogo*, the best and most thorough account of the monster of Okanagan Lake.

There have been a number of reports of footprints of varying sizes and shapes, but as Dr. Roy Mackal comments, "The trouble with footprints is that anyone can fake them easily. Further, to assume that they were made by Natiaka [Mackal prefers the Indian name] is pure conjecture and supposition—certainly possible but without even a circumstantial link to the two cases cited of direct land sightings."

So what we are left with is the uncomfortable fact that there is not a shred of reliable tangible evidence that Ogopogo exists at all. Still, there are all those sightings, made over a long period of time, many by reliable people. This has been enough to produce a virtual orgy of speculation over what Ogopogo might be.

Probably the most mundane explanation, and one that was popular in the 1920s, is that Ogopogo is a monster sturgeon, or perhaps a group of perfectly ordinary sturgeon swimming in a line.

The oarfish, a large elongated fish with a flattened ribbonlike body, has sometimes been suggested as a possible source of sea-serpent sightings, and during the 1920s it was brought up as an explanation for Ogopogo; but it isn't a very good explanation, for the oarfish is extremely rare and, besides, it's a sea animal and Okanagan is a freshwater lake. A manatee, a seal (long necked or otherwise), a school of porpoises, and the ever popular *Plesiosaurus* also have had their partisans.

The most recent challenger to enter the lists is zeuglodon, a long thin primitive form of whale. This is the theory currently supported by Dr. Roy Mackal, who concludes, "a better correspondence of characteristics could hardly be desired." Mackal notes that although whales are thought of as being exclusively sea animals, there is no reason why there could not be freshwater forms of more primitive types for, "It seems probable that adaption to life in the water (in aquatic mammals) proceeds through a freshwater phase."

It also seems probable that the investigation of the Okanagan Lake mystery will not advance much beyond the stage of collecting interesting, but inconclusive sightings until there is some serious scientific interest in the subject.

See also: LOCH NESS MONSTER, MANIPOGO, ZEUGLODON

$ILVER LAKE MONSTER   On the evening of July 13, 1855, a party of six, four men and two boys, were fishing on Silver Lake in Wyoming County in the northwestern part of New York State when they spotted what first appeared to be a large log off the stern of the boat. The log turned out to be the head of what witnesses agreed was "a most horrid and repulsive-looking monster." The monster was thrashing about, and the waves it created nearly swamped the boat. The terrified fishing party reached shore feeling that they had been lucky to escape with their lives.

This was the first appearance of the Silver Lake monster. For the rest of the summer, people reported astonishing close-up encounters with the creature. Somebody interviewed a local Indian, who said that the monster was nothing new to him, his ancestors had known all about it, and that was why they had wisely refrained from fishing and bathing in the lake for generations.

Silver Lake was a remote and undeveloped area in 1855, but this did not discourage hordes of monster hunters from descending upon the region, bristling with harpoons and guns. None of the well-armed parties ever seemed to see the thing, though the creature continued to show itself to isolated boats and fishermen. The monster mania continued right through the following year, when it began to taper off.

The Silver Lake monster might have remained a mystery monster forever had there not been a fire on December 19, 1857, in the Walker House, a hotel in the town of Perry, which borders Silver Lake. In the debris left by the fire was found the remains of the Silver Lake monster. It had all been a hoax cooked up by Truman S. Gillett and A. B. Walker, owner of the hotel. The monster had been concocted out of waterproof canvas and wire, and made to surface by forcing air into the frame with a hose. It was towed around the lake by ropes. Since the Walker House was the only hotel anywhere near Silver Lake, its owner did a booming business from the monster mania.

Walker confessed to the hoax and quietly left town. He returned eleven years later and found that all had been forgiven. The hoaxer was treated as a hero, not a villain. He opened another hotel, which he ran successfully until his death, and every once in a while the Perry Chamber of Commerce stages a Sea Serpent Festival in commemoration of the event.

SLIMEY SLIM   "The serpent was about 50 feet long and going five miles an hour with a sort of undulating movement. . . . His head, which resembles that of a snub-nosed crocodile, was 8 inches above the water. I'd say he was about 35 feet long (on consideration)."

The man who made this report was Thomas L. Rogers, of Boise, Idaho. He reported the sighting in Lake Payette, Idaho, a seven-mile-long lake fed by mountain rivers. The lake is a popular vacation spot and seems an unlikely place for an unknown animal, yet reports of a sea-serpent-like creature have been coming from Lake Payette since the 1930s. The summer of 1941, which was the year in which Rogers reported his sighting, was a banner year, with over thirty people reporting sightings. Newspapers gave the creature the nickname Slimey Slim.

Many people reported the traditional long neck and small head, and others said that the monster appeared to have humps on its back, another feature of other freshwater monster sightings.

After a burst of excitement, and a certain amount of national publicity, Slimey Slim slithered back into obscurity. One might speculate the outbreak of World War II in December 1941 swamped any publicity the monster might otherwise have received.

STORSJÖN ANIMAL   At the museum in the town of Östersund in the mountains of central Sweden there is a display of gigantic hooks and an immense spring trap, which were to be used to catch a monster reputed to live in nearby Lake Storsjön. The lake covers 176 square miles, is the deepest in Sweden, and is frozen over several months of the year. In 1894 a wealthy Östersund widow formed a company to capture the beast. An experienced Norwegian whaler was hired to do the job, and he spent a year on the lake trying various methods of luring the creature into his trap, or getting it to take his hook. The whaler didn't even see the monster, the company went broke, and the Norwegian had to go back to chasing whales.

But if all the stories of the Storsjön animal are to be believed, the Norwegian whaler was one of the few poeple around the lake who didn't see the thing. There are more solid sighting reports of this creature than of any other lake monster, with the exception of the Loch Ness monster itself.

According to the curator of the Östersund museum, the "Great Lake Monster" was seen most frequently between the years 1820 and 1898. According to the curator, "The head is said to be round and smooth like that of a dog, with great eyes . . . the extremities are described as short, stumpy legs or feet, possibly big clumsy fins, possibly long, webbed hind legs. It has great fins on the back of the head, possibly ears, described as little sails, which can be layed tight on the neck." The body is generally described as long and is often reported to have humps which stick above the surface of the water. Except for the "ears," the description is similar to that of many other lake monsters.

Until the 1880s Östersund was just an isolated village and stories of the creature supposed to inhabit the neighboring lake did not travel far. But as the timber industry prospered and a railway was built to the town, the outside world began to hear of the Storsjön animal. One of those who listened to the stories was Dr. Peter Olsson, a zoologist at the Östersund State High School. In 1898 he visited Lake Storsjön to collect all the information he could about the creature. It was a good year to visit; the creature seemed to be exceptionally active. For example, on November 20, 1898, a group of people saw the animal, a mere "two stones' throw" from where they were standing. They estimated it to be twenty or thirty feet long. At first they saw only a head, then it ducked its head and its rear end came up. Then the water was churned up, and the animal took off across the lake at a considerable speed. Two of the group tried to chase it in a boat, but it was too fast for them. After gathering together all of the evidence, Dr. Olsson came up with the theory that the Storsjön animal was a mammal related to the seals. Olsson's theory was undoubtedly influenced by the work of Antoon Cornelis Oudemans, a Dutch biologist who had, a few years earlier, published an enormous volume, *The Great Sea Serpent*, in which he concluded that the sea-serpent sightings were most likely stimulated by an unknown and gigantic long-necked seal. Olsson put his ideas into a little pamphlet that was published at Östersund but generally ignored by the rest of the world.

Though the heyday of Storsjön animal sightings was the late nineteenth century, the unknown creature has not disappeared in modern times. Indeed, sightings are reported quite regularly, particularly in the summer months when tourists flock to the lake in the hopes of seeing the monster. Unfortunately, the best view of the thing that most people get is a mock-up of the monster that welcomes visitors to the town of Östersund.

See also: LOCH NESS MONSTER

WHITE RIVER MONSTER   Where the White River passes the town of Newport, Arkansas, it runs deep—nearly sixty feet deep in some spots. These deep pools are said to be the home of one of America's better-known freshwater monsters, the White River monster.

As with so many American monsters, there were tales of Indian legends of a monster in that very spot. But most of the "Indian legends" surfaced only after the modern monster excitement began—so they are suspect. The modern excitement, however, is well documented.

It began in 1937 when a plantation owner named Bramlett Bateman swore, in an affadavit, that he had seen the thing several times. "I saw something appear on the surface [about 375 feet away]. From the best I could tell, from the distance, it was about 12 feet long and five feet wide. I did not see either head or tail but it slowly rose to the surface and stayed in this position for some five minutes. It did not move up or down the river at this time, but afterward on different occasions I have seen it move up and down the river."

Bateman's motives in reporting his sightings have been questioned, for he owned property on one bank of the White River, and when the inevitable tourists and curiosity seekers flocked to the little town of Newport, Bateman fenced off part of his land and charged twenty-five cents a head for a chance to see the monster. It was a bad bargain because no one saw anything.

Other nonpaying observers did see something. One said, "I just saw a creature the size of a boxcar thrashing in the White River. . . . It was smooth gray and long . . . very, very long. It didn't really have scales, but from where I was standing on the shore, about 150 feet away, it looked as if the thing was peeling all over. But it was a smooth type of flesh . . . the thing was about the length of three or four pick up trucks, and at least two yards across. . . . I didn't see his head, but I didn't have to; his body was enough to scare me bad."

The best recent sighting took place on June 28, 1971.

Cloyce Warren was fishing from the White River Bridge when he saw a foaming and bubbling in the water. "This giant form rose to the surface and began moving in the middle of the river. . . . It was very long and grey colored. It appeared to have a spiny backbone that stretched for 30 or more feet. It was hard to make out exactly what the front portion looked like, but it was awful large. . . . The creature looked like something prehistoric." Warren had his Polaroid camera at hand and took a picture, but it doesn't show much.

Ernest Denks said the creature was gray, weighed over a thousand pounds, and had a big bone sticking out of its forehead. A couple of fishermen, Ollie Richardson and Joe Dupree, had their boat lifted completely out of the water and turned sideways. They didn't see what lifted them, but they were sure it was the White River monster.

There are those who believe that the whole White River monster excitement was a hoax. Dr. Curtis D. MacDougall, a professor of journalism, states in his book *Hoaxes:* "Hoping to intensify interest the Newport Chamber of Commerce really killed business by hiring a Memphis diver with an eight-foot harpoon to descend to the bottom of the eddy and see what he could see. After seventy-five minutes he was compelled to confess he saw nothing, and those who had bet it would be a sturgeon or a catfish or an alligator gar or a cousin of the Loch Ness serpent had to be content to call it even." This failure dampened interest for a while but did not kill it.

Cryptozoologist Dr. Roy Mackal does not believe that the White River monster is a hoax, or an alligator gar, or an unknown creature for that matter. He suggests that it is an elephant seal that has somehow found its way into the White River. The elephant seal, a giant among seals, is found primarily along the coasts of California and Mexico. "It is quite conceivable," he writes, "that occasionally, a wandering individual finds itself in the mouth of the Mississippi, which it follows, finally appearing in the White River, a large branch of the Mississippi."

6

SEA

MONSTERS

COELACANTH No discussion of monsters or unknown animals can go on for long without mention of the coelacanth. While not a monster in any sense of the word, the discovery of this creature has a bearing on every account of the survival of an unknown animal.

The story began on December 22, 1938, when fishermen who had been dredging in shallow water off the tip of South Africa hauled up a large and very odd-looking fish. The fish was about five feet long and weighed over a hundred pounds. It was covered by heavy scales and had big, bulging deep blue eyes. It survived for a long time on the deck of the trawler, snapping viciously at anyone who came near it. It didn't look very edible, and probably could not be sold at the fish market. Under normal circumstances, the unusual creature would have been thrown overboard with the rest of the trash fish. But this trawler's skipper thought the fish was so singular looking that it might have some other value.

By the time the trawler had put into port, the fish had died, and despite rudimentary efforts at preservation it had already begun to rot in the hot African sun. The specimen was taken to a local museum, where the curator, Miss Courtenay Latimer, realized at once that she had been presented with a rare prize. She hurriedly called Dr. J. L. B. Smith, a leading South African ichthyologist. By the time Dr. Smith had arrived at the museum, the fish had become so foul that Miss Latimer had it skinned and the skin mounted. She saved the skull. The rest of the specimen, now alive with maggots, was carried out as quickly and as far as possible. Still, there was enough left for Dr.

Smith to recognize that what he was looking at was a coelacanth fish, belonging to the subclass of the *Crossopterygii*, "lobe-finned fish." It has rather leglike fins, in fact, Dr. Smith nicknamed it "old fourlegs."

While this type of fish was well known to paleontologists, no scientist ever expected to see a living or recently dead specimen. It was a representative of an extremely ancient group of fish, the type from which the first land creatures probably evolved. While the coelacanths had once stood at the pinnacle of evolution, their importance had declined, and ultimately they became extinct at the end of the Cretaceous period, about 60 or 70 million years ago. That was the same time the dinosaurs became extinct. Obviously, the coelacanth had not become extinct, for Dr. Smith found himself confronting the skin and skull of one that had been swimming around in the ocean less than a month earlier.

Clearly, this was not one immortal fish that had somehow survived alone all those millions of years, there must be others. A substantial reward was offered for another specimen, but it was fourteen years before one turned up. The study of this second and considerably more well-preserved example showed beyond a doubt that this indeed was a coelacanth, and that expert opinion which held that this fish had been extinct for 60 or 70 million years had been dead wrong.

Subsequently additional specimens have turned up, and the fish has even been photographed alive by underwater photographers. It isn't as rare as first believed and was not entirely unknown. African fishermen knew of it under the name *Kombessa*, but since it wasn't edible they weren't particularly interested. It was just another big ugly fish as far as they were concerned.

The coelacanth is the best argument in favor of the cryptozoologists' belief that a presumably extinct animal can remain unknown to science well into modern times. If the coelacanth can do it, runs the argument, why not others?

DAEDALUS SEA SERPENT   In October 1848 strange, intriguing and disturbing rumors reached the British Admiralty. It was
said that the frigate H.M.S. *Daedalus* had put into Plymouth Harbor on the fourth, and the men had immediately begun talking about
the enormous sea serpent they had seen while sailing to the East Indies.
A statement about the *Daedalus* sea serpent was even published
in the *Times*. Since such tales tended to reflect discredit on the navy
as a whole, the ship's captain was asked to state openly exactly what
he and his men had seen.

Captain Peter M'Quhae did so, with admirable precision and clar-
ity, and his response constitutes the finest of all the reports of sea-
serpent sightings.

The sighting had taken place on the sixth of August, 1848. After
stating his position, the time of day, the weather, and the condition
of the sea, Captain M'Quhae went on to describe what happened:

Something unusual was seen approaching the ship. "On our attention being called to the object it was discovered to be an enormous
serpent, with head and shoulders kept about four feet constantly
above the surface of the sea, and nearly as we could approximate by
comparing it with the length of what our main topsail yard would
show in the water, there was at the very least 60 feet of the animal *à
fleur d'eau,* no portion of which was, to our perception, used in pro-
pelling it through the water, either by vertical or horizontal undula-
tion. It passed rapidly, but so close under our lee quarter, that had it
been a man of my acquaintance, I should easily have recognized his
features with the naked eye; and it did not, either in approaching the
ship or after it had passed our wake, deviate in the slightest degree
from its course. . . .

"The diameter of the serpent was about 15 or 16 inches behind the
head, which was without any doubt, that of a snake, and it was never
during the 20 minutes that it continued in the sight of our glasses,
once below the surface of the water; its colour a dark brown, with

Daedalus **sea serpent**

yellowish white about the throat. It had no fins, but something like a mane of a horse, or rather a bunch of seaweed, washed about its back. . . ."

All of the officers and several of the crewmen witnessed the passage of this extraordinary creature, and they confirmed Captain M'Quhae's account in all details. Several drawings of the creature were also supplied.

While sailors' tales of sighting sea serpents can sometimes be taken rather lightly, this one cannot. If the officers of the *Daedalus* had decided to cook up a hoax between them, it was a very dangerous sort of hoax, for it meant not only lying to the public but lying to the Lords of the Admiralty as well, a very, very serious offense. If the hoax had been discovered, the career of Captain M'Quhae and all the others who confirmed his story might have been ruined. The risk was far too great for a simple joke; the men of the *Daedalus* had seen something—but what?

There are a couple of odd things about the various accounts of the *Daedalus* sea serpent. Though the creature was seen to be moving rapidly through the water, no one could see how it was propelled. It did not undulate like a snake, nor were there any fins visible. It held to a steady course; it didn't dip or turn its head. Even the picture of the monster is bothersome, for it is shown as having a back as straight as a board. The *Daedalus* sea serpent just does not look or sound like a living creature.

The writer L. Sprague de Camp proposed an interesting theory about this sighting. He suggests that what the men of the *Daedalus* saw was an abandoned dugout canoe. These canoes sometimes have prows painted with the faces of animals. But what was moving the canoe? De Camp believes that the fishermen who had originally used the canoe had harpooned a whale shark. The gigantic shark would then have pulled the canoe out to sea. The fishermen panicked and jumped overboard before they could cut the rope.

There are, of course, objections to such an explanation. Wouldn't the fishermen have cut the rope somehow rather than abandon their canoe? Wouldn't the rope have rotted or broken after a few hours, or wouldn't the canoe have been swamped and sunk? Then there are the witnesses themselves. Could experienced seamen have been so mistaken in their observations?

All such questions are at this late date quite unanswerable.

See also: SEA SERPENT

GIANT OCTOPUS   The giant octopus may be the only modern unknown animal for which we possess physical evidence. The story of the discovery or, to be more accurate, partial discovery of the giant octopus began in Saint Augustine, Florida, in 1896. On November 30, two youngsters were cycling along the beach when they discovered what appeared to be the rotting carcass of something very

large on the beach. The partly decomposed remains of large sea creatures—whales, large sharks, and the like—are not uncommon on the
beaches of the world. But this mass was so large and unusual looking
that when the boys reported their find, the story was soon brought to
the attention of Dr. DeWitt Webb. Webb was a medical doctor with
a passionate interest in natural history and considerable expertise in
the field. He was one of the founders and a longtime president of the
Saint Augustine Historical Society and Institute of Science.

Webb examined the remains and found that they were indeed in
a very poor state of preservation. At first glance, the thing on the
beach seemed nothing more than a shapeless pinkish mass. Webb's
first thought was that he was confronted with the badly rotted carcass
of a whale—the only creature that he could think of large enough to
rot down to such a mass. Upon closer examination, however, Webb
decided that the mass was not a whale at all but the remains of a giant
octopus.

That conclusion was a startling one. True enough the octopus, like
the squid, is a mollusk of the cephalopod class, and the existence of a
gigantic squid was well established and well known by 1896. But the
largest octopus that had even been measured was only twenty feet

Remains of giant octopus

from tip of tentacle to tip of tentacle, and would not have weighed more than about 125 pounds. There were stories of specimens that were a few feet larger and a few pounds heavier. This mass on the beach was quite obviously the remains of something much, much larger and heavier. Webb estimated the weight of the mass to be about five tons. The visible part (it was half buried in the sand) was twenty-three feet long by four feet high and eighteen feet across the widest part.

Just exactly what first led Webb to the octopus identification is not entirely clear, though it may have been the shape of the mass. Photographs were made on December 5 and again on December 7, 1896. The original photographs can no longer be located, but drawings made from two of them show what appear to be the stumps of several tentacles around the central mass. (Photographs taken later have survived, but by that time the remains had suffered further damage.) The squid is a torpedo-shaped creature, with all its tentacles at the head end, whereas the head and body of the octopus form a bulbous central section with the eight tentacles of about equal length radiating starlike around the center. The shape shown in the drawings is vaguely like an octopus.

A man named Wilson, who was digging around the carcass, reported that he had found fragments of tentacles. Said Wilson, "One arm was lying west of the body, twenty-three feet long, one stump of arm, west of body, about four feet; three arms lying south of the body and from appearance attached to same (although I did not dig quite to the body, as it lay well down in the sand, and I was very tired), longest measured over thirty-two feet, the other arms were three to five feet shorter." Unfortunately, Wilson was alone when he did his digging, so there is no other witness to confirm his observations, and a few days later a storm washed the mass out to sea. But it was washed up on the beach again two miles farther south, in a somewhat more battered condition than before. The tentacles, if any, had apparently not survived the second beaching.

There were no professional biologists in the Saint Augustine area at the time, so Webb wrote up his discoveries and sent copies of his report to leading universities in the north. One of his accounts eventually reached the right man, Professor A. E. Verrill of Yale University, a world-renowned authority on the squid, octopus, and the like. Professor Verrill was intrigued by Webb, but his first instinct was to identify the carcass as belonging to a giant squid, a subject in which he had a particular interest. But Webb kept sending additional information, and within a month Professor Verrill had changed his mind and wrote a couple of articles stating that it was his belief that the Saint Augustine mass was a hitherto unknown species of giant *octopus*. Unfortunately, neither Professor Verrill nor any other scientist was able to go to Saint Augustine to examine the specimen at first hand. Webb alone continued to study his rotting prize.

He had a team of horses pull the mass up farther on the beach to prevent it from being washed away once again. This was to no avail, a March storm once again pulled the carcass into the sea. It was washed up at a new location, much the worse for the battering it had received. After that, the Saint Augustine mass disappeared from sight forever.

But before the March storm, Webb had fulfilled a request from Verrill to send some specimens from the remains to Yale for closer study. Webb cut some pieces from the mass, which proved to be very tough and rubbery, placed them in formaldehyde, which Verrill had apparently forwarded to Florida for that specific purpose, and packed them off to Yale. He also sent specimens to Professor William Healy Dall, curator of mollusks at the National Museum (now the Smithsonian Institution) in Washingtion, D.C.

When Verrill looked at the specimens Webb supplied, he decided that he had been wrong about the octopus identification, and even about the squid identification. He concluded that what he had been sent were pieces of blubber from the rotting carcass of a whale. Said Professor F. A. Lucas of the National Museum, "The substance looks like blubber, and smells like blubber, and it is blubber, nothing more nor less." A dead whale was no scientific novelty.

While Verrill publicly withdrew his giant octopus identification, he did admit that there were some difficulties with the whale identification. The tissue samples seemed to contain surprisingly little fat, which whale blubber should have been rich in. He also noted that not all of his colleagues who had examined the specimen sent by Webb agreed that they had come from a whale. Given the badly deteriorated condition of the sample, some disagreement was probably inevitable.

When Webb heard that the carcass upon which he had lavished so much time and attention had been declared to be a perfectly ordinary whale carcass, and not the remains of some monster octopus, he was disappointed and surprised. He expressed his astonishment and disbelief in a letter to Professor Verrill, but could not persuade the professor to change his mind again. And so the matter was dropped—for over fifty years.

It wasn't until 1957 that the giant-octopus controversy was revived. F. G. Wood, a scientist who worked in the Ocean Sciences Department of the Naval Undersea Research and Development Laboratory at San Diego, California, ran across a yellowed clipping with the title "The Facts About Florida." It was one of those illustrated oddity features, much like the popular "Ripley's Believe It or Not." The item contained a drawing and a very brief description of the 1896 Saint Augustine incident. The item noted that Professor Verrill had identified the remains washed ashore as belonging to a giant octopus which, when alive, "had a girth of 25 feet and tentacles 72 feet in length." The item must have been prepared without knowledge of Verrill's change of heart.

Wood was intrigued, for two reasons: at that moment he was working in Florida, a mere sixteen miles from where the carcass had first been washed ashore, and because he recognized Professor Verrill's name and knew that he had indeed been an authority on mollusks, and on the giant squid in particular. Why then, had he never heard of Verrill's giant octopus?

Wood began to do some digging, and found to his surprise that at the time quite a lot had been written both in the popular press and in the scientific journals about the "giant octopus." After Verrill changed his mind, interest in the Saint Augustine mass faded.

From Yale, Wood obtained not only Webb's letters to Verrill, but the photographs he had sent, or the drawings made from them. The deeper Wood looked into the case, the more convinced he became that Verrill's final retraction of the octopus identification had been an error.

The Smithsonian Institution has sometimes been referred to as the nation's attic, because all manner of odds and ends have been stored in it. Wood was soon to have good reason to praise the Smithsonian's reluctance to throw anything out. He heard from an associate that among the thousands of jars of preserved specimens of marine life was one labeled *Octopus giganteus Verrill*. It was the original specimen sent to the Smithsonian by Webb in 1897. The next job was to see if the Smithsonian would part with a piece of its precious specimen. Wood contacted a friend, Dr. Joseph F. Gennaro of the University of Florida, who in turn got in touch with the Smithsonian, where he had contacts. Gennaro was told that he could indeed have a sample of the specimen for examination.

Gennaro went to the Smithsonian personally to pick up his prize. Writing in *Natural History*, Gennaro said, "There by the sink was a glass container about the size of a milk can. Inside was a murky mixture of cheesecloth, formalin (and I think some alcohol), and half a dozen large white masses of tough fibrous material, each about as large as a good-sized roast. We lifted them up with the cheesecloth, then took them out with forceps."

With considerable difficulty, Gennaro cut off two smaller pieces for study in his own laboratory. At first glance, the specimens looked like an undifferentiated mass of tissue, of unidentifiable origin. His first thought was that the tissue had been so badly decomposed that no cellular structure was visable under the microscope. However, when Gennaro examined specimens of known octopus and squid tissue prepared the same way, he found that they also revealed little if any cellular structure. Thus he concluded that the tissue from the Florida monster belonged either to an octopus or a squid—but which?

Gennaro found that there were striking differences in the appearance of the connective tissue of his octopus and squid samples when viewed in polarized light. When he compared the Florida specimen to the contemporary samples, he found that it closely resembled that of the octopus, but hardly resembled the squid tissue at all.

Gennaro concluded, "The evidence appears unmistakable that the Saint Augustine sea monster was in fact an octopus, but the implications are fantastic."

Fantastic indeed, for it now is reasonable to assume that what was washed up on the beach at Saint Augustine in 1896 was the remains of a gigantic octopus that may have measured from 150 to 200 feet across, from tip of tentacle to tip of tentacle. That would make it far and away the largest living invertebrate. The current commonly accepted invertebrate size champion is the giant squid, the octopus's close relative. Squids measuring over fifty feet from tip of tail to tip of tentacle have been confirmed, but they may grow much, much larger. However, a two-hundred-foot octopus would beat even the most generous estimate of squid size.

How could such an enormous sea creature have remained unknown for so long and, indeed, be virtually unknown today? The case of the giant squid is instructive. This monstrous sea creature was unknown to science until the final third of the nineteenth century. It became known to science only when occasional specimens were washed ashore. While the giant squid is a deep-sea dweller, it is also very active, and therefore more likely to appear on the surface and to be washed ashore when sick or injured. The giant octopus, on the other hand, is most likely a sluggish sea-floor dweller, far less likely to be seen on the surface. When one of these monsters dies, its carcass would remain on the sea floor, and only under the most unusual of circumstances would it be washed ashore, as happened at Saint Augustine in 1896. Other specimens may have been washed ashore and gone undetected or at least unrecognized. Professor Verrill, an authority on mollusks, identified the octopus as a whale. Similar misidentifications may have been made elsewhere.

Long before the giant squid was identified, there were legends of the existence of a squidlike monster called the kraken. Some of the kraken stories may have been originally inspired by the sighting of a giant octopus rather than a giant squid. The eccentric nineteenth-century naturalist Denys de Montfort first identified the kraken as a giant octopus, rather than a giant squid.

F. G. Wood, the marine biologist who rediscovered the Saint Augustine incident, found another set of tales which might relate to a giant octopus. Before he had heard of the Saint Augustine mass, Wood had been working in the Bahama Islands. One of his guides told him of the existence of "giant scuttles." *Scuttle* is the Bahamian word for "octopus," and the small octopus is a familiar sight in the waters around the islands. Wood believed that his guide would have known the difference between an octopus and a squid or any other sea creature. Giant squids are also rumored to live in the region, though the evidence is strictly anecdotal. According to the guide, these monster octopus's arms might be as much as seventy-five feet long, but the creatures themselves were not considered aggressive or particularly dangerous.

The commissioner of Andros Island told Wood of an incident that happened when he was a boy. He was out fishing in deep water with his father when his father's line hooked something very heavy. As the line was pulled up, they discovered that a huge octopus had grabbed hold of it. The octopus finally let go and disappeared into the depths from which it had come. The commissioner would not estimate the size of the creature, but it was clearly much larger than the ordinary octopus of the region.

Also from the area of Andros Island come tales of the Lucsa, which may be a giant octopus, but is more probably a giant squid.

The Bahamian stories square away well with the Saint Augustine find. The Florida current sweeps up past the islands toward Florida and could have carried the remains of a giant octopus and deposited it on the Saint Augustine beach in November of 1896.

We may not have to wait for another accidental stranding for further knowledge of this monster of the sea bottom. Deep-sea exploration in the Bahamas region may ultimately establish the existence of the giant octopus.

See also: KRAKEN, LUCSA

GLOUCESTER SEA SERPENT   What could and should have been a significant investigation into the problem of the sea serpent was turned into an embarrassing debacle by overenthusiasm. The case stands as a warning for all future cryptozoological investigation.

During the late summer of 1817 something that looked very much like an enormous snake with a humped back was seen by many apparently credible witnesses swimming in and around Gloucester Harbor in Massachusetts.

A group of scientifically inclined amateurs calling themselves the Linnaean Society of New England quickly organized a committee to collect statements from those who said they had seen the great sea snake. The committee prepared a detailed set of questions to ask every witness, and committee members attempted to get accounts in writing from witnesses as soon after the sightings as possible, so that the information would be fresh. In short, they tried hard to make a competent and thorough investigation.

What emerged from the statements collected by the committee is a fairly consistent picture of a black humpbacked sea snake, perhaps one hundred feet long.

Traps and nets were set out to capture the creature, but nothing was caught. The Linnaeans theorized that the great sea snake had come close to shore in order to lay its eggs on the land. So they abandoned the attempt to catch the snake itself and began a search for sea-serpent eggs. No eggs were found, but some boys brought them a three-foot-long, blackish snake with curious humps down its back. The boys said they had found the snake fifty feet from the shore.

The Linnaean Society's committee had become so enchanted with their theory that the giant snake had come to lay its eggs, that they convinced themselves that what they had before them was a newly hatched baby sea serpent. They gave it a scientific name *Scoliophis atlanticus*, "Atlantic Humped Snake." A report illustrated with excellent plates showing the bones and organs of the "baby sea serpent"

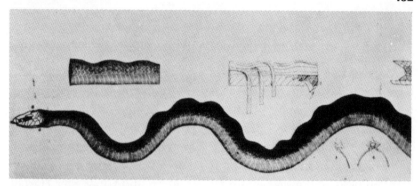

Gloucester sea serpent

appeared in the society's publication. The report contained one observation which should have put the investigators on their guard, the
"baby sea serpent," said the report, bore a remarkable resemblance
to the common black snake.

"On the whole, as these two animals agree in so many conspicuous,
important and peculiar characteristics, and as no material difference
between them has yet been clearly pointed out, excepting that of size,
the Society will probably feel justified in considering them individuals
of the same species. . . ."

It never seemed to occur to anyone in the society that "the baby
sea serpent" *was* a common black snake, and that the humps along
its back were an abnormal condition, the result of injury or disease.
This painfully obvious conclusion was quickly and gleefully pointed
out by the French scientist Alexandre Lesueur after he read the
report. Lesueur's devastating criticism destroyed the credibility of
Scoliophis atlanticus, but it did not provide an answer to the question
of what people saw swimming around Gloucester Harbor in 1817.
Even Lesueur was aware of this, and said that if the giant humped
snake reappeared, he would travel to America to see it.

Unfortunately, if the giant humped snake ever did reappear, no
one was willing to risk the ridicule that might have been involved in
reporting its presence.

See also: SEA SERPENT

KRAKEN   The transformation of the mythical monster the kraken into the very real yet still monstrous giant squid is probably the most instructive story in the entire history of monster hunting.

References to a giant squid are scattered throughout the legends and folklore of many lands. The giant squid may have accounted for the Greek legend of the many-armed Scylla.

Much later, in 1555, Olaus Magnus wrote of "monstrous fish."

"Their forms are horrible, their Heads are square, all set with prickles, and they have sharp and long Horns round about, like a Tree rooted up by the Roots: They are ten or twelve cubits long [twenty to twenty-four feet], very black, and with huge eyes . . . one of these Sea-Monsters will drown easily many great ships provided with many strong Mariners."

"A Tree rooted up by the Roots," is just what a giant squid might look like. But a twenty- or twenty-four-foot monster is a pigmy when compared to the classic kraken as described by Bishop Erik Ludvigen Pontoppidan in his monumental volume *The Natural History of Norway*, written in 1752. Pontoppidan calls the kraken "incontestably the largest Sea-monster in the world." And, as he describes it, it certainly must have been. The bishop wrote that its circumference was a mile and a half, "some say more," but the bishop was disposed to accept the more conservative mile-and-a-half estimate. The kraken was so huge that when resting near the surface it was sometimes taken to be an island, or a series of small islands. The "island beast," that is, a sea creature so large that it was taken to be an island, had been a feature of sea legends since antiquity. It is more likely that the origin of the island-beast legend came from the sighting of a whale or school of whales. Whales may often bask near the surface, giant squids do not.

But aside from the incredible and physically impossible size of Pontoppidan's kraken, his description contains some suggestive features. It is "round, flat and full of arms, or branches.

"As this enormous Sea-animal in all probability may be reckon'd of the Polype, or of the Star-fish kind . . . it seems the parts which are seen rising at its pleasure, and are called arms, are properly tentacles."

Pontoppidan said that while the creature had strength enough to drag down the largest ship, it "has never been known to do any great harm." Except, of course, to those who never came back to tell about it.

Sailors occasionally returned from the sea with firsthand accounts of encounters with the kraken, and fishermen and shore dwellers from the South Sea Islands, South America, and many other places in the world also spoke of a gigantic many-armed sea monster. There were even reports that the remains of some of these creatures (far smaller than those in the stories, but enormous nonetheless) had been washed up on the shore in various parts of the world, and had been examined

Kraken

by the locals before being cut up for bait or reclaimed by the sea. Unfortunately these specimens were generally washed ashore in remote places, there were no cameras, preservation was difficult if not impossible, and so there was no physical evidence to present to recognized scientists and naturalists, who generally lived and worked in cities far from the isolated beaches where the strange giant carcasses were washed ashore. As a result, most scientists and naturalists didn't believe such creatures existed.

There was one exception, an enthusiastic young French naturalist named Denys de Montfort, who did take the reality of the kraken seriously. De Montfort spent a good deal of time with a group of American whalemen who had established themselves in the French port of Dunkirk. From the whalemen, he heard many fantastic stories of encounters with the gigantic many-armed sea beast. One whaling captain told de Montfort of finding what he thought to be a huge sea snake. The "snake" turned out to be the severed arm of an enormous squid or octopus. It was recognizable because of its suckers. The arm alone was forty-five feet long.

De Montfort came to the conclusion that there were really two types of gigantic sea creatures: the kraken octopus—probably a giant squid—and a "colossal octopus"—a true giant octopus. The kraken octopus de Montfort thought to be rather a peaceable creature, whereas the colossal octopus was the raging, ship-sinking monster that had figured in so many sailors' stories.

Just why de Montfort made this particular distinction is unclear. Both squid and octopus are mollusks, of the class Cephalopoda, but they look quite different. The octopus has a sac-shaped head and body, from which radiate eight arms, all roughly equal in length. The squid has a more rigid, torpedo-shaped body with a distinct head at one end. At the head end are eight arms of equal length, and two longer specialized arms or tentacles. The octopus is generally a bottom dweller and not a particularly good swimmer, whereas the stream-lined squid can move with considerable speed by expelling a jet of water. The octopus waits for its prey, while the squid is an active predator. Of the two, the squid would seem to be the more likely

Kraken

candidate for the ship-sinking monster. But de Montfort thought differently.

Both the octopus and squid were well known in de Montfort's time; however, neither were known to grow to giant size. The largest known cephalopod would have been a Mediterranean variety of octopus which might at the very outside have reached a size of twenty-five feet across and a weight of 130 pounds—big but no monster. The known squids were considerably smaller. It is probably because—as far as he knew—the octopus grew larger than the squid that de Montfort was so insistent on identifying so many of the monster tales with a "colossal octopus." In fact, almost all of the stories that de Montfort reported probably originated in encounters with a giant squid. But no matter, de Montfort was closer to the truth than anyone else at the time.

In 1802 de Montfort published a book called *The Natural History of Mollusks* in which he declared that cephalopods are "the most enormous animals that exist on the globe ." Unfortunately for his own reputation, de Montfort was ready to include as gospel virtually any fantastic story he heard. He also included a picture which showed a "colossal octopus" rising up from the sea and wrapping its arms around an unfortunate ship "right to the tops of the masts." De Montfort's drawing was taken from a picture in a church. The story which accompanied the picture told of how the monster attacked the ship, and how the sailors managed to save themselves and their ship with the aid of Saint Thomas. It was the sort of miraculous deliverance story that had been common since ancient times, but was not taken seriously by early nineteenth-century science.

Because his book contained so much of this sort of material, de Montfort was either denounced or ridiculed by other naturalists. De Montfort's own bitter sense of humor didn't help him, and when he once joked, "If my colossal octopus is accepted, I shall make it sink a whole squadron in the second edition," his remark was taken by some as proof that he was a scoundrel and a liar. His reputation never recovered, and he died in poverty and obscurity in Paris around 1820.

Yet despite exaggeration, and a persistent confusion between squid and octopus, de Montfort was basically correct, and he was vindicated less than half a century after his death. There was no single dramatic discovery that at a stroke proved to a skeptical scientific world that the legends of the kraken had been inspired by a gigantic squid; rather it was a gradual accumulation of material, until resistance to the giant squid idea broke down from sheer weight of evidence.

Probably the best evidence came from Newfoundland. An unusually large number of gigantic squids were washed ashore in Newfoundland in the 1870s. The reason for these groundings during this period probably has to do with a change in the ocean currents, but we cannot be sure. Nothing quite like it had happened before or has happened since. The most dramatic case came in 1878 off the coast of a little town with the strange name of Thimble Tickle. On November 2 a couple of fishermen spotted what they thought was a wrecked boat offshore. They rowed toward it and "to their horror found themselves close to a huge fish, having large glassy eyes, which was making desperate efforts to escape, and churning the water into foam by the motion of its immense arms and tail."

The fishermen, who must have been exceptionally brave, managed to slip a line around the thing and tow it to shore. They tied it to a tree, so it couldn't get back in the water. After it died they measured it. The body was twenty feet long, the largest of the tentacles thirty-five feet, a total length of fifty-five feet.

Even before the dramatic Newfoundland groundings, science had been leaning toward recognition of the giant squid. A Danish zoologist, Johan Japteus Steenstrup, interested himself in the giant-squid problem. In 1853 portions of a giant squid that had been grounded in Denmark came into Steenstrup's hands. He published a description of what he called *Architeuthis monachus*, the Latin scientific name for "giant squid," in 1857. Since Steenstrup was a more cautious scientist than de Montfort, and because he had what appeared to be pieces of the creature itself in hand, he was not greeted with the same sort of scorn that de Montfort had faced. But the reality of the giant squid was not fully accepted until the decade of the Newfoundland groundings.

In 1861 sailors on the French gunboat *Alecton* found a giant squid on the surface of the water, hooked it with an anchor, and tried to haul it aboard. Unfortunately, the rope broke and the creature slipped back into the water. Yet when a report of the incident was presented to the highly respected French Academy of Sciences, many refused to accept it, and declared the sailors to have been "mistaken." But after the decade of the Newfoundland groundings all skepticism evaporated.

Since everyone now accepts the fact that the giant squid exists, there is only one question left—how large does it grow? Here there is still considerable room for speculation and controversy. The largest known specimen is the Thimble Tickle squid, which measured approximately fifty-five feet from tip of tail to tip of tentacle. No specimens anywhere near the size of the Thimble Tickle squid or other Newfoundland giants have been beached in the present century. That has led some zoologists to suspect that the late-nineteenth-century Newfoundland measurements may have been exaggerated.

But Bernard Heuvelmans, the Belgian cryptozoologist, thinks that we may actually be underestimating the monster's size. He points to large circular scars found on the skin of some whales. These scars were almost certainly made by the suckers of giant squids. Whales are known to eat squids, and the giant variety doubtless resists becoming a meal, and fights back. The scars are nearly twice as large as those that could have been made by the suckers of the Thimble Tickle squid—indicating that the squid that made them might have been twice as large—perhaps 100 feet in length and weighing, Heuvelmans estimates, as much as sixty-four tons.

Squids, Heuvelmans points out, are active predators. There are stories of fights between a whale and a giant squid. Although the squid was probably just fending off an attack, perhaps the squid *was* the aggressor, and so it is possible that a giant squid might attack and even sink a fair-sized ship, just as de Montfort had once insisted.

Modern accounts of giant squids attacking ships are unknown. Perhaps that is because modern ships are large enough, noisy enough, and fast enough to discourage attack. Or it may be because the giant squid—despite the reputation it has received from such works of science fiction as Jules Verne's *Twenty Thousand Leagues Under the Sea*—is in reality not a very aggressive monster at all.

See also: GIANT OCTOPUS, LUCSA

LEVIATHAN   In several places the Bible mentions a sea creature called leviathan, which has been identified with everything from the great sea serpent to the whale. The translation of the word is unclear, but it has often been rendered as "tortuous monster," a phrase that certainly makes one think of some sort of serpent. But the most complete description of leviathan, that given in Chapter 41 of the Book of Job, presents a rather unserpentlike picture.

"Canst thou draw out leviathan with an hook? . . . I will not conceal his parts, nor his power, nor his comely proportion. . . . Who can open the doors of his face? his teeth are terrible round about. His scales are

Leviathan

his pride, shut up together as with a close seal. One is so near to another, that no air can come between them. They are joined one to another, they stick together, that they can not be sundered. By his neesings a light doth shine, and his eyes are like the eyelids of the morning. . . . In his neck remaineth strength, and sorrow is turned into joy before him. The flakes of his flesh are joined together: they are firm in themselves; they cannot be moved. . . . When he raiseth up himself, the mighty are afraid. . . ."

The description gives many more details of leviathan's power, such as his ability to breathe fire, deflect spear thrusts, and perform other miraculous feats.

It has generally been assumed that leviathan is not an imaginary creature, but it is not at all obvious what animal served as the inspiration for this description. Some of the statements, like "the flakes of his flesh are joined together," which has been taken to mean that leviathan was a creature with webbed feet, and the reference to close-fitting scales and a mouth filled with "terrible" teeth, have led many commentators to the conclusion that the inspiration for leviathan was a large crocodile, a creature with which the ancient Hebrews would have been well acquainted.

If that were the only mention of leviathan, we might be able to content ourselves with the crocodile identification. There is, however, a briefer but much more famous reference to leviathan in Psalm 104, verses 25–26. "So is the great and wide sea, wherein are things creeping innumerable, both small and great beasts. There go the ships: there is that leviathan, whom thou hast made to play therein."

Here the reference clearly is to a creature of the deep sea, but crocodiles are river and swamp dwellers. It is the statement in Psalms which has led to the identification of leviathan with the great whales. But is it likely that the ancient Hebrew would have known about the great whales? The celebrated Jonah and the "whale" story is really the result of a mistranslation. The original reference is to a "big fish" of unspecified variety. Later translators added the word *whale* because it was the biggest "fish" they could think of. Besides, whales just do not fit with the description given in Job; they do not have scales or necks, and the largest don't even have teeth.

Possibly the same word, *leviathan*, is being used to refer to two different creatures. The leviathan of Job is a crocodile, while the leviathan of the Psalms is something else, a whale or some genuinely unknown sea creature.

See also: BEHEMOTH, UNICORN

LUCSA   In the vicinity of Andros Island in the western Bahamas to the south of Florida there are tales of a many-armed monster called Lucsa. This tradition was investigated by George J. Benjamin, a research chemist and underwater explorer. Though Benjamin him-self never saw the creature, he was frequently told about it by island fishermen:

"I remind de time one stop a two-master dead in de water. He wrap all around de rudders and wid de free hahnds he feelin' on decks. Once de hahnd feel a mahn, dey was a flunder in de water, and bot' mahn and Lucsa gone."

Before diving, Benjamin was warned by one of his native helpers, "You go dere and Lucsa, him of de hahnds, sure to catch you. Once de hahnds get hold of you, you dead, mahn."

Biologist Bruce Wright believes that Lucsa might be a giant octo-pus or more probably a giant squid. Wright also found natives who said that these monsters can sometimes be found inland in deep holes in lakes and other deep holes called "banana holes." The squid and octopus do not live in fresh water, but the water found in some of these deep holes may be brackish, and thus the possibility cannot be dismissed out of hand.

See also: KRAKEN, GIANT OCTOPUS

PLESIOSAUR   The ancient animal that comes up most fre-quently in a discussion of water monsters, be they sea or lake mon-sters, is plesiosaur, a gigantic marine reptile from the age of the dino-saurs. This great marine reptile has excited wonder and awe from the time of its discovery in the early nineteenth century. Baron Cuvier, the greatest paleontologist of his day, said of the early plesiosaur fossils:

"We have now reached those of all the reptiles and perhaps of all the animals which least resemble those we know and are most designed to astonish the naturalist by their combinations of structures which without the slightest doubt would seem incredible to anyone who had not been able to observe them himself . . . in the genus *Ple-siosaurus* with the same whale's flippers, a lizard's head, and a long neck like a snake's. . . . The *Plesiosaurus* is perhaps the strangest of

Plesiosaurs (in background)

all of the inhabitants of the ancient world and the one which seems more to deserve the name monster."

Plesiosaur has sometimes been described as looking like a snake that has swallowed a barrel. There are several different known species, but they all possess the same general shape, long thin neck, relatively small head, heavy body, thick but tapering tail, and four powerful flippers. Plesiosaurs attained a length of up to forty-five feet.

Of the known species of *Plesiosaurus,* the elasmosaur, which is the most elongated of the genus, has been mentioned most often in connection with the sea-serpent sightings. With its enormous neck sticking out of the water, it could easily look like a snake.

Plesiosaurs were among the earliest and most sensational of the great reptiles to be discovered. They had been used in stories by Jules Verne and Arthur Conan Doyle. Models of plesiosaurs had been on display at the Crystal Palace during the Great Exhibition of London in 1851. (Indeed, the very same models are still on display in Sydenham Park in London today.) So the image of the plesiosaur was firmly fixed in the public's mind long before the start of the Loch Ness monster excitement, or the reported appearance of many other *Plesiosaurus*-like monsters. How much the well-known image of the great marine reptile influenced what people saw, or thought they saw, is not possible to determine.

There is no fossil evidence to suggest that the plesiosaur survived the wave of extinctions that struck marine reptiles, pterosaurs (flying reptiles), and dinosaurs at the end of the Cretaceous period, some 65 to 70 million years ago. But there has been much speculation that some form of plesiosaur has survived.

See also: LOCH NESS MONSTER, PSEUDOPLESIOSAUR, SEA SERPENT

PSEUDOPLESIOSAUR   Every few years it seems, there is a story that the partly rotted carcass of an unknown sea creature has been washed up on a beach somewhere or dredged up from some great depth. The creature is usually described as being twenty or thirty feet in length with a long thin neck, small head, thick body, long tapering tail, and four flippers. It appears to be the perfect image of the plesiosaur, a large marine reptile from the age of the dinosaurs, and a favorite candidate for everything from the sea serpent to the Loch Ness monster.

Typical of this genre of monster story is one which appeared in newspapers all over the world in mid-1977. It concerned the decaying carcass of a "sea monster" hauled up by a Japanese fishing boat off the coast of New Zealand. The carcass itself was in such a putrid condition that it was thrown overboard before the ship returned to port. But some tissue samples had been preserved, and there were sketches and photographs of the thing. The papers carried a quote from Professor Yoshinori Imaizuni, director of research at the Tokyo National Science Museum: "It's not a fish, whale or any other mammal. It's a reptile and the sketch looks very like a plesiosaurus. . . . This was a precious and important discovery for human beings. It seems to show that these animals are not extinct after all. It's impossible for only one to have survived."

Yet the expected announcement that confirming evidence of the survival of the plesiosaur has been found never appeared. The story died away, and most of those who had first marveled over the report were left to wonder what happened. What happened was that when the tissue samples were examined, they turned out to be from a shark. Looking at the picture of what appears to be a long-necked creature, the layman might wonder how it could possibly be a shark. But anyone familiar with the history of monsters would not have been surprised at this conclusion to the mystery—it had all happened before, many times.

In November 1970 a similar "monster" was washed up on the beach at Scituate, Massachusetts. Photographs of the carcass on the beach show it to be remarkably plesiosaurlike in appearance. Yet the Scituate "monster" also turned out to be a shark. So too did the Stronsa beast, a huge carcass washed up on one of the Orkney islands in 1808—which caused considerable excitement in the scientific community of that day. So too have many lesser-known "monsters" and "beasts" whose rotting remains have sparked short-lived sensations all over the world.

How, you may wonder, can a shark, even one long dead and well on its way to decay, resemble a plesiosaur? As it happens, there is one variety of shark, the basking shark, that is anatomically perfect for the deception, a natural deception, not a man-made hoax. It has hap-

Pseudoplesiosaur

pened so frequently that a basking-shark carcass has sometimes been labeled a pseudoplesiosaur.

The basking shark is one of the largest of all the world's sharks. Males average about thirty feet, and the record length is forty-five feet. But the basking shark, like the even larger whale shark, is a peaceable giant—quite unlike the man-killing monster of *Jaws*. The basking shark feeds entirely on plankton, as do the largest whales. The shark swims lazily along with its mouth open. Water and plankton go in, the plankton are filtered by grill-like structures behind the gills into the digestive system, and the water passes out through the gill slits, which are extremely long and go nearly completely around the neck of the shark.

When a basking shark dies and its carcass begins to decompose, the whole gill apparatus tends to fall away, taking with it the most prominent of all shark features, the enormous jaws. What remains at the front end of the carcass is a small cranium and a long, exposed piece of backbone. These can look like a small head and long neck. Another shark trademark, the triangular dorsal fin, also tends to rot away quickly. The creature's backbone extends into only one lobe of the two-lobed tail, so one lobe will fall off, leaving what appears to be a smooth back and long tapering tail. The pectoral fins remain and look like the front flippers of the extinct marine reptile.

One final joke that nature plays on the enthusiastic monster hunter with this pseudoplesiosaur is that when the shark's skin decomposes, the underlying muscle fibers begin to break up into whiskerlike fibers which tend to give the carcass the appearance of being covered with fur. Never mind that the real plesiosaur was a reptile that did not have fur—the furry appearance further confuses the shark identification.

See also: PLESIOSAUR

$EA APE Georg Wilhelm Steller was one of the pioneer explorers of the northern seas. On August 11, 1741, Steller was aboard a ship in the Gulf of Alaska when he saw swimming alongside the ship an animal the likes of which no one else had ever seen before, and no one has seen since.

It wasn't a giant, being only about five feet in length. "The head was like a dog's," wrote Steller, "with pointed erect ears. From the upper and lower lips on both sides whiskers hung down which made it look almost like a Chinaman. The eyes were large, the body was round and thick, tapering gradually toward the tail. The skin seemed thickly covered with hair, of a gray color on the back, but reddish white on the belly . . . the tail was divided into two fins of which the upper, as in the case of sharks, was twice as large as the lower. Nothing struck me more surprising than the fact that neither forefeet as in the marine amphibians nor, in their sted, fins were to be seen. . . ."

Steller compared the creature he saw to a picture in Konrad Gesner's epic sixteenth-century work on natural history. Steller said Gesner called his creature the sea monkey because of its agility. Steller's creature has more commonly been called the sea ape.

Steller watched the strange animal for about two hours. Then, as naturalists were accustomed to do in those days, he decided to kill it so that he could take the specimen back to Europe. Steller took a shot at it, missed, and the creature fled, never to be seen again by anyone.

Steller's observation has caused nothing but confusion. In the first place, there is no illustration or description in Gesner's well-known work which matches what Steller described, but there are a couple of illustrations that Steller might have recalled imperfectly which could have led him to make the comparison. Steller's description certainly does not match any known animal.

This has led some to conclude that Steller made a mistake, that he was looking at an otter, a seal, or some other kind of known animal. Yet Steller was an experienced and acute observer. He certainly knew what otters and seals looked like and he described them accurately elsewhere. And he had not observed this creature under difficult conditions. On the contrary, he watched it for about two hours, sometimes at very close range.

What, then, did he see? To this day, nobody knows.

See also: STELLER'S SEA COW

$EA SERPENT   For centuries sailors have come back from voyages with tales of the strange and monstrous sea creatures they had seen in the oceans. Today we can identify many of these "sea monsters" as whales, giant squids, or other large but known sea creatures. There remains, however, a considerable body of unexplained sightings generally lumped under the heading of sea serpent. Not all of the sightings refer to a distinctly serpentlike animal, and, indeed, several different sorts of creatures may be involved here. But the traditional name of sea serpent has stuck, and it would be foolish to attempt to change it at this late date.

The first extensive references to what was later to become known as the sea serpent appear in the works of Olaus Magnus, a sixteenth-century archbishop of Uppsala, Sweden. Olaus compiled a history of his northern homeland in which he tried to include descriptions of all the land and sea animals, among them the sea serpent. Olaus described the sea serpent as being two hundred feet long and twenty feet thick. Not only that: "He hath commonly hair hanging from his neck a Cubit long and sharp Scales, and is black, and hath flaming shining eyes. This snake disquiets the Shippers, and he puts his head on high like a pillar, and catcheth away men, and he devours them." No wonder he disquieted the shippers!

Quite clearly Olaus had an active imagination and was willing to treat as gospel the wildest of stories. Yet his book is not entirely fanciful, and many of the creatures that he described, while exaggerated, are quite real.

The first really good eyewitness account of a sea serpent we have comes from a Norwegian Protestant missionary named Hans Egede. In 1734 Egede was on his way to Greenland, when he saw a huge sea creature, that was not really a serpent, but certainly was an unknown.

"This monster was of so huge a size," he wrote, "that coming out of the Water, its Head reached as high as the Mast Head; its Body was bulky as the Ship and three or four times as long. [Unfortunately,

Hans Egede's sea serpent

we do not know the dimensions of Egede's ship, but Egede probably thought the creature was at least one hundred feet long.] It had a long pointed Snout and spouted like a Whale-Fish; great broad Paws, and the Body seemed covered with shell-work, its skin very rugged and uneven. The under part of its Body was shaped like an enormous huge Serpent, and when it dived again under the Water, it plunged backwards into the Sea, and so raised its Tail aloft, which seemed a whole ship's length distant from the bulkiest part of the Body." A sketch of the monster, made by another missionary, accompanied Egede's account of his voyage. Everything that we know of Egede indicates that he was a competent and trustworthy observer, one not given to hysterical exaggeration. Unfortunately, we have little information concerning the conditions under which this sighting was made, so we can't be sure how good a view Egede got of his monster. Much later, a skeptic named Henry Lee, in his book *Sea Monsters Unmasked,* concluded that what Egede had really seen was a giant squid with its tail sticking out of the water. Lee believed that Egede had mistaken the squid's tail for a head and a tentacle for the tail.

It was yet another churchman who took the next major step in sea-serpent history. In 1752 Erik Pontoppidan, bishop of Bergen, compiled a massive book called *A Natural History of Norway.* In his chapter on the wondrous creatures of the northern seas, Pontoppidan published a lot of previously unknown sea-serpent reports. The bishop made a clear distinction between the "true" legless sea serpent and all of the other monstrous creatures of the sea, like that of Hans Egede, which possessed legs or "paws."

Pontoppidan was an uncritical collector who included obviously fabulous as well as possibly factual accounts, and made no attempt to distinguish between the two. One of the more believable stories is that of Captain Lorenz von Ferry, who recounted for Pontoppidan how he shot at a large sea snake in August 1746. "As the snake swam faster than we could row, I took my gun, which was loaded with small shot, and fired at it; on this it immediately plunged under water. We rowed to the place where it sank down (which in the calm might be easily observed) and lay upon our oars, thinking it would come up again to the surface; however, it did not. Where the snake plunged down, the water appeared thick and red; perhaps the small shot might have wounded it, the distance being very little.

"The head of this sea serpent, which it held more than two feet above the surface of the water, resembled that of a horse. It was of a greyish colour, and the mouth was quite black, and very large. It had large black eyes, and a long white mane, which hung down to the surface of the water. Besides the head and neck we saw seven or eight folds, or coils, of this snake, which were very thick, and as far as we could guess there was a fathom's distance between each fold."

The nineteenth century was in many respects the heyday of the sea serpent. Sightings of the creature, which at one time seem to have been limited to the Scandinavian countries, began coming in from all parts of the world. At least a few of these reports appeared to be beyond reproach. Yet the scientific community in general failed to take much of an interest in the subject of the sea serpent. In addition, scientists got themselves involved in a couple of well-publicized errors and frauds, and so they tended to treat the subject of the sea serpent with extreme caution, and even derision. Certainly, few scientists were going to invest their time and prestige in attempting to investigate the subject, which by the end of the nineteenth century had become something to laugh about.

One exception to this generally hands-off attitude on the part of scientists was Antoon Cornelis Oudemans, a Dutch biologist and expert on ticks and mites. Perhaps as a relief from the study of these tiny pests, Dr. Oudemans turned to collecting information about the great unknown giant of the sea. Oudemans, who was an extremely methodical man, gathered an impressive number of sea-serpent sightings from around the world and then tried to make some sense out of the mass of material.

His conclusion was a rather surprising one for the time. The sea serpent was real, he said, but it wasn't a serpent at all, it was a mammal, probably a gigantic long-necked seal with small flippers. Oudemans's seal resembled the ancient reptile plesiosaurs more closely than it did any modern seal, both in size and shape. The Dutch biologist had rejected reptiles because of the worldwide distribution of the unknown sea serpent. Reptiles, he pointed out, could not survive in the far northern waters where the sea serpent seemed to be particularly active. Besides, there were many mentions of fur, whiskers, and a mane, definitely not reptilian characteristics.

Oudemans massive tome was rather roughly treated by the popular press and the scientific community. He brought part of this treatment upon himself by trying to explain so many different kinds of sightings with his theoretical long-necked seal. That required too much stretching and bending of the evidence. Still, there were those who praised his courage for tackling so controversial a subject, even if they did not share his opinions.

Interest in the sea serpent declined rapidly after the publication of Oudemans's book, not because of it, of course, but simply because there were fewer and fewer sea-serpent reports coming in. By the outbreak of World War I, sightings of gigantic snakelike marine animals had dropped off to near zero. But there was one sea monster that allegedly fell victim to the war.

U-boat Captain Georg Gunther Freiherr von Forstner reported that in 1915 he sank the British steamer *Iberian*. Shortly after the ship went down, there was a tremendous underwater explosion and among the objects thrown to the surface was a violently struggling sea monster. Von Forstner described the monster as looking like a sixty-foot crocodile with a long neck. The report, however, is highly suspect because of inconsistencies and contradictions, and would not be mentioned at all if there were other good accounts of this era to chose from, but there are not.

After the war the sea serpent never again regained its popularity as a monster to be wondered over and speculated upon. There was a brief flurry of enthusiasm in 1930 with the publication of a book called *The Case for the Sea Serpent*, written by Lieutenant Commander Rupert T. Gould. Gould was a retired naval officer, radio broadcaster, and tireless collector of odd facts and unexplained phenomena. Gould had dug up a considerable number of previously unpublished sea-serpent reports, but he was so aggressively partisan about the creature that he hurt his own case by jumping to conclusions.

The inescapable fact was that people were reporting fewer and fewer sea serpents, and that by the 1930s the Loch Ness monster had replaced the venerable sea serpent in public interest.

While most people had either decided that the sea serpent did not exist at all, or did not care whether or not it existed, cryptobiologist Bernard Heuvelmans toiled patiently away, checking out all possible information on the sea serpent. In 1968, after nearly a decade of what he described as, "the hardest work I have ever done," Heuvelmans's massive book *In the Wake of the Sea Serpents* was published.

Heuvelmans reviews all of the classic cases cited by Oudemans, Gould, and the others, and brings the catalog of sea serpent events up to date. But Heuvelmans is no mere collector of data. In his final chapter, "Disentangled and Classified at Last," he attempts to determine the kind of creature or creatures that were responsible for all of the sea-serpent stories. While Oudemans tried to attribute all sea-serpent sightings to a single long-necked mammal, Heuvelmans does the opposite, indeed, one may say he goes to the other extreme. He postulates nine different sorts of large unknown sea animals, five giant sea mammals, two huge reptiles, a colossal eel, and something called the Yellow-belly, which is of an unknown type. In practice, Heuvelmans is willing to drop two of the nine, one of the reptiles and the Yellow-belly, for the reports concerning them, he believes, are too infrequent and too vague to inspire much confidence. But he sticks by the other seven: the long-necked sea serpent, the many-humped sea serpent, the many-finned sea serpent, the merhourse, and the super otter—all mammals—plus the super eel and the reptilian marine saurian.

Oudemans floundered upon getting us to believe that so many characteristics could be displayed by a single animal. Heuvelmans stretches our credulity by asking us to believe that there are not one or two but a veritable zooful of large, unknown, and very unique-looking creatures swimming around in the sea.

While the seas are not realms of total mystery to us anymore, it is quite true that we know a great deal less about them, and the creatures that live in them, than we do about the land. But is it reasonable to believe that we have overlooked all of these different kinds of animals? It is particularly difficult to accept Heuvelmans's theory because the majority of his sea serpents are mammals. Of all creatures, the mammals should be the most obvious and easy to identify. They are air breathers and must come to the surface frequently. Many basically marine mammals spend much of their time on land. Mammals are intelligent and curious and should show more interest in passing ships than the sea-serpent reports seem to indicate that it does. An anatomical objection is that while most marine mammals, whales, seals, sea cows, and the like tend to have torpedo shapes and necks that are either severely reduced or entirely absent, at least some of Heuvelmans's theoretical mammalian sea serpents have long necks and elongated bodies.

In the more than ten years since Bernard Heuvelmans first advanced his theories about the many unknown species that contributed to the legend of the great sea serpent, no additional evidence has turned up to support the theories. The seas, particularly the great depths, have been explored more intensively than ever before. Many new and utterly surprising life forms have been discovered. But there is no trace of Heuvelmans's theoretical sea serpents or of any other unknown sea creatures that could possibly have accounted for any of the classic sea-serpent sightings.

We must recall that the evidence for the existence of a large and unknown serpentiform animal in the sea rests entirely upon reported sightings. Not a single one of these creatures, as far as we know, has ever been washed ashore. Nor has there ever been an even vaguely credible photograph of any sort of sea serpent. Beachings of "sea serpents" have been recorded, but these have either turned out to be mistakes or the alleged sea-serpent remains were never examined by persons competent to determine what they might be. The surprisingly few sea-serpent photographs that have been shown are either so vague they are worthless as evidence, or are clearly hoaxes.

An intriguing bit of possible evidence turned up in 1969. An Alaskan shrimper picked up what appeared to be a distinctly plesiosaur-like shape that might have been as much as 150 feet long on its echo sounder, while dragging for shrimp off Raspberry Island in the Shelikof Strait. Cryptozoologist Ivan Sanderson got wind of the story and gave it considerable publicity. The publicity attracted the attention of the Norwegian firm that manufactured the echo-sounding device. After examining the paper strip upon which this astonishing echo "picture" had been traced, a company official said that it had been tampered with. In short, the tracing was a fake. Sanderson refused to accept this verdict. He wrote, "I have to say simply, that until and unless somebody comes up with a lot more accurate and provable facts to the contrary and much better ones than the manufacturers of Simrad [the echo-detection device] offered, we have here the first concrete proof of the existence of a marine longneck." But alas, nothing has been heard from the marine longneck since.

Still, it is not wise to completely shut our minds to the possibility that some form of "sea serpent," possibly even several forms, might yet be found. The oceans have surprised us before, and doubtless will do so again.

See also: DAEDLAUS SEA SERPENT, GLOUCESTER SEA SERPENT, KRAKEN, PLESIOSAUR, PSEUDOPLESIOSAUR, ZEUGLODON

$TELLER'S SEA COW   Vitus Bering, a Danish mariner, had been hired by Peter the Great of Russia to find out if Siberia was attached to America. He found it wasn't and the body of water that separates the two continents is now called the Bering Strait in his honor. Bering might better have declined the honor, for during the course of the expedition, in 1741, his ship was wrecked on the coast of a desolate island between Kamchatka and the Aleutians. Bering died on the island of scurvy and cold. But a number of his crew survived the cruel winter and were able to salvage enough of their old ship to make a new and smaller one and sail back to Europe.

Among the survivors was Georg Wilhelm Steller, a German naturalist and surgeon. Steller was the first man with scientific training to visit the remote regions of the Arctic, and he kept a careful record of his observations. Steller told of how, during the time he was shipwrecked, he saw what appeared to be the dark-colored hulks of overturned boats drifitng near the shore. Periodically, a snout would appear above the water and expel a great gust of air. His first thought was that this was some kind of whale or even a large shark. But closer observation proved that it was neither whale nor shark, but an enormous sirenian or sea cow, a relative of the gentle dugongs and manatees of southern waters, but much larger than these familiar beasts. This northern sea cow reached a length of thirty-five feet. The great sea cows grazed on seaweed that is surprisingly abundant in Arctic waters.

The peaceable, slow-moving animals proved to be a boon to the shipwrecked mariners, who easily slaughtered them for food. Other explorers and hunters followed in the wake of the Bering expedition and they too found the huge sea cow an excellent and easy source of fresh meat. They were slaughtered not only for survival but for convenience, and by 1768 no more of these gentle giants could be found. It had taken a mere twenty-seven years from discovery to extinction. Indeed, there is not even a complete skeleton or good contemporary

Manatee

drawing of Steller's sea cow available today.

But did Steller's sea cow really become extinct in 1768? There are some accounts which indicate it might have survived longer, indeed that it, or something very like it, may still survive today.

The exact date of extinction (if the creature is indeed extinct) has long been a matter of controversy, with at least one authority, A. E. Nordenskjold, insisting that the giant sea cow had survived at least until 1854. As late as 1963, Russian whalers reported seeing a small herd of sea animals that were neither whales nor seals. From the description they might—just might—have been a few surviving specimens of the Steller's sea cow.

Bernard Heuvelmans also thinks that Steller's sea cow could have accounted for at least a few northern sea-serpent observations. "It sometimes lifts its head above the water and is not in the least shy of approaching man. Its blackish skin, with irregular creases, looks like the bark of an oak and could remind one of a reptile's scales. And its fat forms a series of great rolls round its body which might look like a series of humps out of the water. Someone ignorant of anatomy might think they were a serpent's coils."

See also: SEA APE

ZEUGLODON   The zeuglodon is a primitive form of whale that is not only suspected of being several types of modern monster, but its remains were actually passed off as a monster during the nineteenth century.

A variety of these creatures roamed the seas during the Miocene, some 25 million years ago. Though they were ancestors of the modern whale, they didn't look much like them. The zeuglodons were long and fairly thin, the longest being possibly seventy feet from snout to tail. They had long pointed snouts, big mouths, and a wicked-looking set of teeth. The zeuglodon is so unwhalelike in its superficial appearance that when fossil remains were first found in the 1830s they were thought to be the remains of a marine reptile and were given the name *Basilosaurus*. This misidentification was corrected long ago, but the term *Basilosaurus* is still occasionally used.

A zeuglodon skeleton looks very much like one would imagine the skeleton of the traditional sea serpent to look. When "Dr." Albert Koch, a talented but none too honest collector of fossils, unearthed the skeletons of several zeuglodons in Alabama, he got the idea that he could improve on nature. Koch put the pieces from four different skeletons together and wound up with a monster some 114 feet long, impressive indeed. Koch exhibited his creation around the country as the remains of a sea serpent and leviathan of the Bible. "Dr." Koch, whose academic credentials appear to have been self-conferred, did not neglect to observe the scientific proprieties. He felt he had the right to give his creation a Latin scientific name, *Hydrargos silli-manii,* "Silliman's water king." Benjamin Silliman was a professor at Yale who had once said some nice things about Koch. As soon as sci-

Dr. Koch's sea serpent

entists got a look at the 114-foot-monstrosity, they knew it was a fake and began saying that only a silly man could believe in *Hydrargos sillimani*. Silliman, stung by the gibe, asked Koch to change the creature's name. He did, to *Hydrargos harlani*, in honor of Dr. Richard Harlin, a pioneer American paleontologist, who also happened to be safely dead and unable to decline the honor.

Conventional scientific opinion holds that the zeuglodon has been extinct for some 20 million years, but cryptozoologist Dr. Roy Mackal has suggested that surviving zeuglodons may not only be the source of many sea-serpent sightings, but that their freshwater descendants may be the Loch Ness monster, Ogopogo, and other monsters that have been reported in many northern lakes.

See also: LOCH NESS MONSTER, SEA SERPENT, OGOPOGO

7

VISITORS

FROM

STRANGE

PLACES

ALIENS IN THE FREEZER   The most persistent of all of the rumors of contact with alien creatures from UFOs is this one: Sometime back in about 1947 or 1948 when the flying-saucer sightings began, one (or in many accounts two) of the flying saucers crashed somewhere in the western desert. The crew of the alien craft was killed in the crash. The air force immediately descended upon the crash scene, hauled away the wreckage of the flying saucer, and took the corpses of the little men found inside of it. These alien corpses were put in a cold storage unit at some air force base out West. There they remain to this day, though the government will always deny and ridicule this fact. For years the government has been covering up the momentous information of alien contact because officials are afraid that if it leaks out, the news will create a worldwide panic.

With variations, this rumor has been the basis of a popular film, and at least one apparently serious book. In one form or another, the rumor resurfaces every few years, accompanied by the promise that the "lid will finally be blown off the cover-up and the full and shocking truth will be revealed." Of course it never is, but this does not stop the same rumor from being repeated again in a slightly different form a few years later, and it fascinates a new group, hearing it for the first time. Yet the origins of this particular legend are well known, or should be. It began in the late 1940s with a fellow by the name of Silas Newton, who, among his other activities, gave lectures on flying saucers.

The centerpiece of Newton's talk was the story of the crashed saucer, the aliens in the freezer, and the government cover-up. Newton

191

said that he had learned all of these details from a friend of his, a mysterious Dr. Gee, a "magnetic expert," who had been called in by the government to investigate the saucer crash, because these flying saucers seemed to be propelled by some kind of magnetic force.

In Newton's account there were two separate crashes, one of a larger craft, the other of a small "scout ship," both taking place in the same general area. Inside the craft, according to Newton, were several little men from Venus who had been killed in the accident. They were miniature replicas of human beings, and they were perfect, that is, they showed none of the defects, such as tooth decay, that humans suffer from.

According to Newton, Dr. Gee told him that after examining the craft and its occupants the government had everything moved to a secret location, and then denied that the crash had ever taken place. Newton said that Dr. Gee deplored the cover-up and was trying to get the story out.

Newton repeated his tale to audiences all over the West, but he never achieved much more than local fame, until his tale reached the ears of a writer named Frank Scully, who had spent the bulk of his career working for the show-business newspaper *Variety*. Scully built a book called *Behind the Flying Saucers* around Newton's account. The book, published in 1950, became the first in a long line of flying saucer best-sellers.

Even at that time a lot of people who believed in flying saucers were highly suspicious of the Newton-Scully story. Today it is generally acknowledged to be a complete hoax. Silas Newton, who, among other things, had tried to portray himself as a Texas oil millionaire, was in truth a promoter of a variety of questionable schemes, including a device for finding oil. Selling that device earned him a conviction for fraud. The mysterious Dr. Gee was no government scientist; he was a radio repair man and sometime associate of Newton named GeBauer. Whether Frank Scully knew, or cared, that there was no foundation to the story that he had made famous can not be determined, for Scully died shortly after the publication of his book.

Copies of *Behind the Flying Saucers* can still be found today, but most of those who repeat the tale of the aliens in the freezer are quite unaware of its origins. It has become a genuine and prominent feature of American folklore.

ALIEN KIDNAPPERS   On the night of September 19, 1961, Betty and Barney Hill, a couple from Portsmouth, New Hampshire, were driving home from a vacation in Canada. The drive took them down a deserted highway in the White Mountains of New Hampshire. At about ten o'clock they saw a bright object in the sky, and Barney got the idea that it was a UFO, which seemed to be following the car. He stopped a couple of times to look at the object through binoculars. When he drove on, it still seemed to be following the car, and that worried him.

At approximately twelve o'clock, Barney stopped the car again. Now the light seemed closer, and he could see a craft—a sort of a wingless plane behind the light. The thing seemed to be about to land, and that prospect absolutely terrified Barney. He rushed back to the car and drove off.

Approximately two hours later Barney saw a road sign that he figured was about thirty-five miles from where he had last stopped his car. Neither he nor Betty had any clear recollection of what had happened during the previous two hours.

After weeks of being troubled with headaches and nightmares, the Hills went to see a psychiatrist and underwent a series of hypnotic sessions. Under hypnosis, the Hills told of being stopped on the road by the occupants of a spaceship, taken aboard the ship, given a physical examination, and then released, with the memory of their experiences erased or partially erased from their minds. The memory, they believed, had been retained in their unconscious minds and released by hypnosis.

The descriptions that both Betty and Barney Hill gave of their alien kidnappers were rather vague. The aliens appeared to wear black shiny jackets. Betty said they had faces with large slanting eyes and big lipless mouths. A hypnotized Barney Hill drew pictures of strange insectlike faces. It was the eyes that he remembered most clearly and horribly. During one hypnotic session he cried out, "Ohhh, those eyes! They're in my brain! Please, can't I wake up?"

Were the Hills really kidnapped by the strange-looking aliens? They apparently thought so, but there was no tangible evidence to back up their story. Even the psychiatrist who hypnotized them did not think there had been an actual abduction. He believed that after the drive home Betty had begun to have nightmares about being taken aboard a spaceship. She had some previous interest in UFOs. Gradually she convinced first herself and then Barney of the truth of these nightmares—and so when the Hills were hypnotized they thought they were telling the truth—but the whole thing had never happened.

Still, the case became extraordinarily famous. It has inspired hundreds of similar accounts of UFO abductions over the last two

Betty and Barney Hill

decades. The slanting-eyed, lipless creatures of the Hills' experience or fantasy has become part of our national consciousness, and since 1961 a lot of other people have reported seeing them.

See also: PASCAGOULA CREATURES

DEROS   In 1943 Raymond Palmer, the editor of the science fiction magazine *Amazing Stories*, received a long letter from a Pennsylvania welder named Richard S. Shaver. Shaver claimed that he had discovered the key that would unlock the secret ancient language of the lost continent of Lemuria. Palmer was intrigued and asked for more details, and was rewarded with a bulky manuscript entitled "Warning to Future Man." Thus began what some have called "the Great Shaver Mystery" and others labeled "the Great Shaver Hoax."

In a long series of stories written by Shaver, and heavily edited and rewritten by Palmer, the "hidden history of earth's past" was spun out in a melodramatic fashion. According to Shaver, the earth had once been inhabited by two godlike races, the Titans and the Atlans, who built enormous civilizations. A change in the sun's radiation forced the superbeings to retreat underground to protect themselves from the harmful rays. But even that solution was only temporary and the Titans and Atlans were forced to abandon earth, leaving the planet in possession of the inferior human race.

Some humans found their way into the underground caverns of the superraces and began meddling with the marvelous machinery that they left behind. The results were disastrous, for the radiation from the machines affected these people, turning them into what Shaver called "detrimental robots," or "deros." The evil deros came to control the machinery, and used it to cause accidents, disappearances, and all sorts of other unpleasant things on the surface of the earth. Almost all evil could be attributed to the actions of the deros.

Shaver's stories turned out to be enormously popular, and boosted the circulation of *Amazing Stories*. Moreover, a lot of people began writing to *Amazing Stories* saying that they agreed with Shaver's theories, that they too had seen the underground caverns and had been subjected to the evil rays of the deros.

Whether Palmer himself really believed in Shaver's deros is difficult to determine. But after being editorially noncommittal for many months, he openly began to support the truth of the "mystery." Shaver almost certainly believed a good deal of what he was writing. He finally got into a dispute with Palmer, complaining that the editor had given his scientific research an "occult slant" with the rewriting. Up until his death in 1975, Shaver continued to try to illuminate earth's hidden history by translation of what he called the "rock books," the records of the ancients written on rocks and stones all over the world but scattered and nearly obliterated by the biblical Flood.

For several years the Shaver mystery was big news in the science fiction world, and had begun to attract considerable attention beyond. The deros had become the modern equivalent of demons. But science fiction fans turned against Shaver, labeling his mystery a hoax, and Palmer was attracted by the newer mysteries of flying saucers. Though Shaver labored on, he was taken seriously by fewer and fewer, and the deros, which once seemed destined to become a permanent part of American folklore, were forgotten.

DOVER DEMON   At first young Bill Bartlett thought it was a cat on the wall. But as the headlights of his car illuminated the little figure more completely, he realized that it was not cat. He didn't know what it was. The creature's most prominent feature was a huge head, dominated by large, shiny orange eyes. The body was tiny and frail in comparison, though the fingers and toes seemed extraordinarily long. It appeared to be hairless, with a rough, peach-colored skin. The total length, head to foot, Bartlett estimated, was about four feet.

"Did you see that," Bartlett yelled. The two other boys who were in the car with him had been looking out the other window, and saw nothing. They persuaded Bartlett to drive back to the spot where he saw the creature, though he was frightened and did not want to do so. By the time they got back to the wall, whatever it was had disappeared.

This sighting took place in the town of Dover, Massachusetts, about fifteen miles southwest of Boston. The date was April 21, 1977, the time approximately 10:30 P.M.

About two hours later, fifteen-year-old John Baxter was walking home when he saw a small figure coming toward him. As he got close to it, the figure ran off into a wooded area. Baxter gave chase but was not able to catch it. He did get close enough to get a pretty good look at it. The figure he saw had a thin monkeylike body and a large head shaped like a figure eight. When it stopped and turned to stare at him with its enormous eyes, Baxter became nervous and backed off. Within a few seconds he found himself running away.

Both Bill Bartlett and John Baxter made drawings of what they saw, or said they saw. The drawing looked as if they were of the same creature, though both boys insisted they had not heard of the other's experience until after they made their drawings.

The following evening several other teenagers in the area reported catching a glimpse of the thing. The newspapers got hold of the story and began calling the thing "the Dover demon."

But the Dover demon was a short-lived phenomenon, as are so many monsters. After two days no one else reported seeing the Dover demon and interest died away. However, monster buffs continued to speculate over what this thing, assuming that it had been anything more than the result of teenage hysteria, might have been. The most common explanation was that it had come from a UFO, not that any UFOs had been seen in the vicinity, just because it looked as if it *should* have come from a UFO.

Someone also mentioned the Mannegishi, creatures from the mythology of the Cree Indians of Canada. They are supposed to be little people with big round heads, small skinny bodies, big eyes, and no noses. Their main purpose in life, according to the Cree legends, was to play jokes on the big people.

FLATWOODS MONSTER   The first well-publicized UFO
monster was reported in the small town of Flatwoods, in Braxton
County, West Virginia, on September 12, 1952. That was a mere four
years after the start of the modern UFO, or flying-saucer, era, and it
took place at a moment when interest in the subject was greater than
it had ever been, or perhaps ever was to be again.

Early in the evening a couple of teenagers saw what they first
thought was a meteor flash through the sky and crash into a nearby
hill. Gathering a few of their friends and one adult, a Mrs. Kathleen
May, a party of seven hurried up the hill to where they estimated the
meteor had fallen.

It was dark. There was mountain fog around. The group was
excited. And above it all there had been a great deal of talk and speculation in the newspapers and on the radio about flying saucers and
creatures from outer space.

When they got to the top of the hill, they did not find a meteor
crater as they had expected; rather they were confronted with, "a fire
breathing monster, ten-feet-tall with a bright green body and blood-
red face."

Mrs. May said, "It looked worse than Frankenstein [sic]. It couldn't
have been human."

Such descriptions are more hysterical than helpful, but it was a hysterical moment, and details of the appearance of the Flatwoods monster are difficult to come by. One thing all the witnesses seemed to
agree on was that the top had a roughly triangular shape; "like the
ace of spades," was how one witness described it. It has been theorized
that this was some sort of helmet or hood. The face, particularly the
eyes, were luminous, though details of the face are vague. The rest of
the body seemed to be swathed in a dark cloak, and the feet, or bottom, of the creature were not visible at all because of the fog and
darkness.

It moved toward the little group with "a bouncing floating motion."

Though it didn't make any overtly hostile moves, the group was not inclined to hang around long enough to find out if it was friendly or not. Panic broke out and they dashed madly down the hill. One account tells of Mrs. May clearing a high fence in a single leap to get away from the thing.

When they got back to Mrs. May's house, they called the sheriff. The sheriff was skeptical and unsympathetic, but he investigated anyway. As he expected, he found nothing. It was the opinion of the sheriff and other local skeptics that the whole affair was the result of over-excitement. It was suggested that when the group arrived at the top of the hill, they had seen the eyeshine from a raccoon or some other animal sitting in a tree some ten feet above the ground. Since the group was mostly young, and they really expected to see something, imagination did the rest.

Despite such skeptical grumbling, the story caught on. Accounts of the Flatwoods monster appeared in newspapers throughout the coun-

Flatwoods monster

try. Mrs. May and one of the other witnesses were invited to New York City to appear on a radio program that specialized in UFO reports. Their story was very popular, and for a short time these people from the small West Virginia town were celebrities.

No more was ever seen of the Flatwoods monster, and years later those who had been involved in the original sighting seemed unwilling to discuss it further. But the Flatwoods monster still has the distinction of being the first of the major UFO-monster incidents.

See also: MOTHMAN

H OPKINSVILLE GOBLINS   One of the early UFO "contact" cases took place in August 1955 at a farmhouse about eight miles from the town of Hopkinsville, Kentucky. The farm was occupied by a Mrs. Lenny Langford and her son Cecil "Lucky" Sutton and his family. On the night of August 21, 1955, they also had visitors—so the house was crowded. Shortly after 7:00 P.M. they got more visitors, these entirely uninvited, unexpected, and unearthly.

First there was a light which came to rest a short distance from the house. When one of the men went out to investigate, he found that the light was coming from some kind of a craft—a flying saucer or UFO. And also coming from the craft was the first of some strange and frightening-looking creatures. Later, people began referring to them as "goblins."

The creature was about three and one-half feet tall with a roundish outsized head and huge pointed ears. Its large eyes were set wide apart almost on the sides of its head. The creature's mouth was slitlike, and it had no external nose, only a couple of nostrils in the middle of its face. The creature's arms hung almost to the ground and ended in large clawlike hands.

It seemed to be clad in a silvery sort of garment, and according to one witness it floated rather than walked. Another said that when the creature ran it dropped down on all fours. Obviously there was a good deal of confusion, for the witnesses were excited and more than a little

bit frightened. They ran back inside the house. The men grabbed
their guns and waited.

When a pointy-eared head popped up at the window, Lucky Sutton fired at it with his shotgun. The blast tore out the screen, and

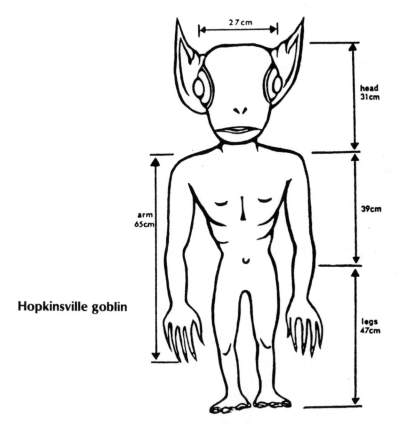

Hopkinsville goblin

should have shattered anything standing directly in its line. But the
little creature seemed relatively unharmed. It was knocked backwards, rolled over a couple of times, and then scuttled away on all
fours.

One of the men stepped outside the back door only to discover that
a goblin had climbed onto the roof of the house and made a grab for
his hair or head. The man was able to shake himself out of the creature's grasp.

Dozens of the goblins seemed to be prowling around the house or climbing all over it. During the next four hours a battle of sorts erupted between the humans and goblins as shots were fired wildly and ineffectively at the ducking and dodging little creatures. At one point one of the creatures was hit full in the body at close range. But it simply rolled up into a ball and floated away in the direction of the "flying saucer" from whence it had come originally. The creatures didn't seem capable of being hurt, but on the other hand, they didn't seem capable, or willing, to hurt the humans either.

When the "battle" was over, and the little creatures in the silvery suits seemed to have disappeared, all the members of the Sutton family and their friends piled into cars and drove to the Hopkinsville police station. The police investigated, but could find nothing unusual in the dark. While they did not necessarily believe the stories told them by Sutton and the others, they were convinced that something had happened, for all of the witnesses were genuinely frightened and excited.

Sutton and his family returned home, but about three-thirty in the morning the alien creatures returned too, and one of them was peering through the window. More shots were fired with the same results—nothing. The police went back to the farm, but the only evidence of anything unusual that they could find were a few stray bullet holes.

The United States Air Force, which was still investigating UFO reports in 1955, conducted a quick and informal investigation. Air force investigators dismissed the incident as hysteria or hoax. Other groups that were interested in UFOs were more thorough, and more impressed, but no one was able to come up with any tangible evidence that the "attack" at Hopkinsville had ever really taken place and that the goblins existed. They did discover that Sutton and his family were generally well thought of by their neighbors, and were not considered to be the sort of people who told lies or had hallucinations.

Once the story got around, the family was besieged by curiosity seekers. At first the Suttons tried to make a little money off their notoriety by charging admission to their land and a fee for photographing the house. This inevitably led to more charges of fakery. All the attention and ridicule was too unwelcome and disruptive, so within a few days the entire family packed up and left without telling anyone where they were going. At the time there were a lot of rumors that they had been "kidnapped" by the aliens or silenced by the government. But none of these rumors had any basis in fact. The family simply moved to get away from the publicity—but they continued to stick to their story about being attacked by goblins from outer space.

LITTLE GREEN MEN   "People keep insisting that they've seen little green men." .

That statement was attributed to Captain Robert White, spokesman for Project Blue Book, the U.S. Air Force's UFO investigation project in the mid 1950s.

The statement is quite wrong, for while the idea of the "little green men from outer space" became a popular cliché and a joke, in reality very few people have ever reported seeing little *green* men. Just how the concept of little green men became synonymous with creatures from outer space is far from clear.

Probably the best early story of the little green men from space comes from Europe. It concerns an encounter that is supposed to have taken place on August 14, 1947, less than two months after the modern era of UFO's or flying saucers began in June of 1947, with a flying-saucer sighting in the state of Washington.

By August 14, the term *flying saucers* had become pretty well known in the United States, but it was apparently unknown to Professor Rapuzzi Luigi Johannis, an Italian artist who was on a hiking trip in the mountainous region between Italy and Yugoslavia.

As he was walking along, Johannis spied, through the rocks, what appeared to be a large, bright red, round object, about ten feet in diameter. Standing next to the object were a couple of figures that Johannis first took to be boys—but they were very odd boys, for they had green skin.

The pair was a little under three feet tall, with outsized heads. Their faces were completely hairless, lacking even eyelashes and eyebrows. Their yellow green eyes were huge, round, and prominent, and seemed to have no eyelids. Their mouths were wide and slitlike and, all in all, with the green skin their faces reminded the artist of a frog. There was no sign of hair on their heads, but it might have been

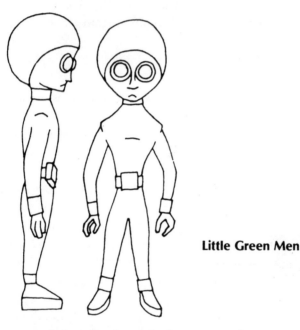

Little Green Men

concealed under the tight-fitting caps they wore. They were clothed in tight-fitting brown suits.

At first Johannis did not see the two figures clearly and he walked toward them, but when he got a good look at those green faces, he froze. Johannis was carrying a geologist's pick, for he was an amateur rock collector. He waved the pick in the direction of the figures, in what they may have taken to be a threatening gesture. One of the creatures touched his belt, which gave off either a ray or some sort of puff of smoke, Johannis wasn't clear. Whatever it was, it struck the artist with the force of an electric shock, and knocked him to the ground. He was momentarily stunned.

"I felt myself deprived of all my strength and all my efforts to raise myself meant an expenditure of energy that was beyond me.

"Meanwhile the two midgets were coming toward me . . . I managed to roll over to one side and I saw one of them bend down and pick up the tool [the geologist's pick he had dropped], which was longer than he was. And this was how I was able to see his green 'hand' quite distinctly. It had eight fingers, four of them opposable to the others! It wasn't a hand: it was a claw, and the fingers were without joints.

"I also noticed that the chests of the two beings were quivering: like a dog's chest when it pants after a long run."

Too weak to even rise, Johannis watched helplessly as the two little green men went back to their craft, which then took off silently and disappeared. They took his geologist's pick with them, and Johannis commented:

"I believe that that old pick of mine is now in a museum on some other planet. I hope that somebody up there is trying to decipher the marks cut in the handle, my name and a mountaineering motto, and a pair of stylized alpine flowers, and an eagle. And I hope they rack their brains to a standstill trying to make it out."

Johannis said that it was several months before he first heard of the flying-saucer excitement which had begun in the United States. If the date given for Johannis's encounter is accepted, his is the first known little-green-man sighting.

In a discussion of this case in *The Humanoids*, Gordon Creighton asks, "Do we have here the creatures that gave rise to the stories about 'little green men'?" That is a hard question to answer, for while the Johannis case has never received extensive publicity, it is the *only* good early contact case involving little green men. The idea of creatures from other planets being little green men may actually have come from science fiction rather than from any reported contacts with UFO occupants.

See also: ALIENS IN THE FREEZER

MAD GASSER OF MATTOON   In 1944 a number of people in the town of Mattoon, Illinois, got up in the morning feeling ill. Some reported severely upset stomachs, while others complained of a temporary paralysis. Doctors could find no obvious reasons for the illnesses. The possibility that the illness might be caused by some sort of noxious fumes was discussed, and the afflicted houses were checked for escaping gas. Everything appeared to be normal. Yet the reports of the mysterious illness continued.

Then a rumor began that someone had awakened during the night and seen a strange figure in a tight-fitting dark suit and wearing some sort of gas mask standing outside the open window. The figure was spraying a gas into the room, and the gas made the person feel ill. When the figure saw that his victim was awake, it fled. During the scare, there were several other reports of this figure dubbed the phantom anesthetist or, more popularly, the Mad Gasser of Mattoon. No mad gasser was ever found, nor was there ever a full explanation of the strange illness.

Some psychologists put the mad gasser scare down as a classic case of mass hysteria, and say the hysteria itself caused the illness. Others, including the more radical Forteans and UFO buffs, suspect that there really was some sort of "mad gasser," but that he was a creature from another world or another dimension. Why was this creature gassing people in Mattoon, Illinois, in 1944? No one will even venture a guess.

See also: SPRING-HEELED JACK

MEN IN BLACK   The mysterious Men in Black, or MIBs, are the extreme personification of a sense of paranoia that sometimes pervades the world of Ufology. In its broadest sense, the Men in Black can be an entity (earthly or unearthly) that for unknown reasons persecutes, harasses, confuses, or otherwise interferes with those who say they have seen UFOs, or people who believe that they are in possession of important information regarding UFOs. MIBs also are blamed for stealing evidence that would prove the existence of UFOs.

Usually these entities are described as men wearing new black suits, black hats, and often sunglasses. Commonly, they are rather short in stature, have olive complexions, and straight dark hair. Indeed, they are said to look "like gypsies." When their sunglasses are removed, they sometimes reveal strange "glowing" eyes. Typically the Men in Black arrive in shiny new black cars—usually Cadillacs. The newness of the cars is stressed, people saying that the cars even "smell new." The MIBs may claim to be on some sort of official mission (they often flash official-looking cards or badges), but attempts to trace the individuals are invariably fruitless. They appear to come from nowhere. Though the MIBs are never reported to have done physical harm to anyone, a visit from them tends to leave an individual badly shaken and feeling physically ill. Some people have reported that after receiving a visit from the MIBs, they have had to seek psychiatric help to overcome insomnia, loss of appetite, and depression.

This is one of those cases where the origin of a belief is well known. Without any question, the saga of the Men in Black began in 1953 with a man named Albert K. Bender. Bender was head of a small organization with the grandiose title of the International Flying Saucer Bureau. He edited a little publication called *Space Review*, which was read by a few hundred hard-core saucer believers.

In the September 1953 edition of *Space Review*, Bender printed two rather surprising announcements. The first said that the flying-saucer "mystery" was nearing a solution. It was commonly believed at that time that there was a single "key" to the flying-saucer "mystery," and as soon as that "key" was found, all would be known. Promises that the solution was close at hand would have been familiar fare to the readers of *Space Review*.

The second notice was more surprising. It announced that the flying saucer mystery had in fact been "solved," but that the solution was being withheld on orders from "a higher source." Bender said, "We advise those engaged in saucer work to be very cautious." He then suspended publication of *Space Review* and dissolved the IFSB.

Bender's friends and fellow saucer buffs were shocked by his actions, but at first he wouldn't tell them why he had taken such drastic action. After a few weeks Bender gave an interview to a local newspaper in which he stated that he had been "emphatically" warned to stop publishing by "three men in dark suits." Later they became men in black suits.

From the beginning, many of those who knew Albert Bender simply did not believe this story. They knew that *Space Review* and the IFSB were shoestring operations, always tottering on the verge of financial extinction. They assumed that Bender got out of the flying-saucer business because he ran out of money and time, but didn't want to say so, so had invented the tale of the three men in dark suits as an excuse for making an exit. It was a more dramatic way to go.

There was, however, another school of thought about the story. In the 1950s a lot of people in the flying-saucer world assumed that the air force or the government was trying to "cover up" the "truth" about flying saucers. That they would send some of their agents wearing dark suits to attempt to silence a man who knew the "truth" was not entirely implausible to this line of thinking. Indeed, Albert Bender's own comments about his mysterious visitors strongly supported the belief that they were agents of the U.S. government. In an interview with his friend Gray Barker, recorded shortly after he closed down the IFSB, Bender was asked, "Why can't you talk freely about this thing?"

Bender responded, "Just before the men left, one of them said, 'I suppose you know you're on your honor as an American. If I hear another word out of your office you're in trouble!'"

"What will they do with you if you give out information?"

"Put me in jail and keep me shut up."

So the original men in black sounded like they were government agents.

Soon these entities, whose very existence was based entirely on the unsupported word of Albert Bender, began to take on an independent life of their own. Bender retired from the Ufological world for nearly a decade. But others began to report visits from the Men in Black, only now they were less and less like government agents, at least like agents of any earthly government. The MIBs began to take on a distinctly otherworldy, even supernatural air.

In 1963, a decade after he had begun the tale of the three men, Albert Bender decided to enlarge upon it in a book called *Flying Saucers and the Three Men in Black*. This time the Men in Black were distinctly extraterrestrial. They were accompanied by women in "tight white dresses." It is a fairly standard work of the UFO contactee, which means it is a difficult, rambling, confused, and in some respects a rather troubling book. *Flying Saucers and the Three Men in Black* had no impact at all on the general public and very little within the community of UFO believers, who are quite used to stories of contacts with beings from other worlds. The book could not even find an American publisher. People were not interested in Albert Bender anymore, but they were very interested in the Men in Black.

All manner of things were being blamed on them. When Maurice K. Jessup, a well-known Ufologist, committed suicide in 1958, there were rumors and at least one published hint that he might have "ignored the warning of the dark trio."

A bizarre, but not untypical MIB story was reported by Ivan Sanderson in his book *Uninvited Visitors*. It concerned an unnamed family who had made a UFO sighting. A short time after the sighting they were visited by a very strange individual. He was described as being "almost seven feet tall, with a small head, dead white skin, enormous frame, but pipe stem limbs." This odd-looking fellow arrived at the family's isolated home one evening saying that he was an insurance investigator and he was looking for someone who had the same name as the husband in this family. The "insurance investigator" hinted that the man he was looking for had inherited a great deal of money. Continued Sanderson, "This weird individual just appeared out of the night wearing a strange fur hat with a vizor and only a light jacket. He flashed an official-looking card on entry but put it away immediately. Later on he removed his jacket and disclosed an official looking gold shield on his shirt which he instantly covered with his hand and removed."

The visitor's line of questioning was as odd as his appearance, and sometimes very personal. He didn't even mention UFOs. The strangest and creepiest moment in the whole affair came when the eldest daughter of the family noticed that the "insurance investigator's" tight pants had ridden up his skinny leg, and she saw a green wire running out of his sock up his leg and into his flesh at two points. After the interview was over, the "insurance investigator" got into a large black car which contained at least two other persons and seemed to appear on a dirt road that led from the woods. The car drove off into the night without headlights.

Though the "insurance investigator" in this case wasn't wearing black, and never specifically discussed UFOs, this is unhesitatingly classed as an MIB case. So too is what happened to Rex Heflin.

Heflin was a California highway inspector. On August 3, 1963, he took a series of what were to become some of the most widely reprinted flying-saucer pictures ever. Heflin said that he was sitting in his car near the Santa Ana Freeway when he saw the UFO quite close by. He grabbed his Polaroid camera and took four shots of the craft before it disappeared. The pictures show an object that looks rather like a straw hat floating above the ground.

Naturally, there was some suspicion that the photos had been faked, and when a major government-sponsored UFO study was carried out, the investigators wanted to get a look at Heflin's original prints, on the theory that they might show something less distinct copies did not.

But Heflin said he didn't have the originals, he had already given them to a man who claimed that he represented the North American Air Defense Command, NORAD. NORAD denied that it had ever sent anybody to Heflin, or that it had the slightest interest in his photographs.

Later, Heflin said that he received another mysterious visitor, this one also claiming he came from the air force. The second visitor asked all sorts of strange and apparently unrelated questions. While the interview was going on, Heflin said that he saw a car parked in the street in front of his house. It had some sort of lettering on the front door, but he could not make it out. A report on the incident states, "In the back seat could be seen a figure and a violet (not blue) glow, which the witness attributed to instrument dials. He believed he was being photographed or recorded. In the meantime his FM multiplex radio was playing in the living room and during the questioning it made several loud audible pops." The identity of this second "investigator" was never established either, and of course the original pictures were never seen again.

In neither of these cases were the men actually wearing black. But these too have been classified as MIBs.

John Keel, an author who has written extensively about UFOs and particularly about the sightings of a weird UFO-related creature called Mothman of West Virginia, reported that while the Mothman excitement was going on, dozens of witnesses were visited by MIB types. In some of the rural areas, it was said the MIBs drove around in shiny new black pickup trucks instead of the traditional black Cadillacs.

Keel was called by Ufological researcher Dan Drasin and told, "You know, this probably doesn't mean anything, but the other day I was walking through midtown Manhattan and an Indian took my picture. He wasn't even wearing a black suit."

Stories of alleged encounters with MIBs are frequently spoken of among UFO buffs, and such encounters are sometimes reported in the more sensationalistic weekly supermarket tabloids.

See also: ALIENS IN THE FREEZER, MOTHMAN

MOTHMAN   The extraordinary series of events that became known as the Mothman phenomenon began on the night of November 14, 1966. Two young couples from Point Pleasant, West Virginia, were driving through an abandoned ammunition dump known locally as the TNT Area. It was located approximately seven miles outside of the town.

As they passed the empty power plant they saw something "shaped like a man but bigger" standing alongside the road. The thing seemed to have large wings folded against its back, and bright, almost luminous red eyes. The driver of the car slowed down and the four stared at it for about a minute, but it didn't seem to have any interest in them. The thing then turned away from the road, and walked, with a strange shuffling gait, back towards the door of the power plant. The sight filled the four occupants of the car with a sense of uneasiness, almost dread, and they didn't feel like hanging around to see what would happen. The driver stepped on the accelerator and sped away down Route 62.

Imagine their horror when they looked up in the sky and found that the "thing" was following them. It was flying overhead, and seemed to be pacing the car though the driver swears he was doing 100 mph after he spotted it. The thing made a squeaking noise "like a big mouse." At the city limits, the flying creature veered off and disappeared.

The frightened quartet drove directly to the sheriff's office, and a deputy was dispatched to the TNT Area and the abandoned power plant, but nothing out of the ordinary was found.

While the two young couples may have been frightened by the creature, they were not shy. The very next day they held a press conference and the story of their encounter was picked up by one of the wire services. "The Bird," as it first was called, became known throughout the nation.

The title "the Bird" was not grand enough for a creature that was described as being seven feet tall and having a wingspan of at least ten feet. It couldn't be called "Big Bird," because that was the name of a character on the popular children's TV show "Sesame Street." But another popular TV show at that time was based on the comic strip Batman, and somewhere some newspaperman began calling the thing seen near Point Pleasant "Mothman," and the name caught on. That has led to a lot of jokes about people finding gigantic holes in their clothes. In fact, the creature was never described as having a particularly mothlike appearance.

Usually it was described as a big gray manlike thing, with folded wings and reddish staring eyes. That's how it was described by Mrs. Marcella Bennett. Just a few days after the initial sighting, Mrs. Bennett was out for a visit with her friends Mr. and Mrs. Raymond Wamsley. Mrs. Bennett was holding her infant daughter. They were driving out to see the Ralph Thomas family, who happened to live in one of the few houses in the TNT Area.

They stopped the car in front of the Thomas house, and Mrs. Bennett, carrying her baby, was the first to get out. Then she saw it. "It seemed as if it had been lying down. It rose up slowly from the ground. A big grey thing. Bigger than a man, with terrible glowing eyes."

Mrs. Bennett was so startled that she actually dropped her baby, but she soon recovered, scooped up the child, and along with the Wamsleys ran for the house. Only the Thomas children were home, but they let in the terrified visitors and locked the door behind them. Mothman followed slowly. It shuffled up onto the porch and peered in the window. No one inside was brave enough to try and get a good look at it. Wamsley called the police, but by the time they arrived, the creature had already disappeared.

Mothman sightings started coming in from all over the Point Pleasant area, and beyond. Most of the reports were from people who had been driving along some relatively deserted stretch of road. The creature, almost always described as being between six and seven feet tall and gray in color, was seen standing at the side of the road. At the approach of the car, it might unfold its wings and rise straight up in the air "like a helicopter" according to one witness. Sometimes it flew away, but on other occasions, like the one described by eighteen-year-old Connie Carpenter, it made straight for the car. It flew directly at the windshield; she thought there was going to be a collision, but Mothman veered off at the last second.

"Those eyes!" she said. "They were a very red and once they were fixed on me I couldn't take my own eyes off them. It's a wonder I didn't have a wreck."

Most people could only remember the eyes. Connie Carpenter got a closer look at the creature's face, though her description isn't too helpful. "It was horrible . . . like something out of a science-fiction movie."

Police in nearby Clarkton, West Virginia, received a call from a man who insisted that "Batman" was standing on the roof of the house next door.

The exact number of Mothman sightings made over the next few weeks is a matter of some controversy. Estimates range from the dozens to the hundreds. Police gave out the lower number; independent investigators say the vast majority of sightings were never reported to the police, who tended to be skeptical and unsympathetic. Whatever the real number, there is little doubt that the Mothman stories generated considerable local excitement, and in addition, accounts were carried in newspapers and on TV and radio stations throughout the nation. Mothman had become a celebrity.

Explanations for the sightings were also advanced. Dr. Robert Smith of the West Virginia University biology department suggested that the excitement might have been set off by sightings of a rare sandhill crane. The sandhill crane is a large gray bird, with a bald red forehead. It also has a reputation for being an aggressive bird which might run or fly after people. The sudden appearance of one of these creatures could startle an unwary witness, particularly since such a creature is not native to West Virginia.

However, there is a wildlife station in the Point Pleasant region, and the rangers there discounted the sandhill-crane theory, insisting that if such a bird had been in the area, they certainly would have known about it.

John Keel, a writer who spent a great deal of time interviewing witnesses in the Mothman case, carried pictures of a sandhill crane and other large birds that had been suggested as the inspiration of the Mothman excitement and showed them to people who had reported seeing the monster. Not one of the witnesses thought the sandhill crane resembled what they had seen in the least. The other birds were even less satisfactory.

Mothman was rapidly linked to UFOs. While no one had ever

claimed they had seen the creature stepping out of a UFO, UFOs had, from time to time, been reported in the Point Pleasant area. In addition, several of those, like Keel, who had done a great deal to research and publicize Mothman, had a long-standing interest in UFOs, and many of the Mothman accounts were published in UFO-oriented magazines. There also is a natural human tendency to lump mysteries together, even if there is no compelling reason to do so. Somehow it seems more intellectually satisfying, though in reality it may simply confuse the issue. So the connection between Mothman and UFOs became an accepted "fact."

After the initial burst of Mothman publicity, the number of reported sightings of the creature dropped off but still continued at a somewhat lower level until December 1967. On December 15, 1967, some thirteen months after the Mothman sightings began, there was a terrible disaster near Point Pleasant. The Silver Bridge, an old suspension bridge which spanned the Ohio River between West Virginia and Ohio, collapsed in the middle of an afternoon rush hour. Forty-six vehicles plunged into the river, and nearly fifty people died as a result of the disaster.

Engineers who prepared a report on the bridge collapse pointed out that the structure had been erected in 1928, was unsuited to the needs of modern traffic, and had been poorly maintained to boot. They insisted that the collapse was completely attributable to natural causes.

But believers in Mothman thought differently. They whispered that the disaster was somehow connected with the appearance of the flying monster. In past ages the sighting of a sea serpent or some other strange or unnatural creature was considered to be an omen of impending disaster. Some thought that Mothman too had been an omen of doom.

Omen or not, Mothman sightings fell to near zero after the Silver Bridge disaster. Whatever it was seems to have disappeared.

See also: FLATWOODS MONSTER

OANNES   There has been endless speculation over the possibility that in some time long past, the earth was contacted by superior beings from outer space who imparted to the then primitive human race some of the arts of civilization. This would help to explain why the human race has made so much progress over the past seven or eight thousand years, after stagnating for tens of thousands of years.

Most of this speculation has been sheer fudge, and most of the theorizers have been either cranks or charlatans. But there is one bit of speculation that cannot be so easily brushed aside, for those who proposed it are neither cranks nor charlatans. One of them is a noted Soviet astronomer, Dr. I. S. Shklovsky, the other the now celebrated American astronomer Dr. Carl Sagan. In 1966 these two scientists collaborated on a book called *Intelligent Life in the Universe*. In this admittedly highly speculative work, the astronomers discussed the possibility of ancient contact, and how memory of such a contact might have been transmitted from generation to generation in mythological or legendary form. The authors found one ancient story which in their view "more nearly fulfills some of our criteria for a genuine contact myth."

It is the story of Oannes, a half-man, half-fish creature. The story comes to us from the Babylonians of the third or fourth century B.C., but it is much, much older, perhaps going back as far as the Sumerians, the first known civilization in the world. About six thousand years ago the Sumerians, who lived in the valley of the Tigris and Euphrates rivers, made a leap from the simple village life that mankind had lived for thousands of years to full urban civilization. The sudden appearance of civilization seems to be freakishly abrupt—though it may not be. Perhaps archaeologists have just not dug in the right places yet, and somewhere there still exists evidence of the slow development of Sumerian civilization.

But there is another possibility: that Sumerian civilization did begin explosively after the people of the valley of the Tigris and Euphrates came into contact with superior beings. And that is where Oannes comes in, for, according to the myths, that is just exactly what happened.

This half-man, half-fish being appears suddenly from the Persian Gulf. The Babylonian version of the story continues: "This Being, in the day time used to converse with men; but took no food at that

Oannes

season; and he gave them insight into letters, and sciences and every kind of art. He taught them to construct houses, to found temples, to compile laws and explained to them the principles of geometrical knowledge. He made them distinguish the seeds of the earth, and showed them how to collect fruits. In short, he instructed them in everything which could tend to soften the manners and humanize mankind. From that time, so universal were his instructions, nothing material has been added by way of improvement. When the sun set it was the custom of this Being to plunge again into the sea, and abide all night in the deep; for he was amphibious."

See also: MERMAID

PASCAGOULA CREATURES   Charles Hickson and Calvin Parker, a couple of Mississippi shipyard workers, said that they were kidnapped briefly by weird-looking creatures that had landed in a UFO. This is their story:

On the night of October 11, 1973, Hickson and Parker were fishing from an abandoned pier in the Pascagoula River. Without warning, a strange craft landed about thirty yards from where they were sitting.

A door opened and three grotesque-looking creatures floated out. According to Hickson, who did most of the talking about the incident, the creatures were about five feet tall and covered with grayish wrinkled skin. It was like "the skin of an elephant," he said. They didn't have any real faces; where the nose should be there was a carrotlike growth. Two similar carrotlike growths were where there should have been ears. The mouth was just a hole, and there were no eyes at all.

The creatures had what looked like two legs, but the legs were stuck together so they could not walk in any normal fashion. Their two arms ended in clawlike pincers. Hickson also felt that there was something rather robotlike about the way they acted.

Hickson and Parker said that they were too terrified by the sight of these escapees from a science-fiction horror film to try to run away. "Calvin done went hysterical on me," Hickson complained.

The creatures floated toward them, making buzzing noises, as if they were communicating with one another. Hickson and Parker felt as if they had been hypnotized and were unable to move. The creatures took hold of them and floated them into the ship. Once inside the brightly lighted ship, the creatures examined the two men with a machine. Hickson said, "It looked like a big eye, and it went all over my body, up and down."

The examination didn't hurt, but during the fifteen or twenty minutes the men were in the ship they were still unable to move. When the examination was over, the creatures floated the two men back outside their craft and then took off, disappearing into the night sky.

At first Hickson and Parker were badly confused, but when they gathered their wits they decided that they had better tell someone what had happened. So they went to the local newspaper. It was closed. Their next stop was the sheriff's office. As news of the "abduction" spread, these two "good 'ol boys," as they have often been described, rapidly attained celebrity status. They even appeared on a couple of nationally televised talk shows to repeat their story. Artists' renderings of the carrot-nosed, elephant-skinned aliens were widely circulated.

However, aside from the word of the two men, there is absolutely no evidence to suggest that the story they told was true. No one else saw the creatures, no one else even saw the strange craft, though the alleged landing had taken place just a few blocks from the center of the city of Pascagoula, and the abandoned pier was near a busy highway. Very near the place where the spaceship was supposed to have landed is a drawbridge, and the bridge operator was on duty throughout the entire period of the landing and abduction. He should have been able to see a brightly lighted spaceship nearby. He saw nothing.

Hickson took and passed a lie-detector, or polygraphy, test about his story, but the lie detector is not an infallible guide to reality. The accuracy of a lie-detector test depends in large measure on the skill of the machine's operator. The man who tested Hickson was a relative novice. More highly trained polygraph operators were found closer by, but Hickson chose to go all the way to New Orleans to employ this particular operator. Hickson also turned down an offer to take another polygraph test with a more experienced operator. Even if Hickson told the truth, that does not mean that the events he described happened as he described them. A person who has a hallucination may really believe what he has seen, and would be able to pass a lie-detector test. But that does not mean that the hallucination was a physical reality.

See also: ALIEN KIDNAPPERS

$PRING-HEELED JACK   In 1888 all London was terrified by a series of particularly gruesome murders. The unknown murderer was never caught; the press gave him the name Jack the Ripper, a name that the murderer himself seems to have adopted and a name that is still famous today. But Jack the Ripper was not the first mysterious "Jack" to terrorize London; a half century earlier, terror had spread by someone or something called Spring-Heeled Jack.

Now it must be admitted that this earlier Jack was nowhere near as bloodthirsty as Jack the Ripper. His activities seemed to consist of jumping in front of people, frightening them badly, and then disappearing with great leaps and bounds before anyone could lay hands on him. It was this apparent leaping ability which gave rise to the name spring-heeled.

Rumors of Spring-Heeled Jack began to circulate in London late in 1837, and they were obviously tinged with hysteria and exaggeration. While some stories said that Spring-Heeled Jack looked like a powerfully built man in a strange, shiny, tight-fitting suit, others contended that he had wings, or horns, or that he breathed fire.

The London police apparently didn't take the stories very seriously at first. Then one day in early 1838 a very respectable-looking man, accompanied by this two equally respectable-looking daughters, walked into the police station in Lambeth Street and told an astonishing story.

He said that he lived with his daughters on Bearbind Lane, at that time a rather isolated and out-of-the-way spot. The previous evening one of his daughters went to the front gate to answer the bell. It was dark and foggy, so she couldn't see the figure at the gate too clearly, though she got the impression of a tall man wearing a cloak. The figure at the gate said that he was a policeman who had been hunting Spring-Heeled Jack, and had finally located him in that neighborhood. "For God's sake, bring a light!" he cried. The girl ran to the house and got a candle and gave it to the cloaked figure. Suddenly he threw back his cloak, revealing a "hideous and frightful appearance." He seemed to be wearing a helmet, and a shiny white suit. He slashed at the girl with metallic claws, tearing her dress. Blue and white flames shot from his mouth. Naturally, the terrified girl screamed and her screams brought people running, but the creature bounded away before anyone else could get a good look at it.

A few months later the men of the Lambeth Street police station heard a very similar story from a butcher named Squires. He said that his two sisters had been walking along the street when they were accosted by a cloaked figure. The cloak was pulled back to reveal a shiny suit. The thing then appeared to squirt blue flames in the younger girl's face. She was uninjured physically, but had been frightened half to death. As usual, Spring-Heeled Jack bounded away before help could arrive.

As these stories circulated, people demanded that the police protect them. The police felt helpless. What were they trying to protect people from? No one was sure, and the mystery made the whole affair more frightening than ever.

There was another report that a strange and ghastly figure had been seen climbing the spire of a London church. It spent several minutes glaring down at the crowd below before leaping agilely from its high perch and disappearing into the darkness. There was a rumor that the same figure had been seen at the Tower of London.

Excitements of this kind inevitably inspire hoaxes, and in Warwickshire the police caught a young man wearing a sheet and mask trying to jump about with the aid of springs attached to his boots.

The major Spring-Heeled Jack excitement died down after a few months, but for decades there were minor Spring-Heeled Jack flaps. In the 1860s there was a rash of Spring-Heeled Jack sightings around London. According to one report, the monster had been cornered by an angry mob but got away by jumping over a hedge. People kept their children off the streets for fear that they would somehow be harmed by the thing.

In 1878 an athletic army officer was arrested in the town of Aldershot on the charge of impersonating Spring-Heeled Jack, though the charge appears to have been a false one and the officer was let go.

Meanwhile, Spring-Heeled Jack had undergone sort of a popular metamorphosis in those cheap and sensationalistic Victorian publications known as "penny dreadfuls." The penny dreadfuls were the literature of the poor. They cost only a penny and you got your money's worth, plenty of action and thrills, even if the stories often didn't make much sense. The Spring-Heeled Jack of the penny dreadfuls was no longer an evil monster; he had become a sort of strange-looking superhero, a bit like the popular comic book and TV superhero the Incredible Hulk. Amid flashes of lightning and rolls of thunder, Spring-Heeled Jack would arrive to frighten the evil doers.

Spring-Heeled Jack stories kept on appearing for years. In 1863 there was a popular play on the London stage called *Spring-Heeled Jack; or the Felon's Wrongs*. It and a couple of lesser-known Spring-Heeled Jack plays ran for several seasons, indicating the general public's fascination with the mysterious subject.

The Spring-Heeled Jack excitement never had a dramatic ending. It just petered out. No one really knows what happened, or how the excitement began in the first place. Some believe that it began as the work of a prankster, aided by public hysteria and a sensationalistic press. Others think it was hysteria and sensationalism alone. Still others are not sure, and point out that the shiny suit so often reported on Spring-Heeled Jack sounds very much like some kind of a space suit, and the "fire" that squirted from his mouth may really have been an exaggerated and imperfect recollection of the action of a ray gun. Spring-Heeled Jack is sometimes mentioned in discussions of UFO contacts, or creatures from another dimension.

See also: MAD GASSER OF MATTOON

8

WEIRD

CREATURES

IN

FOLKLORE

ALLIGATORS IN THE SEWER   Stories that alligators live in the sewers of New York City have circulated for decades. The story runs like this: At one time, baby alligators were widely sold as pets in Miami and other Florida cities. Vacationers returning to New York City brought baby alligators with them, but they proved to be troublesome pets, and so many of them were simply flushed down the toilet. A few survived the experience and in the warmth and darkness of the sewers of New York thrived, feeding on rats. In some versions of the tale a new breed of blind albino alligator had developed. Sewer maintenance workers were said to fear meeting one of these creatures, and to have publicly protested the additional on-the-job hazard of having to face hungry alligators.

Most people have never taken the alligators-in-the-sewer stories very seriously, however, researcher Loren Coleman has unearthed a factual-sounding story in *The New York Times* of February 10, 1935. Writing in the *Journal of American Folklore,* Coleman states: "The incident may or may not have taken place, but its publication in a no nonsense fashion in a highly regarded and respected newspaper must have lent much credibility to the story."

According to the *Times* article a group of teenaged boys were shoveling snow into a manhole on East 123rd Street near the Harlem River. One of them saw something moving down where the manhole drop merged with the sewer conduit, which led to the river. The moving thing turned out to be a seven-and-a-half-foot alligator. The boys dropped a rope around it, pulled it to the surface, and then proceeded
225

Alligator

to beat it to death with their snow shovels. The alligator, said the *Times*, "was in no mood for a struggle after its icy incarceration. It died on the spot."

The article is very specific about times, places, and names of witnesses. It reported that the dead creature was taken to the Lehigh Stove and Repair Shop, where it was found to weigh 125 pounds. Unfortunately, the story ends, "A Department of Sanitation truck rumbled up to the store and made off with the prize. Its destination was Barren Island and an incinerator."

The *Times* speculated that the creature might have been dumped from a passing ship into the East River and, attracted by the relatively warm water flowing out of the sewer, swam a short way up the conduit to the place where it was discovered.

As far as Coleman has been able to determine, this is the earliest published report of an alligator in the sewer, and it may even be true.

BASILISK   To Aristotle the basilisk was the "king of snakes." To the Roman naturalist Pliny it was simply a snake that had some sort of crownlike structure on its head. But by the late Middle Ages, the basilisk had become something quite a bit more wonderful and terrible. A book printed in 1480 states: "There is a kind of lizard that is called Basilisk in Greek and Regulus in Latin and Isidorus says that it is the king of all the snakes and serpents. Even serpents flee the Basilisk because its breath is deadly and so is its appearance."

According to one medieval version of the already elaborate basilisk story, it had to be born of an egg laid during the days of the dog star Sirius by a seven-year-old cock. Such an egg was easy to recognize: it did not have the normal ovoid shape but was spherical. It had no shell, but was covered by a thick skin or membrane. The egg then had to be hatched by a toad, and the result was an unbelievably poisonous monster which was basically a serpent but with some of the characteristics of the toad and the cock as well.

Despite all the fabulous characteristics, the basilisk was widely believed in during the Middle Ages. Many mysterious deaths were attributed to the presence of a basilisk, and more than one basilisk hunt was organized. Those brave enough to attempt such a hunt would carry a mirror, for just to look directly at a basilisk was a death sentence, and in order to strike it with a sword, you had to view it in a mirror. Alternately, the mirror was an excellent weapon, for if the basilisk looked at itself in the mirror it would be killed by its own poisonous glance.

In 1587 there was a big basilisk hunt in Warsaw, perhaps the world's last major basilisk hunt. Two small girls had been found dead in a cellar and it was assumed a basilisk was responsible. A condemned prisoner was the only "volunteer" to hunt the monster.

Fitted with a leather suit and mirrors, the condemned man entered the cellar. A short time later he merged carrying what looked like an ordinary snake. But a physician proclaimed it to be a basilisk.

The basilisk legend was kept alive by the sale of manufactured

Basilisk

monsters called jenny hanivers which were often sold as basilisks and
influenced the popular view of what a basilisk was supposed to look
like. But in the sixteenth-century naturalist Konrad Gesner had
already denounced the creature as "gossip," and belief declined
rapidly.

See also: DRAGON, JENNY HANIVERS

DRAGON   Of all the world's monsters, the dragon appears to
be the most universal, and its history the most complex. Yet the origin
of the idea of the dragon in the West is quite simple and straightforward. The word *dragon* itself can be traced back to a Greek word
meaning "sharp-sighted one," an appropriate epithet for a beady-
eyed snake. In Latin, the Greek word was converted to *draco*, and it
came to mean "giant snake." To the Romans the dragon was a giant
snake, probably a python from India or Africa.

Very few Romans had ever seen a real python, for their information they had to rely on travelers' tales which tended to be both exaggerated and inaccurate. These exaggerations and inaccuracies found
their way into standard works on natural history and were reported
and believed for nearly two thousand years. The greatest of the
Roman naturalists, Pliny, said of the dragon of India that it was "so
enormous a size as easily to envelop the elephant with its folds and
encircle them with its coils. The contest is equally fatal to both; the
elephant, vanquished, falls to the earth and by its weight crushes the
dragon which is entwined about it."

Pliny added a few more details about dragons. There were dragons
in Ethiopia, he said, but these were a mere thirty feet long, and therefore much smaller than the great elephant-killing Indian dragons.
Actually the longest Old World snake is the reticulated python of
India, which reaches a length of thirty feet. Pliny had greatly exaggerated the length of the python. But as with the traditional fish story,
length tends to increase the more often a story is retold. Encircling
their prey and squeezing it to death is what pythons and a number of

other large snakes do. However, no python would be foolish enough to attack an elephant, even a small one, and despite what is often shown in films and described in books, pythons do not attack full-grown human beings either. There have been a couple of reports of pythons attacking small children, but such attacks, if they occur at all, are extremely rare.

Pliny added a few exotic tales about African dragons which he said had crests on their heads, and would use them to go sailing. "Four or

Dragon

five of them twisted and interlaced together . . . setting sail with their heads erect, they are borne along upon the waves to find better sources of nourishment in Arabia." Pliny didn't seem to take this dragon tale too seriously.

Pliny's work remained the standard compilation of natural history for centuries. At the time of his death, Konrad Gesner, the first compiler of a work on natural history since the days of the Romans, was working on a volume on snakes. While he never finished the book, his manuscript was later edited and published by others. It is clear that Gesner believed dragons were giant snakes of the python variety. He got most of his information from Pliny and even repeats some of Pliny's dragon stories.

In an English version of Gesner's work, *Historie of Serepents*, published in 1608, translated and edited by Edward Topsell, we once again meet the elephant-killing dragon:

"They [the dragons] hide themselves in trees, covering their head and letting the other part hang downe like a rope. In those trees they watch until the Elephant comes to eate and croppe of the branches;

then suddenly, before he be aware, they leape into his face and digge out his eyes. Then doe they claspe themselves about his necke, and with their tayles or hinder parts, beate and vexe the Elephant untill they have made him breathlesse, for they strangle him with theyr fore parts as they beate him with the hinder. . . . And this is the disposition of the Dragon that he never setteth upon the Elephant but with the advantage of the place, and namely from some high tree or rock."

Pliny had the struggle end as a draw, but over the centuries the dragon seems to have come out the winner.

Other evidence that the dragon was a large snake comes from the early pictorial representations of dragons. They were almost always shown as large snakes. Gesner had noted that the old German word for "dragon," *Lindwurm*, really meant "snake-worm," or just "snake, snake." The old Anglo-Saxon word *Wyrm* has been translated as meaning equally "dragon," "serpent," or "worm." In *Beowulf* the dragon is called the Worm, and in old English ballads dragons are called the "laidly (loathly) Worm." Throughout Ireland dragonlike monsters were called "direful Wurms."

A popular English folktale which may date back to the early fifteenth century recounts the fight between Sir John Lambton and "the Worm." It is a traditional knight-versus-dragon story. From the sixteenth century onward, artists showed "the Worm" with legs. But the original legend says nothing of legs.

So the direct dragon-snake identification is unarguable. Yet the dragon has become much more than a large snake, for a variety of reasons. The principal reason is that the dragon is mentioned prominently in the Bible. Sometimes the words *dragon* and *serpent* are used interchangeably, but this itself became a source of confusion, for the snake was the animal that the Hebrews hated and feared the most; the snake, and thus the dragon, became identified with evil and the Devil. And so, by the time we reach the Book of Revelation, the final book of the New Testament, we find:

"And the great dragon was cast out, that old serpent called the Devil, and Satan, which deceiveth the whole world: he was cast out into the earth, and his angels were cast out with him" (Rev. 12:9).

This interchangeable use of the words *dragon* and *Devil* gave us the name for one of the most popular fictional monsters, Dracula. The fictional vampire Dracula was very loosely based on a fourteenth-century Transylvanian ruler, Vlad IV. Vlad belonged to a knightly order, the order of the Dragon. (In the West dragons were usually, but not always, considered evil. Occasionally they were admired for their power and the dragon could be a symbol of power.) The word for both dragon and Devil was *dracul*, and Vlad was called Dracula. Since he had such a fearsome reputation, people tended to use the Devil, rather than the dragon, connotation of the name.

Dragon

Just how the dragon picked up all its other attributes—the legs, the wings, the ability to breathe fire and the rest—is not clear. They seem to have been added bit by bit over the centuries by people who thought that a simple snake, no matter how large, was not a sufficient symbol of pure evil. Gesner's incomplete volume on snakes and dragons displays the confusion. He discusses how the dragon was really a large constricting snake, and then immediately the text jumps to dragons with feet and wings. Something has been left out, and had Gesner lived to complete his work, we might know a lot more about dragon history than we do now.

The fire-breathing attribute may have come from the many poisonous snakes, though the python is not poisonous. The spitting cobra from India, a snake which actually spits its venom, may have influenced the fire-breathing concept, but we really cannot be sure.

The belief that a dragon was a creature with feet and wings was reinforced, even if it was not begun, by medieval monster makers, those clever forgers who pieced together parts of different animals and sold the exotic results to collecters of wonders and curios. A dragon, being such a well-known monster, would have been in demand. Of course, manufactured dragons were necessarily small, and had to be passed off as "baby dragons."

Several of these showed up in Paris in 1557. An Italian mathematician who saw the "baby dragons" described them thus: "Two footed creatures with wings so small that, in my opinion they could hardly fly with them. Their heads were small and shaped like the heads of snakes, they were of a pleasant color without feathers or hair and the largest of them was as large as a wren."

Dragon

At about the same time, a Frenchman named Pierre Belon printed a picture of a winged dragon which was to become the standard source for many later dragon pictures. In 1640 a book called *The History of Serpents and Dragons* by Ulisse Aldrovandi was published and it contained a drawing of a two-footed dragon that was clearly a more elegant rendering of Belon's sketch. The Aldrovandi dragon has been reprinted countless times.

So it is possible that the fakers who sewed bat wings on lizard's bodies to produce "baby dragons," may have influenced all later visions of the dragon. Many kinds of weird creatures were passed off as dragons. The Bible speaks of the seven-headed dragon of the Apocalypse, and apparently a group of fourteenth-century monks, trying to attract pilgrims to their monastery, sewed seven weasels' heads onto a snake's body and displayed the result as the seven-headed dragon of the Apocalypse. Later this monstrosity was sold as an example of another monster, the hydra.

For centuries, people had been finding gigantic bones of unexplained origin. These were attributed to humanoid giants, unicorns, behemoth and leviathan of the Bible, and of course to dragons. The bones belonged to extinct giant mammals that had once roamed much of the world but had died out at the end of the Ice Age. Dinosaur bones contributed little if anything to belief in dragons. The strange relationship between dragons and dinosaurs will be discussed shortly.

How dragon legends were spun from the bones of extinct mammals has been beautifully illustrated by Willy Ley. In the marketplace in the city of Klangenfurt in Austria, says Ley, is a rather impressive monument. "That monument fashioned about the year 1590 shows a naked giant in the act of slaying a dragon with a big spiked club. The dragon has a body similar to that of a crocodile, with bat wings attached, and is furiously spitting at a giant—fire in the legend, water in the monument. It is the skull of the dragon that is interesting. Aside from its somewhat incongruous leaf ears, it displays very clearly the outlines of the skull of woolly *Rhinoceros antiquitatis,* one of the contemporaries of the woolly mammoth. Chroniclers state that the skull of the 'dragon' was found near Klangenfurt about the middle of the sixteenth century, three decades before the monument was erected. The skull itself was kept in the Town Hall. It has been repeatedly examined by modern scientists and found to be the skull of a woolly rhinoceros."

Several learned treatises were written on the "dragon bones" and "dragon skulls" found throughout Eruope. Examined in the light of today's knowledge, it is obvious that the "dragons" were really extinct mammals. The learned seventeenth-century Jesuit Father Athanasius

Kircher developed an elaborate theory about how dragons lived underground—because their bones were usually found underground. He said that they lived in caves and, being subterranean creatures, were rarely seen on the surface. It was only when their return to the underground was blocked by an earthquake or avalanche that they were forced to remain on the surface. That is why so few dragons were seen.

Even after the real origin of the many strange bones was established, there were still those who refused to believe that the dragon was just a myth-encrusted snake. They looked for some sort of large lizardlike animal that might have inspired the dragon stories. One man, Charles Gould, was able to describe this theoretical monster in some detail: "We may infer that it was a long terrestrial lizard, hibernating and carniverous, with the power of constricting, with its snake like body and tail; possibly furnished with winglike expansions of its integument . . . and capable of occasional progress on its hind legs alone, when excited in an attack. . . . "

Most modern lizards are small, generally sluggish creatures that are unlikely candidates for inspiring the dragon myths. Then in 1912 a great monitor lizard that lives only on the island of Komodo in the East Indies was discovered by Europeans. It looked so much like what people thought a dragon should look like that the lizard was named the Komodo dragon. But the range of the Komodo dragon is very restricted, and as far as we know always has been. Nor is there any other modern lizard that seems to have served in any way as the model for the dragon myth.

Well if not a modern, or recent lizard, how about a very ancient one—the dinosaur. Dinosaurs aren's really giant lizards—they may not even have been giant reptiles—but when first discovered, people thought they were gigantic lizards, and the name dinosaur itself means "terrible lizard."

When dinosaurs were first being discovered during the latter half of the last century, the dinosaur-dragon identification was made frequently. Even today people who gaze on the awesome skeletons or reconstructions of dinosaurs are often struck with the feeling that here is the origin of the worldwide dragon story.

But that identification runs into serious problems. The first is time; the dinosaurs, as far as we know, died out completely 65 or 70 million years ago. That is long before human beings, or anything vaguely resembling human beings, existed on this earth. In the days of the dinosaurs, our own ancestors were little furry ratlike things running between the legs of the great dinosaurs.

Could the date for the extinction of dinosaurs be wrong? Could dinosaurs have survived until a time when they would have met human beings face to face? Unlikely, but even if it is possible, the dinosaurian survivors would have been extremely rare and unlikely to have inspired a widespread myth.

The fact is that dinosaurs don't really look like the traditional dragon—which in its early days looked like a snake, and later like a winged lizard. Indeed, the influence has probably run the other way. Many of the early reconstructions of dinosaurs were influenced by the popular view of dragons. But we now know that most dinosaurs, instead of crawling about in a lizardlike fashion, stood nearly erect and moved on two long and powerful legs. Dinosaurs looked more like a kangaroo or an ostrich than the traditional dragon. (There are a couple of medieval and Renaissance drawings of bipedal dragons, but these are quite untypical.) The four-footed dinosaurs—the sauropods—such as the brontosaurus did not look dragonlike either.

What is now happening is that our view of the dinosaur has influenced our view of the dragon, and some modern representations of dragons look more like a tyrannosaurus than the traditional dragon.

There is no authentic connection between dinosaurs and dragons.

See also: DRAGON OF THE ISHTAR GATE, ORIENTAL DRAGON

FAIRIES   "The word 'fairy' is used in various ways," explains the British folklorist Katharine Briggs. "There are a number of slang and cant usages of the word, varying from time to time, which are beside the point. . . . "

The usage preferred by Briggs and others is an old one dating back at least to the seventeenth century describing the fairies as creatures "of a middle nature between men and angels." To update that a bit, the fairies have been regarded as a separate race of beings, neither human nor divine, nor, we may add, diabolical—just different. Though they inhabit some of the same space on earth as human beings, the lives of the fairies are separate and quite distinct and the two races interact only occasionally.

In Victorian times fairy lore was debased into children's stories, and the fairies portrayed as tiny winged creatures flitting from buttercup to buttercup. But that was only because people, at least those who wrote and read Victorian "fairy stories," no longer believed in fairies. In earlier times, and in rural areas of the British Isles and parts of continental Europe, up to about the turn of the century, belief in fairies remained strong, and they weren't all Tinkerbell either.

The fairy folk could come in a variety of sizes, some quite as large as the average human being. While they were rarely considered actively malevolent, they were regarded as potentially dangerous, for they did not much like human beings, particularly humans who entered their territory or pried into their secrets. The fairy folk were quite powerful, and capable of severely punishing those who irritated them. They might also aid those who had gained their favor, but good deeds from the faries were relatively rare. The fairies were so feared that their name could not be uttered aloud. They were referred to as "The Good People" or "The People of Peace" or "The Good Neighbors." Such names expressed more hope than reality, rather like saying "good dog" to a large and ferocious-looking animal confronting you.

The body of fairy lore is large and extraordinarily complex. Most scholars believe that belief in fairies grew out of the ancient belief in nature spirits and pre-Christian religions in which many gods and spirits were worshiped.

However, there are a small number of scholars who are of the opinion that fairy lore grew from authentic memories of contact with a small-statured, secretive race of forest dwellers. According to the theory, these small people were the early inhabitants of the British Isles and perhaps other parts of Europe. They were conquered by invading tribes—the Celts in Britain and the Germanic tribes in northern Europe. The original inhabitants were submerged, but not destroyed. Instead, they retired to the inaccessible woods and continued to live a secretive existence around the towns, farms, and fortifications of the invaders. They may have dwelt in low turf-covered houses that resembled green hillocks. Fairies were traditionally supposed to live inside of hills. The green costume so often attributed to the fairy folk may have been a form of camouflage.

Such a people would surely hate their conquerors and take every opportunity to strike back at them. They could never risk an open attack. They would have relied on guerrilla warfare, the murder of isolated travelers, kidnapping, cattle poisoning, and other hit-and-run tactics to revenge themselves. From these activities would grow the legends of changelings and the dangers associated with traveling at night through regions supposed to be the home of the fairy folk and of the hazards to livestock posed by angry fairies.

The small and elusive people would probably have had a difficult time eking out a living in the forest. They may have lived by robbing their larger neighbors, and there are plenty of legends to indicate that fairies were confirmed robbers. In order to stay in the good graces of the fairies, people living on isolated farms customarily left food out at night for them.

Elusive as they were, these little people could not have remained entirely isolated from their larger neighbors. There are many stories of men taking "fairy wives" who brought good or ill fortune depending on the circumstances. In the castle of Dunvagen on the Isle of Skye, off the coast of Scotland, a visitor will be shown the ancient "fairy flag," which according to legend was given to one of the early leaders of the Clan McCloud by his fairy wife, and when carried into battle always brought victory.

There are stories of tiny children like Tom Thumb (not the famous circus midget, but the Tom Thumb of *Grimm's Fairy Tales*) and Hop o' my Thumb, who were born to normal-sized parents. The stories may reflect the fact that some families had the "little people" in their hereditary background.

Ultimately, the little people would have either died out or have been completely absorbed by the dominant elements of the population. But memories of the small hidden forest folk would remain, and as stories of them were retold they would slowly be transformed from human to supernatural beings.

Professor Margaret Murray, an early twentieth-century British Egyptologist who became interested in the Middle Ages and who propounded a number of influential if eccentric theories, suggested that what we call witchcraft started with these small folk. They were, she said, followers of the old pagan gods and doubtless resisted Christianity. With their secretive ways, they were able to keep their ancient beliefs alive. And like many primitive people, they were skilled in the use of herbs and poisons, which gave them their reputation for being magical.

It is an attractive theory, but for one shortcoming, there is not a shred of physical evidence to back it up. Margaret Murray wrote, "The dwarf race which at one time inhabited Europe has left few concrete remains but has survived in innumerable stories of fairies and elves." That is an understatement; they left *no* concrete remains. Not an artifact, not a bone, not the ruins of a hovel, can be attributed, even remotely, to this theoretical small-statured race. Until such time as some tangible evidence turns up, the idea of a real race of little people must be regarded as sheer unfounded speculation.

There is an even more bizarre theory regarding the origin of fairy beliefs. The British writer Leslie Shepard, when reviewing some of the work of the British Fairy Investigation Society, commented:

"I have a strong suspicion that in the newer mythology of flying saucers, some of those 'shining visitors' in spacecraft from other worlds might turn out to be just another form of fairies."

UFO theoretician Jacques Vallée has suggested that the beliefs about UFOs and fairy lore spring from the same source. He is, however, quite unclear as to just what this source may be. But he has been able to point to an extraordinary number of parallels in the accounts of persons who say that they have encountered fairies and those who say they encountered beings from outer space.

FEARSOME CRITTERS   "Fearsome critters" is a term used
by Richard Barber and Ann Riches in their book *A Dictionary of
Fabulous Beasts* to describe "the fabulous fauna of the American
West." Most of these critters were born in the tall tales of the lumberjacks and other frontiersmen. The creatures were part of storytelling sessions where the participants tried to top one another in telling
the most outrageous and outlandish lie. But while the tellers knew
they were lying, some of their listeners did not. The essence of a tall
tale is that it be told as if it were true. No matter how ludicrous the
story might seem, it is told with a straight face; it is told to be believed.
That is the difference between a tall tale and a joke.

The favored victims of these tall tales were "greenhorns," newcom-
ers to an area. As the critters became part of the general folklore of
the country, the primary victims were children, perhaps those going
on their first outing in the woods. Under these circumstances, many
of the fearsome critters of the tall tales were believed in—at least for
a while.

The tall-tale tradition was also taken up in newspapers or other
publications intent on creating or promoting some local monster.

Of all the fearsome critters, the one that has received the widest
currency is probably the hoop snake. This is the fabulous snake that
grasps its tail in its mouth and can roll down a hill at tremendous
speed. The only way to escape such a snake is to jump through the
hoop. Barber and Riches comment that the hoop snake "may derive
from the eternity-serpent symbol known in Egyptian and Greek art."
Most children appear to believe the hoop snake story when it is first
told to them, and some may carry this belief into adulthood. Another
fearsome serpent is the horn snake, which has a poisonous spur on the
end of its tail.

A popular creature known under a variety of names was the guyascutus, sidewinder, hunkus, ricaboo racker, side-hill gouger, prock
gwinter, or cutter cuss. The most notable feature of this creature was

that the legs on one side of its body were longer than the legs on the other side, so that it could graze in steep mountain pastures. There were many variations of this theme. Some said there were either right-sided or left-sided guyascutuses, and that they could go around the hill in only one direction. Others insisted that the creature had telescoping legs so that when it wanted to go one way it made one set of legs longer, and when it wanted to go the other way it elongated the other set. It is possible that this tale originated in an old belief that the badger has one set of legs shorter than the other. An alternate name for badger is brock, and one of the names for this creature was prock.

Guyascutus was also used as a name for a far larger and more dangerous animal. The size and appearance of this particular beast was never made clear, but it was certainly something to be feared. There are a number of stories connected with showmen who put one of these truly fearsome critters on display. In one story, a couple of showmen came into a Midwestern town and advertised that the ferocious guyascutus, or guyanoosa, would be shown, for a fee of course, that evening. The local people dutifully paid their fee and took their seats, and as they waited with some anxiety for their first sight of this terrifying creature, one of the showmen rushed in shouting, "De guyanoosa am loose!" The audience fled in panic, and the showman pocketed the money without ever having to show the local yokels anything.

Mark Twain improved the tale a bit by telling how the showmen came to town advertising that they would be displaying a guyanoosa and a prock. As the moment for showing the two fabulous beasts approached, the showman rushed in shouting, "De guyanoosa am loose, and it's eaten de prock!"

The hodag was a monster of the Wisconsin swamps. The creature had huge claws, bulging eyes, large horns, and a line of sharp spikes which ran down the middle of its back. But the most unusual feature of the hodag was that it could never lie down, for it had no joints in its legs. It slept by leaning against a tree and the best way to catch one was to cut into its favorite tree so that when the hodag leaned against it to sleep, both monster and tree fell over.

The jointless legs were a characteristic also attributed to the achlis, a creature mentioned in the works of the ancient Roman naturalist Pliny. Pliny's beast, however, was an inoffensive vegetarian, not a ferocious killer like the hodag. Whether the characteristic of being unable to lie down was carried straight from the pages of Pliny to the swamps of Wisconsin or whether the hodag received his jointless legs as the result of independent invention is unknown.

A live hodag was supposedly captured near Rhinelander, Wisconsin, in the late nineteenth century. The whole hodag capture was a hoax planned and executed by a man named Eugene S. Shephard who threw a spike-studded horsehide over a large dog and then charged admission to see the "hodag" that was housed in a dimly lighted cage. When the story of the hodag's capture was sent to the

Hodag

newspapers, the theory was advanced that the hodag was "the long sought missing link between the ichthyosaurus and the mylodon of the Ice Age"—a statement that is meaningless double-talk.

According to Curtis D. MacDougall in his book *Hoaxes*, "After the original hodag's death a stuffed successor was exhibited at fairs for two years. Whenever a convention meets at Rhinelander the fame of the monster lives anew, stuffed hodags being manufactured for floats and other displays. Luke Sylvester Kearney in 1928 published a book *The Hodag*. W. J. Lemke, head of the news bureau of the University of Arkansas, states that during his boyhood at Wausau, Wisconsin, 'large photographs of the hodag on a fallen log, surrounded by a group of his captors armed with axes pitchforks, etc., were fairly common. Many of them were used as decorations in the saloons.'"

The growrow, so named because of the terrible growling sounds it made, was a monster from Arkansas. A copy of the Arkansas *Gazette* of Little Rock in 1897 mentions the killing of one of these creatures by a posse in Search County, Arkansas, after the monster had terrified the countryside and killed off a large number of cows and horses. According to the paper, the creature was twenty feet long, with a ponderous head, two enormous tusks, short legs, webbed feet with claws, green scales, a back bristling with short horns, and a long thin tail. Around the turn of the century the newspaper hoax—an absolutely ridiculous story, reported straight without any indication of its fictional origin—was a popular and nearly respectable style of journalism. The newspaperman's cynical attitude was if the reader fell for such nonsense, that was his problem. We can assume that the Arkansas growrow falls into the hoax category.

Some of the popular fearsome critters were not really meant to be taken seriously at all, and they are examined here in order to give something of the flavor that these tall tales possessed. There was, for example, the argopelter, which lives in hollow trees and amuses itself by throwing pieces of wood at passers-by. It throws so hard that it sometimes causes injury, and it is so fast that it has never been seen. The mysterious whirling whumpus has been seen only as a blur, because it constantly spins around at a tremendous rate of speed. The splinter cat eats raccoons and bees, both of which live in hollow trees. It extracts its prey by charging at the tree and smashing it with its hard forehead. The results of a hungry splinter cat's work is often attributed to lightning or wind damage.

The sliver cat is a killer; it eats people. It's an evil-looking thing with slanting red eyes and a long tail with a hard knob on the end. One side of the knob is spiked, the other side smooth. The creature would lurk in the branches of trees and when a likely-looking meal passed underneath, it would knock him down with the knob and pick him up with the spikes.

Another danger lurking about in trees was the hidebehind. It got its name because it hid behind trees ready to carry men off to its lair and eat them. No one knew what a hidebehind looked like because it was always hiding behind something. When a lumberjack failed to return to camp, it was assumed that a hidebehind had gotten him.

The rumpifusel was a thin furry creature that wrapped itself around trees and looked rather like a fur scarf. An inexperienced lumberjack might actually try to put a rumpifusel on, and be strangled by it.

The flitterbick is a flying squirrel that flew so quickly it could kill a man if it hit him between the eyes. Flitterbicks were considered exceptionally dangerous because you couldn't see them coming.

From the Southwest came the cactus cat, which looked very much like an ordinary cat except that it had hair like thorns and a clump of thorns over each ear. Sharp knifelike spurs of bone protruded from above its feet, and it had a three-branched tail. It used the blades on its legs to slash giant cactuses and allow the sap to ooze out, thus getting a drink in the dry desert. But there was a danger, for after several days the oozing sap would ferment in the desert heat and when the cactus cat drank it, the creature became intoxicated and rushed around the desert uttering horrible shrieks.

In an even more lighthearted vein there was the goofus, a bird that only flew backwards, because it was not interested in where it was going, only where it had been. Its aquatic counterpart, the goofgang, was a fish that swam backwards to keep the water out of its eyes. The phyllyloo was an American variety of stork that flew upside down to keep warm and avoid rheumatism, and the gillygaloo was a bird that nested on hilly ground and therefore had to lay square eggs so that they would not roll downhill. Hardboiled gillygaloo eggs were used as dice by the lumberjacks.

Giddyfish were small and elastic. In the winter they could be caught in a rather unusual way through holes in the ice. The trick was to hit one of them on the head with a paddle, so that it would begin to bounce up and down. All the other giddyfish would imitate it. When they had all bounced through the hole in the ice, fishermen could just pick them up.

There are almost an endless number of other local monsters or incredible creatures bearing such names as the billdad, treesqueak, cross-feathered see, and snoligostus, but of all of them the most melancholy was the squonk. This was a beast from the hemlock forests of Pennsylvania. It was extremely ugly, and so ashamed of its appearance that it kept out of sight and wept continuously from self-pity. It could be traced by the trail of tears that it left, but if captured was liable to dissolve entirely, leaving behind only a puddle of tears and some bubbles.

See also: FUR-BEARING TROUT, JACKALOPE, JERSEY DEVIL

FUR-BEARING TROUT   The fur-bearing trout, that is, a perfectly ordinary mounted trout wrapped in a white rabbit pelt or some other fur, was a common ornament at bars in the upper Midwest and parts of Canada. Specimens of this fake were sometimes shown at fairs throughout the country. They were said to be examples of a very rare fish that was found only in deep cold lakes and rivers. Often these mounted fish looked realistic enough to fool, or at least puzzle, the young or the inexperienced.

In his book *Animal Fakes & Frauds* Peter Dance describes a fur-bearing trout that was brought by a lady to the Royal Scottish Museum in Edinburgh. Under the fish was this engraved label:

FUR BEARING TROUT
Very Rare
Caught while trolling in lake Superior off Gros Cap, near Sault Ste. Marie, district of Algoma. It is believed that the great depth and the extreme penetrating coldness of the water in which the fish live has caused them to grow their dense coat of (usually) white fur. Mounted by ROSS C. JOBE, Taxidermist of Sault Ste. Marie, Ont.

Dance indicates that the woman who brought the fish into the museum had bought it in good faith and "the *idea* of a fur-bearing trout did not seem outlandish to her."

See also: JACKALOPE

GIANTS   Most peoples have tales of giants somewhere in their mythology. The fact that giants are mentioned prominently in the Bible has made many people believe that even if giants no longer exist today, they did at some time in the history of the human race.

Some of the biblical references to giants, most notably the story of Goliath, can be explained by assuming that Goliath was just an exceptionally tall and powerful individual whose size and strength tended to be exaggerated as the story of his defeat by David was retold over the centuries. How much more wonderful it is to defeat a giant, rather than a tall man.

Other references are not quite so easy to explain. In Numbers (13:33) there is the tale of the Israelites who had been sent ahead to spy on the inhabitants of the Promised Land: "And there we saw giants; and we were in our own sight as grasshoppers, and so we were in their sight." This thoroughly unsettling report plunged the Children of Israel into a state of despair.

Another reference to giants comes in Deuteronomy (3:11) and speaks of Og, king of Bashan, as the last of the race of giants. We are given some idea of Og's size by being told that his iron bedstead was about fourteen feet long and six feet wide.

In both of these cases, we might again explain the giants away by assuming that they are exceptionally tall individuals or races whose size had been exaggerated as stories about them were retold. But the reference that has always excited the most speculation about the existence of a race of real giants is the one that appears very early in the Bible, Genesis 6:4: "There were giants in the earth in those days."

This passage begins one of the most enigmatic and widely discussed sections of the Bible. It is connected with the ancient Jewish story of the watcher angels, and some believe with the story of the fall of Satan. One possible interpretation of this section of Genesis is that the giants were the result of a union between human females and fallen angels—though such an interpretation is by no means obvious. But it is beyond dispute that the ancient Hebrews believed that at one time there were giants in the world.

It is also possible that the Hebrews got the idea of giants from occasional observations of the bones of giant animals of past ages. Unquestionably, some of the belief in giants was kept alive in later eras by finding such bones. An ingenious theory holds that the giant cyclops that appears in Homer's *Odyssey* was inspired by the finding of the skull of an extinct variety of elephant. Homer, or the people from which this story of the cyclops originally sprang, may never have seen a living elephant. So when they found the huge skull of one, the enormous nasal passage looked to them like a gigantic single eye socket, right in the middle of the creature's forehead.

When the Spanish reached Mexico, they were told that the land had once been inhabited by a race of giants. These giants had been evil creatures, the Indians said, and had been defeated by the Indians' ancestors.

Bernal Díaz del Castillo, whose chronicle of the Spanish conquest of Mexico is considered accurate and reliable, wrote: "And in order that we might judge their [the giants] size, they brought us a thighbone of a man of this race. It was so large that when placed upright it was as high as a man of average size. I stood beside it, and found that it was as tall as myself, though I am as tall as most men. They brought also other pieces of other bones of great size, but much decayed by time, but the one I have mentioned was entire; we were astonished at these remains, and thought they certainly proved the former existence of giants." One of the best samples of bones was sent to Charles V of Spain, but there is no record that it was ever received, or if it was what happened to it. It would be nice to have the specimen, but even without it we are quite safe in assuming that Bernal Díaz's interpretation of what he saw was wrong. He was almost certainly looking at the thighbone of a long-extinct mastodon, and not a bone from the leg of a humanoid giant, though both the Spaniard and the Mexican Indian thought that's what it was.

The confusion continued for centuries. When an enormous tooth and some very large bones were uncovered in 1705 on the Hudson River near the town of Claverack, N.Y., the discovery inspired Joseph Dudley, governor of Massachusetts and a keen student of natural history as well as of the Bible, to write: "I am perfectly of the opinion that the tooth will agree only to the human body, for whom the Flood could only prepare a funeral."

Dudley wrote those words to the Reverend Cotton Mather, who is known today primarily for his part in the notorious Salem witchcraft trials. But in his own time, Mather was highly respected intellectual, and one of the best-educated men in the country. He was very interested in the remains of giants that had perished in the Flood, and had sent a description of a "giant's tooth" to the Royal Society in London, the world's leading scientific organization. It was an elephant's tooth, but most of the members of the Royal Society didn't know that.

The biblical giant explanation for the bones of long-extinct giant mammals went out of fashion completely in about the middle of the eighteenth century. But the search for giants in the earth did not end then; there was even talk of living giants.

Patagonia, the southern part of Argentina that has so often been the setting for tales of bizarre creatures, was also supposed to be the home of giants. Antonio Pigafetta, who wrote the chronicle of Ferdinand Magellan's around-the-world voyage, said that in Patagonia Magellan's crew had encountered giants. "This man was so tall that our heads scarcely came up to his waist, and his voice was like that of a bull." Other early travelers to Patagonia reported meetings with similar giants and the Patagonian giants became world famous. But they did not much impress the young naturalist Charles Darwin, who met them during his around-the-world voyage on the *Beagle*.

"We had an interview at Cape Gregory with the famous so-called gigantic Patagonians who gave us a cordial reception," Darwin wrote in his journal. "Their height appears greater than it really is, from their large guanaco mantles, their long flowing hair, and general figure. On an average their height is about six feet, with some men taller and only a few shorter; and the women are also tall; altogether they are certainly the tallest race which we anywhere saw." Darwin had not encountered the Watusi of Africa, who are even taller. Though the Patagonians were tall, Darwin believed that the impression of truly colossal size they had given to many travelers was more of an illusion. No one since Darwin has spoken of meeting Patagonian giants.

There are rumors that the people met by Darwin and later travelers were not the real Patagonian giants. The real giants, according to the rumors, have slipped away into the interior where they cannot be found, and they may be lurking there still.

Patagonian giants

There are tales, fairly recent ones, of giants in the interior of South America. This item appeared in the *London Daily Mirror* on May 16, 1966:

"A ferocious band of savages more than seven feet tall are terrorizing neighboring tribes in the Amazon jungle. The existence of the savages was revealed by a group of Brazilian air cadets who went on a course of adventure-training in the jungle.

"According to the cadets the giants are known locally as the Krem-Akaore."

Closer investigation revealed that these "giants" in fact averaged only six feet or less in height. They were only somewhat taller than the average member of the surrounding tribes.

The newspapers, particularly the more sensationalistic ones, occasionally carry reports of the discovery of the dried and mummified remains of "red-haired giant cannibals" in places throughout the American West. While naturally dried and mummified remains have been found in the American West, such giant stories are based on exaggeration, misinterpretation, and downright falsehood.

Another piece of evidence often cited for the existence of a now vanished race of giants are huge and ancient structures found in various parts of the world, which, according to some, could not possibly have been built by ordinary mortals with simple tools. Such structures are often called "cyclopean," a reference to the giant Cyclops of Greek mythology. Stonehenge is the best known of these "cyclopean" structures, and at one time it was known as the Giant's Dance. However, the theory that any of these great structures were built by giants can no longer be taken seriously by anyone.

Another area that has been explored in the search for the "giants in the earth" is our own evolutionary heritage. In the 1930s Ralph von Koenigswald, a Dutch geologist, found the teeth of a creature that he believed belonged to a long-extinct giant ape that he named *Gigantopithecus*. One of von Koenigswald's friends and associates, Franz Weidenreich, decided that the teeth belonged to a giant man, or *Giganthropus*, not a giant ape. He linked this up with some other fossil fragments and concluded:

"I believe that all of these [giant] forms have to be ranged back in the human line and the human line leads to giants the farther back it is traced. . . . In other words the giants may be directly ancestral to man."

Weidenreich got very little scientific support for his giant-ancestor theory, and the multitude of fossil finds made since he first developed the idea point strongly in the other direction—our ancestors were not giants—they were in fact quite small, and the human race is bigger today than it has ever been.

One cannot leave the subject of giants without at least a brief mention of one of the more spectacular and funnier hoaxes in American history—the Cardiff giant. The hoax was pulled off by George Hull, a tabacconist from Binghampton, N.Y. Hull apparently got the idea after losing an argument to a traveling evangelist about the existence of giants in biblical times.

If they want to believe in giants, Hull appears to have thought, then I'll give them giants. He had a giant figure carved out of gypsum by Edward Salle, an Iowa stonecutter. He then had the figure brought in by cart and buried secretly on the farm of one of his relatives, William C. Newell of Cardiff, New York. All in all, the hoax cost the conspirators about one thousand dollars, a considerable sum in those days, but they looked on it as an investment.

The conspirators were in no hurry. A full year was allowed to pass before some of Newell's neighbors "accidentally" unearthed the figure while digging a well on Newell's property. The figure was about twelve feet long, four feet broad, and twenty-two inches thick. It was a nude man with his legs drawn slightly upward and with one hand placed modestly to cover his genitals.

As word of the remarkable find spread, Hull and his associates acted rapidly. They set up a tent and began charging admission to see "the American goliath." Many people did indeed believe that they were seeing proof positive of the biblical statement about giants in the earth, and that this petrified figure was one of a race of giants that had existed before the Flood.

Incredibly, an Indian "legend" was also brought out to explain the

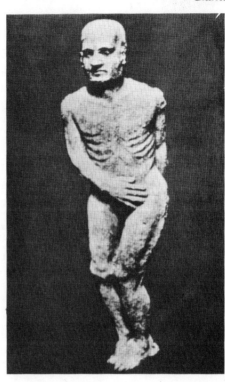

Cardiff giant

fake. An Onondaga woman was said to have declared that Cardiff giant was really the body of a gigantic Indian prophet who had said upon his death that his descendants would see him again. Others thought that the giant was a Phoenician idol, and still others insisted it had been made by the Jesuits, who had once been in the region. The great paleontologist Othniel Charles Marsh of Yale would have none of this speculation. He flatly declared the thing to be a modern fake, and his word carried great weight. Finally Hull himself admitted to the hoax.

The Cardiff giant was the victim of a double hoax. The showman Phineas T. Barnum tried to buy the thing, but Hull refused to sell, so Barnum just had his own fake made and exhibited it at Wood's Museum in New York City as the genuine article. What could Hull do—sue for fraud? It would have made an interesting legal case.

GRIFFIN   The origins of the griffin—that fabulous half lion, half eagle—are obscure. Griffins often appeared in the art of the nomadic Scythians, who used all sorts of fabulous animals for decoration. The Scythians, however, probably didn't invent the griffin. The Romans heard rumors of griffins in central Asia. The depredations of these wild creatures were cited by refugees who came to Rome from the East as one of the major reasons for fleeing their homeland.

The Roman naturalist Pliny wrote about griffins, but he made it quite clear that he did not believe such monsters existed. Those who compiled medieval bestiaries, or books of beasts, were a good deal more credulous than Pliny. One book warns men to stay away from the griffin "because it feasts upon them at any opportunity." The warning continues: "It is also extremely fond of eating horses."

Throughout the Middle Ages, objects reputed to be "griffin's claws" were brought to the markets of Europe. Those that came from the north were often the tusks of long-extinct mammoths, or the horns of the equally extinct woolly rhinoceros. Those "griffin's claws" from southern regions were usually the horns of antelopes.

Unlike the dragon, which has been the subject of serious speculation, the griffin has long been recognized to be an entirely mythical creature.

HYDRA   The second of Hercules' twelve labors was to vanquish the many-headed Hydra. This monster had nine heads, one of which was immortal. Every time you cut off one of the heads, two more quickly grew to replace it. Hercules managed to prevail over the monster by having his servant cauterize the stump as he severed each head, and then burying the immortal central head under a big rock.

The Hydra was almost certainly inspired by the eight-tentacled octopus: the ninth immortal head would have been the octopus's real head. There are several pieces of Roman art which show Hercules struggling with a distinctly octopuslike Hydra.

However, the Hydra-octopus identification was lost and both Konrad Gesner in the sixteenth century and Edward Topsell in the seventeenth century wrote of the Hydra as a real, many-headed monster,

Hydra

specimens of which existed in private collections. Said Topsell in 1607, "I have also heard that in Venice in the Duke's treasury, among the rare Monuments of that City, there is preserved a Serpent with seven heads, which if it be true, it is more probable that there is a Hydra, and that the Poets were not altogether deceived that say Hercules killed such a one."

What happened to this "Hydra" is unknown, but a couple of other preserved "Hydras" turned up. The most famous of these was kept in a collection in Hamburg, and was regarded as authentic by many naturalists for years. This monster, in fact, was a fabrication made up of weasels' heads and paws and snakeskin. It had probably begun as a monkish forgery of the seven-headed dragon of the Apocalypse, but had somehow been transformed into a Hydra in an age when people no longer believed in the dragon of the Apocalypse. By the early eighteenth century, even the Hydra identification could no longer be sustained. The young naturalist Carl Linnaeus, who was to become the acknowledged father of systematic biology, took one look at the fabled creature and exclaimed, "Great God, who never put more than one clear brain in one of thy created bodies."

The day of the Hydra was over. It is now the name of a multitentacled miscroscopic creature.

See also: DRAGON

JACKALOPE   Throughout the Western United States, you can buy postcards with a photograph of the fabulous jackalope. Stuffed specimens of this creature can sometimes be found on display, usually in bars. The jackalope is said to be a rare, nearly extinct antlered species of rabbit. Up close, the jackalope looks like a stuffed rabbit with a pair of horns or antlers stuck onto it. And, of course, that is exactly what it is.

The jackalope appears to be strictly an American invention, for the

Jackalope

creature is often made up of a combination of jackrabbit and antelope (pronghorn) horns. However, the combination of stuffed rabbit and horns has a wider popularity. Daphne Hills of the British museum tells of a letter from a Frenchwoman who said that she had seen a hare with deer's antler attached in a shop in Scotland.

In his book *Animal Fakes & Frauds*, Peter Dance adds this information: "Henry Tegner discovered that it [the jackalope] probably originated in Central Europe many years ago. Commenting on a jackalope exhibited in a small Canadian town recently (it was a 'horned cotton-tailed rabbit' as far as he was concerned), he mentioned a discovery he had made in one of the Seine-side open-air bookstalls in Paris. There he found a series of old German prints 'beautifully painted by an artist called Haid and dated 1794.' The series included pictures of a number of antlered hares. 'The antlers of these nonexistent creatures' he says, 'appeared to resemble those of immature roebucks.' Whether or not the Scottish and American jackalopes have connections with these German examples I have not been able to discover."

See also: FEARSOME CRITTERS, FUR-BEARING TROUT, JENNY HANIVERS

JENNY HANIVERS   Sailors would bring them home to amaze their friends. Sometimes they would be sold at curio shops in seaports. They were called baby dragons, basilisks, devil fishes, or some other suitably monstrous name. But those who knew what they were called them jenny hanivers, though no one really knew why.

They were small dried, ugly creatures, with rather diabolical faces, wings, tails, and often legs. They looked extremely monstrous, but in fact they were only fish of the ray or skate tribe which had been carved in various ways, dried, and varnished.

No one knows when the practice of turning skates and rays into miniature monsters began, but it must have been centuries ago. Konrad Gesner's historic work on the animals of the world, *Historia Animalium*, published in 1558, contains a picture of a creature that is clearly a jenny haniver, and a couple of others that might be.

It isn't hard to see how the practice began; you just have to look at the underside of a skate or ray to get the idea. Said science writer Willy Ley, "Anyone who has ever seen a ray swimming in an upright position near the glass of a large seawater aquarium will recall the quite unpleasant sensation of having faced an evil living mask.

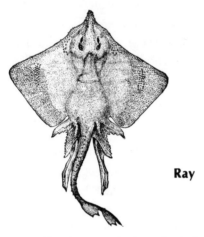

Ray

Actually the staring 'eyes' of the face are but the nostrils. The real eyes are on the dark back of the fish and are rather inconspicuous." Our imagination turns the nostrils into eyes. So while the ray looks harmless enough from the top, which is practically featureless, the "face" on the bottom looks distinctly evil.

At some time someone looked at a dead ray turned up on the beach and decided that its evil appearance could be improved upon. Here, according to the Australian ichtyologist Gilbert P. Whitley, is how it can be done: "By taking a small dead skate, curling its side fins over its back, and twisting its tail into any required position. A piece of string is tied round the head behind the jaws to form a neck and the skate is dried in the sun. During the subsequent shrinkage, the jaws project to form a snout and a hitherto concealed arch of cartilage protrudes so as to resemble folded arms. The nostrils, situated a little above the jaws are transformed into a quaint pair of eyes, the olfactory *laminae* resembling eyelashes. The result of this simple process, preserved with a coat of varnish and perhaps ornamented with a few dabs of paint, is a jenny haniver, well calculated to excite wonder in anyone interested in marine curios. The front aspect of the finished article is really the under surface of the skate, whose back and true eyes are hidden by the curled pectoral fins."

The fins can be cut and stretched so as to appear to be wings or legs

Jenny haniver

or both. Thus a rather harmless and ordinary-looking sea creature can be transformed into a monster. The only real mystery is the origin of the odd name, which has proved quite untraceable. The best guess is that the second word is a distorted form of Anvers, the French name for Antwerp, a port city in Belgium where many of these fraudulent monsters were made.

Jenny hanivers were extremely popular and valued specimens during the sixteenth and seventeenth centuries, and they frequently turned up in the collections of amateur naturalists. The jenny hanivers greatly influenced the popular conception of the appearance of a purely mythical monster, the basilisk. By the eighteenth century, however, the fraudulent nature of these creations was generally recognized by knowledgeable people, though they were still collected as oddities.

The once thriving trade in jenny hanivers isn't completely dead, even today. New specimens turn up now and then. The most common place of origin today is the Gulf of Mexico. Usually they are crudely made when compared to their old prototypes, and they are no longer displayed as basilisks and dragons, but as "devil fish" and, at least on one occasion, as a little man from outer space.

See also: BASILISK, NONDESCRIPT

JERSEY DEVIL   The Pine Barrens of New Jersey are a surprisingly isolated and sparsely populated region, located in the midst of one of the most heavily populated and highly industrialized places in the world, southeastern New Jersey. The Pine Barrens, which are unsuitable for farming, enjoyed a measure of prosperity during the late eighteenth and early nineteenth century when iron ore was mined there. But the mines closed down over a century ago when their product could no longer compete with the higher grades of iron ore being mined in the West, and the population of the Pine Barrens shrank. Those "Pineys" who remained slid into isolation and extreme poverty.

From this region come tales of the monster known as the Jersey Devil. No one is quite sure when the Jersey Devil stories began. Some think they go back to colonial times while others insist the story is less than 150 years old. There are also many versions of what the Jersey Devil is, and where it is supposed to have come from. In his book on the Pine Barrens, the writer John McPhee recounts the most popular tale concerning the birth of the monster.

In about 1735 a poor woman known as "Mother" Leeds had eleven children. When she found out she was to bear a twelfth, she cried out that she was sick of children, and that this next one could be the Devil. And so, according to the legend, it was.

The Leeds Devil was another popular name for the monster of the Pine Barrens; yet another version of the legend places the birth of the "Devil" at Leeds Point, between the Pine Barrens and the Atlantic Ocean. "Mother" Leeds is not mentioned. Still another variation sets the birth of the monster as late as 1850, and says that it was born as the result of a Gypsy's curse on a young girl. According to all the versions of the legend, the monster escaped into the woods shortly after its birth and still survives there.

Descriptions of the monster also vary a good deal, though certain basic characteristics remain fairly constant: a large horselike head, wings, and a long serpentine body. People said they could hear its screams coming from deep in the woods at night, and its appearance was generally regarded as a harbinger of evil.

The Jersey Devil would probably have remained an obscure local legend, and have faded away entirely by now, were it not for a series of events that took place during the week of January 16 to 23, 1909.

These events are chronicled in detail in *The Jersey Devil*, a book by James F. McCloy and Ray Miller, Jr. According to the authors, thousands of people saw the Devil or its footprints during that week. Fairly typical was the sighting of E. W. Minster of Bristol, N.J.

"As I got up I heard an eerie, almost supernatural sound from the direction of the river. . . . I looked out upon the Delaware and saw flying diagonally across what appeared to be a large crane, but which was emitting a glow like a fire-fly.

"Its head resembled that of a ram, with curled horns, and its long thick neck was thrust forward in flight. It had long thin wings and short legs, the front legs shorter than the hind. Again it uttered its mournful and awful call—a combination of a squawk and a whistle, the beginning very high and piercing and ending very low and hoarse. . . . "

In addition to this and other equally fantastic sightings, many people found what they took to be the hoofprints of a strange animal in the snow. The mysterious tracks appeared in the oddest places, even on the roofs of houses. The prints seemed to be particularly thick around chicken houses, and indeed the death or disappearance of many chickens and some larger animals were blamed on the Jersey Devil. The Jersey Devil was no longer a local legend of the Pine Barrens; stories about it appeared in papers all over the country. And sightings were reported well beyond the boundaries of the Barrens. The newspaper accounts contained ridicule and awestruck speculation, in about equal measure. Like most monster stories, people were unsure about whether to take them seriously.

But after a week, the Devil seemed to disappear as suddenly and as mysteriously as it had appeared. Interest, however, did not die down at once. The curator of the Philadelphia Zoo, with tongue firmly in cheek, offered a $10,000 reward for the monster.

Jacob F. Hope, an animal trainer, and Norman Jefferies, a publicist, claimed that they had actually captured the Jersey Devil. It was, they said, a rare Australian vampire which Hope had in his possession and intended to put on display, when the creature escaped and created all the Jersey Devil excitement. Hope and Jefferies said it had been recaptured after "a terrific struggle," and was put on display in a dime museum. What was put on display was a large kangaroo with false wings attached to its back and painted with green stripes. The public was only given a quick look at this bogus monstrosity. Jefferies later gleefully confessed to his part in the hoax.

Since 1909 there have been occasional Jersey Devil "flaps," but none approaching the great 1909 outburst. The Jersey Devil did create quite a furor among the teenagers in the area of Gibbstown in November 1951. There were the familiar tales of strange sounds in the woods, rumors of killed and maimed birds and animals. Most of those who reported seeing the Devil were teenagers, and the local police and school authorities firmly denounced the excitement as a mixture of hoax and hysteria.

See also: DEVIL'S FOOTPRINTS

MERMAID   "As well as yearning to fly like a bird, we humans have always wanted to swim like a fish, and that may be one reason for the existence of the mermaid legend, prevalent in all ages and in almost all countries." So writes Peter Dance of the British Museum, author of *Animal Fakes & Frauds*.

Unfortunately, the historical record for the mermaid contains an enormous gap. We know that the first civilizations of the Middle East worshiped a variety of fish-tailed gods. The earliest known was Oannes, Lord of the Waters, whose worship began some 7,000 years ago, about the same time civilization itself began. There are also fish-tailed gods of one sort or another to be found in the beliefs of India, China, Japan, and Greece.

The connection between these ancient gods and the mermaid frequently reported by European seamen from the fifteenth century onward, however, is unclear. The mermaid tradition does not appear to have been drawn directly from the ancient beliefs but is the product of relatively modern seafaring lore.

According to Richard Barber and Anne Riches, authors of *A Dictionary of Fabulous Beasts:* "The seal is at the root of the many Norwegian and Hebridean legends about mermaids; and she has been confused again with the seal-maid proper, who comes ashore and casts her skin. If her skin is removed she is compelled to remain in human shape. . . . Mermaids who took human lovers more frequently exacted a vow of secrecy from them, which if broken meant their return to the water."

But this is the purely legendary mermaid; there are also plenty of sightings of "real" mermaids. In 1608 two of Henry Hudson's crew saw a mermaid. "This morning," wrote Hudson, "one of our companie looking over boord saw a Mermaid, and calling up some of the companie to see her, one more came up, and by the time shee was come close to the ships side, looking earnstly on the men: a little after, a Sea came and overturned her: From the Navill upward her backe and breasts were like a womans [as they say they saw her] her body as big as one of us; her skin very white; and long haire hanging down behinde, of the colour blacke; in her going downe they saw her tayle, which was like the tayle of a Porposse, and speckled like a Macrell."

Mermaid sightings were reported right into the nineteenth century. In 1881 a Boston paper ran a description of a preserved mermaid that was brought to New Orleans:

"This wonder of the deep is in a fine state of preservation. The head and body of a woman are very plainly and distinctly marked. The features of the face, eyes, nose, mouth, teeth, arms, breasts and hair are those of a human being. The hair on its head is of a pale silky blonde, several inches in length. The arms terminate in claws closely resembling an eagle's talons instead of fingers with nails. From the waist up, the resemblance to a woman is perfect, and from the waist down, the body is exactly the same as of the ordinary mullet of our waters, with its scales, fins and tail perfect."

What are we to make of such reports? Even during the nineteenth century there were a few zoologists who took the mermaid accounts quite seriously. Of course, we now know there are no such creatures. As far as the sightings like the one reported by Henry Hudson's crewmen, they may have been deliberate tall tales, or they may have been mistakes. It has often been suggested that seals, or more probably sirenians like the manatee and sea cow, were mistaken for mermaids. How these rather ugly creatures could have been seen as the traditionally beautiful mermaid is unclear to anyone who has not spent a long period at sea. However, the manatee will sometimes nurse its young in a surprisingly human manner.

The report in the Boston paper of the mermaid that had been brought to New Orleans may have been a complete hoax. Hoaxes of that type were quite common in newspapers. But it was more probably a different sort of hoax. The manufacture of "mermaids" was a small, though vigorous, industry from the sixteenth to the nineteenth centuries. Not that these manufactured mermaids were very good looking. Writes Peter Dance:

"Ideally the mermaid needed to be—well, like a mermaid is supposed to be—good to look at. The reality, as concocted by the mermaid manufacturers, fell far short of this ideal. It is as if they knew they could not produce anything even remotely satisfying as the legendary mermaid and abandoned the attempt in favour of a grotesque parody of it."

Dance speculates that the manufacture of mermaids probably began in ancient times, though there is no proof of this. The earliest recorded reference to a manufactured mermaid appears in a work written in the late sixteenth century, and by the late eighteenth century there was a virtual "mermaid craze" which continued well into the nineteenth century. It was an age of showmen who exhibited displays of "curiosities of nature" for a fee in public halls all over the world. Along with the two-headed snakes and three-legged dogs there was often a preserved mermaid.

Most of these "mermaids" were quite small, being made up of the head and shoulders of a shaved monkey stitched to the body and tail of a fish. Occasionally, a larger specimen used the head and shoulders of an ape, like an orangutan, and the tail of a porpoise. These manufactured mermaids were invariably ugly and often obviously faked. It took a great deal of imagination to see the beautiful mermaid of legend in such specimens.

P. T. Barnum, America's prince of humbug, described in detail how he took what he described as "an ugly, dried up, black-looking

Fejee Mermaid

and diminutive specimen," that he called "the Fejee Mermaid" and promoted it into an enormous financial success. In 1842 thousands of people in New York paid 25 cents each (a considerable sum in those days) to view the tiny fake.

A large number of these nineteenth-century manufactured mermaids are still in the hands of private collectors, or in museums where they are valued, not as mermaids, but as interesting examples of historical fraud.

See also: OANNES

ORIENTAL DRAGON   When Westerners first came into contact with the civilization of China, they discovered that Chinese mythology and art was rich with tales and pictures of a large, powerful reptilian creature that looked remarkably like the large, powerful reptilian dragon with which they were already familiar. The Chinese called the creature the *lung*. Westerners called it the dragon. This has led to a belief that the dragon is a universal symbol in both East and West, based on memories of the dinosaur or some other great "lizard" of the past. In reality there is no evidence to support this view. The Western and Oriental dragon have quite different origins.

The two forms of dragons really have few things in common aside from being generally long and rather fearsome in appearance. In mythology both Western and Oriental dragons are reputed to be powerful and the guardians of great fortunes. (In both East and West the figure of a dragon is commonly displayed at entrances and on doors. From its treasure-guarding activities, the dragon has come to be used as a protective symbol.) There the similarities end. Western dragons were evil misers, while one rarely encountered an Oriental dragon without coming away with a generous gift.

Oriental dragons could occasionally be capricious and even malevolent, but they were usually benevolent. Unlike the Western dragon, which was a symbol of evil, closely allied to the Devil himself, the Oriental dragon was often a symbol of royalty and good luck. Western dragons were notoriously solitary, while Oriental dragons lived in crowded Chinese-style societies. There was, for example, a hierarchy of dragon bureaucrats.

As with the Western dragon, many once believed (and a few still do) that the stories of the Oriental dragon began with a real, but

Oriental dragon

unknown, giant reptile. Dr. N. B. Dennys, a nineteenth-century expert on Chinese mythology, held that there was "little doubt" that there once had been real dragons in China.

Thrilling as Dr. Dennys's suggestion was, there is "little doubt" that there never was a real dragon in China. The form of the mythical Oriental dragon was probably taken from a much more ordinary creature, but not the snake, which is at the core of the Western dragon myth. The snake also figures heavily in Chinese mythology, and, like most other peoples in the world, the Chinese hated snakes and regarded them as symbols of evil, quite unlike the usually benevolent dragon.

One clue to the possible origin of the Oriental dragon is that it is intimately associated with water. Dragons lived in lakes and rivers and seas, even in raindrops. Dragons controlled the tides and waves, created or stopped floods, and were the guardians of the rainfall. For the ancestor of the Oriental dragon, we should look to a water animal.

The best candidate is the Chinese alligator, *Alligator sinensis*.

Today the creature is rare and its range highly restricted. But in historical times it was widespread throughout eastern China. Although not quite as large as the American alligator, it is sufficiently large and powerful to inspire legends. Of course, as with the snake in the West, the Chinese alligator was only the starting point.

Like the Europeans, the Chinese also mistook the bones of ancient and extinct mammals for those of departed dragons. While the bones of the evil Western dragons were regarded as mere curiosities, the bones of the benevolent Oriental dragon were supposed to have great healing powers. The Chinese pharmacopoeia, accumulated over the long centuries of Chinese civilization, is a marvelously long and detailed collection of remedies. Virtually every known substance, if properly prepared, was thought to be a cure for some disease. But of all the cures, dragon bones were supposed to be the most effective.

Dragon bones and teeth, that is, the bones and teeth of extinct animals, were once prominently displayed in the drugstores of Peking, Hong Kong, and other metropolitan centers in China. There they were ground up and sold as medicine, often at very high prices. During the late nineteenth and early twentieth centuries, Western paleontologists could also be found browsing among the bins of dragon bones. They were not looking for a cure for stomach trouble, they were looking for valuable fossils, and they found some, including some teeth that ultimately led to the discovery of Peking man.

See also: DRAGON

UNICORN   The unicorn, a horselike creature with a single horn in the middle of its forehead, is the most glorious of all mythological animals. Today we are in the midst of what must be called a unicorn revival. We find the symbol of the unicorn on everything from stationery to sheets—it is more popular than it has ever been.

How did belief in this extraordinary beast begin? Is it possible that somewhere, sometime there was a real unicorn?

The first mention of the unicorn comes in the writings of the Greek historian Ctesias, onetime physician to the King of Persia. Ctesias returned from Persia around the year 389 B.C. and proceeded to write a lengthy history of that land, and another of India. Only fragments or abstracts of Ctesias's original works survive, but it is in one of these that the unicorn first enters written history:

"There are in India certain wild asses which are as large as horses and larger. Their bodies are white, their heads dark red, and their eyes dark blue. They have a horn on the forehead which is about a foot and a half in length. The dust filed from this horn is administered in a potion as a protection against deadly drugs. The base of this horn, for some two hands breadth above the brow, is pure white, the upper part is sharp and a vivid crimson; and the remainder or middle portion is black. Those who drink out of these horns made into drinking vessels, are not subject, they say, to convulsions or to the holy disease [epilepsy]. Indeed, they are immune even to poisons if, either before or after swallowing such they drink wine, water, or anything else from these beakers. . . . "

Ctesias was writing about India, a land he had never seen, so his account had to be based on hearsay, not firsthand knowledge. The

Rhinoceros

basic animal being described is almost certainly the Indian rhinoceros, for the rhinoceros is the only one-horned animal in the world. (Strictly speaking, the rhinoceros does not have a true horn, but that is a distinction that would bother only professional zoologists.) The key to the rhinoceros identification is the almost magical properties attributed to the horn. Even today rhinoceros horn is regarded as both a universal remedy and powerful aphrodisiac throughout much of the Middle East, an unfortunate honor for the rare and hard-pressed rhinoceros. So long as rich and superstitious men are willing to pay enormous prices for illegally obtained rhinoceros horn, there will be poachers willing to kill the protected animal and drive it to extinction.

In addition to the rhinoceros, Ctesias apparently mixed a couple of other creatures into his description of the unicorn, for it is difficult to imagine a cumbersome rhino being described as a form of wild ass. But this sort of confusion was common enough in travelers' tales. The unicorn was just one of a number of mythical beasts that were built up from an exaggerated and inaccurate description of a real animal.

Mention of the unicorn appeared in the writings of Pliny and other Romans, but what really insured the survival of the unicorn concept into modern times was its mention in the Bible. The primary reference to the unicorn comes in the Book of Job (39:9–12), the same book in which the monsters leviathan and behemoth are described. The unicorn is treated very much in the same way as these other creatures.

"Will the unicorn be willing to serve thee, or abide by thy crib?

"Canst thou bind the unicorn with his band in the furrow? or will he harrow the valleys after thee?

"Wilt thou trust him, because his strength is great? or wilt thou leave thy labour to him?

"Wilt thou believe him, that he will bring home thy seed, and gather it into thy barn?"

It is more than probable that the use of the word *unicorn* is the result of a mistranslation from the original Hebrew. The animal being described is really a form of wild cattle that was unfamiliar to the translators, so they used the name of another animal that was reputed to be fierce and intractable—the unicorn. In any case, once the name of the unicorn was inserted into the Bible, it was guaranteed a high degree of respectability in Europe during the Middle Ages. Saint Bernard railed against the "ridiculous monstrosities" that often adorned even church walls, but he could not bring himself to denounce the biblical unicorn. Christian artists who would have hesitated depicting "pagan monsters" had no such reservations about the unicorn. The unicorn was sometimes even used as a symbol for Christ.

Throughout the Middle Ages there were two attitudes toward the unicorn. One emphasized its wildness, as seen in this 1587 translation of a Roman description of the beast:

"But the cruellest is the Unicorne, a monster that belloweth horrible, bodyed like a horse, footed like an elephant, tayled like a Swyne, and headed like a Stagge. His horn sticketh out the middle of hys forehead, of a wonderful brightness about foure foote long, so sharp, that whatsoever he pusheth at, he striketh it through easily. He is never caught alive; kylled he may be, but taken he cannot bee."

Yet the unicorn had a romantic side too. The myth grew that while no man could capture the unicorn, it would immediately become slave to a virgin.

The unicorn never completely shook off its rhinoceros origins. Like the horn of the rhinoceros, the horn of the unicorn, called the alicorn, was credited with miraculous healing powers when ground up and

Unicorn

taken as a powder. Most of the "true" unicorn horns that were offered for sale were the tusk of the narwhale, which like the unicorn of myth has a single "horn." In most medieval drawings of the unicorn, the horn was clearly inspired by the narwhale tusk. Sometimes mammoth

Narwhale

tusks were sold as unicorn horns, but even in the Middle Ages they were denounced as "false."

When travelers went to the Orient looking for the fabled unicorn, they were often shown a rhinoceros, a great disappointment. Marco Polo, after seeing a rhinoceros unicorn, complained, "It is a hideous beast to look at, and in no way like what we think and say in our countries, namely a beast that lets itself be taken in the lap of a virgin. Indeed, I assure you that it is quite the opposite of what we say it is."

Belief in the unicorn that is the beautiful yet ferocious horse with the horn in the middle of its forehead began to fade during the Renaissance, and the use of unicorn horn as a cure was questioned. Alicorn was last listed by London pharmacies in 1741.

By the beginning of the nineteenth century, the unicorn was declared to be a biological impossibility by no less a figure than Baron Cuvier, the most distinguished and influential anatomist of his day.

There was a brief reprise for a belief in a real unicorn in the early 1900s when the remains of an extinct relative of the modern rhinoceros was discovered in Siberia. But the scientists soon recognized what they were dealing with and the unicorn was once again placed firmly in the world of myth—permanently this time—despite occasional excitements about the birth of one-horned goats and bulls.

See also: BEHEMOTH, LEVIATHAN

VAMPIRE   Our modern conception of the vampire as an ele-
gantly dressed, erotically attractive, and supremely evil "undead"
creature represents the blending of a number of different folkloric
traditions with a heavy influence of nineteenth-century fiction and
twentieth-century filmmaking.

Some sort of blood-sucking spirit or demon is a part of the mythology of many lands. Such spirits were not necessarily or even usually
associated with the dead. However, blood has always been considered
a substance with magical properties, and blood sacrifices were commonly made to appease the dead. In the *Odyssey*, Odysseus descends
to the underworld, but is unable to speak to the shades of the dead
until he feeds them with the blood of a sacrificed sheep. Without the
blood, the dead are too weak and insubstantial to be heard.

Another tradition that figures importantly in the vampire story is
the belief that under some circumstances a corpse, not a spirit or
ghost, but the physical body itself, could rise out of the grave and walk
about.

A twelfth-century English chronicle by William of Newburgh tells
several stories of such animated corpses. The most interesting is about
an evil man who died without confessing his sins but was nevertheless
given a proper Christian burial which "he did not deserve and which
profited him nothing."

This evil man could not be held in his grave: "For by the power of
Satan in the dark hours, he was wont to come forth from his tomb
and to wander about all through the streets, prowling round the
houses, whilst on every side dogs were howling the whole night long."

Since this creature was a real corpse, it was rotting and its presence
infected the air with a terrible plague so severe that "there was hardly
a house that did not mourn its dead."

Finally, two brothers decided to dig up the body and burn it. Opening a grave was a mortal sin, but in this case it seemed to be a sin
committed in a good cause. This particular story has many of the

overtones of a modern vampire tale, for the brothers found the corpse, "gorged and swollen with a frightful corpulence, and its face was florid and chubby, with huge red puffed cheeks."

When the corpse was struck with a spade, "there immediately gushed out such a stream of warm red gore that they realized the creature had fattened in the blood of many poor folk." The corpse was burned and the plague ended.

Other animated corpse accounts from the same era do not mention the apparent blood-drinking activities of the corpse.

The various traditions about blood-sucking spirits, the magical properties of blood, and animated corpses seemed to merge most completely in central Europe. By around the seventeenth century, printed accounts of vampires began to appear. These were not meant as fiction but were supposed to be true accounts. In 1732 a typical vampire was exhumed near Belgrade in what is now Yugoslavia:

"It leaned to one side, the skin was fresh and ruddy, the nails grown long and evilly crooked, the mouth slobbered with blood from its last night's repast. Accordingly a stake was driven through the chest of the vampire, who uttered a terrible screech whilst blood poured in quantities from the wound. Then it was burned to ashes."

Vampire beliefs were occasionally given a Christian veneer with the claim that a vampire was a dead witch, or a corpse animated by a demon. But in general, vampirism was not of much concern to church authorities, who appeared to regard it as just another primitive superstition. In werewolf cases, people were actually brought to trial and executed, but no one was ever tried for being a vampire, so no important theological decisions had to be rendered, except possibly concerning the exhumation of corpses.

The various vampire tales from central Europe were doubtless read in western Europe and the British Isles, but there was no deep indigenous belief in vampires, indeed, the word itself did not even appear in English until 1734. The modern, Dracula type of vampire is strictly a recent and completely literary development.

The first great vampire in English fiction, Lord Ruthven, appeared in a novel written in 1819. At one time the writer of this sensational

CHAPTER I.

———" How graves give up their dead.
And how the night air hideous grows
With shrieks !"

MIDNIGHT. — THE HAIL-STORM. — THE
DREADFUL VISITOR.—THE VAMPYRE

THE solemn tones of an old cathedral
clock have announced midnight—the air is
thick and heavy—a strange, death like
stillness pervades all nature. Like the
ominous calm which precedes some more
than usually terrific outbreak of the elements, they seem to have paused even in
their ordinary fluctuations, to gather a terrific strength for the great effort. A faint
peal of thunder now comes from far off
Like a signal gun for the battle of the winds
to begin, it appeared to awaken them from
their lethargy, and one awful, warring hur-
ricane swept over a whole city, producing
more devastation in the four or five minutes
it lasted, than would a half century of ordinary phenomena.

It was as if some giant had blown upon
some toy town, and scattered many of the
buildings before the hot blast of his terrific

Illustration from Varney, The Vampyre

story was believed to be the poet Lord Byron, but the real author of *Vampyre* was Dr. John Polidori, Byron's personal physician and friend, though it is probable that Byron first suggested the idea.

In 1847 *Varney, The Vampyre,* a long, confusing, but incredibly popular tale of vampirism and adventure began appearing as a series of penny dreadfuls. But it was the publication of Bram Stoker's novel *Dracula* in 1897 that set the standard for all later vampires.

It has often been said that there was a "real" Dracula, and in a sense there was. Stoker drew the name of his vampire and some of the background characteristics from Vlad IV, a mid-fifteenth-century Transylvanian ruler. Vlad had a reputation for exceptional cruelty, and his nickname, Dracula, could mean either dragon or devil. But there is nothing in Vlad's history to indicate that anyone thought of him as being a blood-sucking corpse. In a sense Dracula the vampire is what Vlad is supposed to have become after he died. But this is entirely Stoker's invention.

Another figure historically linked with vampirism is Elizabeth Bathory, the so-called vampire countess of Hungary. In 1610 Elizabeth Bathory was suspected of killing several hundred peasants and often using their blood in potions that were supposed to help her retain her youth. She was convicted of sorcery, rather than vampirism. Later ages stuck her with the title of "vampire."

The idea that a vampire might be able to change itself into a bat is also a fairly recent and apparently completely literary development. There were tales of vampires that changed themselves into wolves, for there has always been an intermingling of vampire and werewolf lore.

During the eighteenth century there was some serious discussion, particularly among the occult minded, about "real" vampires. Dr. Johannes von Lobel participated in vampire hunts in Serbia, and maintained that he could even feel a slight pulse in a vampire corpse.

The last of the vampire hunters was Dr. Franz Hartmann, a scholar of occultism and later a member (and for a while president) of the Theosophical Society. But Hartmann's views leaned away from the physical, and he spoke of such creatures as "astral vampires."

From the movie *Nosferatu*

Since Hartmann's time there has been only one serious believer in vampirism—he was Montague Summers, a highly eccentric Catholic clergyman who may well have been self-ordained. Summers looked upon vampires as just another Satanic manifestation.

A few modern vampire-hunting, or Dracula, societies profess to treat the subject seriously, but one can not help suspect that there is a smile behind all the assumed gravity.

The vampire has become the most popular of all the folklore-fictional monsters—it is nothing more than that and hasn't been for a long time.

See also: VAMPIRE BAT

WEREWOLF   The werewolf and other *were*, or "man," animals are creations of both folklore and modern fiction and filmmaking. Belief that humans could be transformed or transform themselves into animals of one sort or the other is extremely ancient and very widespread. It has been theorized that the lore of the *were* animal began with hunting magic. An early cave drawing shows a human figure, apparently a sorcerer, wearing the skin of a deer. This is one of the very few human figures ever to appear in cave art.

In modern hunting societies, the sorcerer, shaman, or witch doctor will sometimes put on the skin of the animal that is to be hunted. When the shaman looks like an animal, this is supposed to establish a magical connection with the real animal, which gives the shaman some power over the real animal's movements and helps him guide it to the hunters' spears or traps. This is called sympathetic magic. The shaman dressed like an animal is caught by the hunters. The shaman looks like the animal to be hunted and, since like produces like, the hunters will catch the animal.

Under the hypnotic influence of dancing, chanting, or perhaps some form or narcotic, the shaman or any other individual who put on an animal skin or mask might begin to feel that he had actually taken on the characteristics of that animal, that for the period of the ceremony he had magically or mystically become whatever creature it was that he was imitating.

In many primitive societies, different tribes or clans possess what is called a totemic animal. This is the particular sort of animal from which the tribe or clan is believed to be descended, or to which it has some other special relationship. In ceremonies tribesmen will put on the costumes that make them look like their totem. They then begin to act like the animal because they believe they have become the animal.

Among the ancient Norsemen there were the berserkers—men in bear shirts. These warriors would wear the pelts of bears, not only for the warmth and appearance of ferocity they gave but because such a shirt was supposed to impart to the wearer the courage and strength of a bear. Here is a clear case of sympathetic magic. The berserkers were the most feared fighters among the warrior Norsemen, for they fought with the insane courage of wounded bears. No one could stand against them. Ultimately the word *berserk*, which can mean anyone who is violently insane and imagines himself to be a wild animal, came into our language.

The transformation from man to animal might also take place in

Madman thinking himself to be a werewolf

secret. In many primitive societies there are secret cults whose activities are deliberately shrouded in mystery and fear. Meeting in hidden places, the cult members don the skins of the cult animal to perform the rites specified by membership. These rites may include acting like the cult animal. If the animal happens to be a vicious one, such cults can represent a danger to the community. In the middle of the twentieth century, several members of an African leopard-man cult were convicted of murder. They put on leopard skins armed with sharp metal claws and clawed their victims to death, just as a leopard might. There was some suspicion that the cult had lost its original purpose, which was religious and magical, and had degenerated into a gang of professional killers who used the leopard costume to hide their identity and spread terror among those who might betray them.

In Roman times the werewolf idea was firmly established. A well-known Roman story that describes how a young man watched his companion turn into a large gray wolf, later wounded the wolf, and found his companion dying of the very same sort of wound, could be

Wolf

used as the basis for a modern werewolf film. Sophisticated Romans probably didn't believe the werewolf story any more than modern moviegoers do, but it was an established part of the folklore of the time.

In the Middle Ages, however, the werewolf story was believed, and many individuals were executed for being werewolves. The medieval attitude toward the werewolf represents a mixture of pagan lore about shape shifting and Christian theology.

The medieval werewolf was not merely a man changed to a wolf. The werewolf was some sort of demon or servant of the Devil. Werewolf and witchcraft were closely intertwined in the medieval mind. Such unnatural transformation had to be the work of the Devil. A particularly vicious witch might be "rewarded" by his master the Devil, and allowed to become a werewolf. The change from man (or, less frequently, woman) to wolf was the result of diabolical magic. The Devil gave the werewolf a magic wolf skin, or wolf "ointment," that was rubbed on. Eating roasted wolf flesh or drinking water from a cup made from the skull of a wolf might also effect the transformation.

The wolf was a particularly powerful symbol in Christian Europe. It was the largest and most dangerous animal the average European was ever likely to meet. In addition, the wolf was a conspicuous symbol of evil in the Bible: "Beware of false prophets, who come to you in the clothing of sheep, but inwardly they are ravening wolves. . . . Behold I send you as sheep in the midst of wolves. . . . I know that after my departure, ravening wolves will enter in among you, not sparing the flock."

However, the Bible did not specifically mention werewolves, and that gave theologians considerable trouble. Some proposed that the man did not change into a wolf, but that under diabolical influence he was able to project the illusion of being a wolf. Others said that he was not a wolf at all, but a demon in the shape of a wolf. While still others insisted that there had been no actual transformation, but that an individual's spirit left his human body and temporarily took over the body of a wolf.

Such quibbling hardly mattered when a suspected werewolf was brought to trial. The "evidence" was usually based on a collection of old superstitions such as werewolves having hair on the palms of their hands, long index fingers, eyebrows that grew together, etc. As far as one can determine from the scanty trial evidence, most of those who were convicted and executed as werewolves were actually madmen who killed their victims in fits of insane savagery. Perhaps they actually were convinced that they had become wolves, or became convinced of the transformation during their trial. Most seemed to confess freely.

There is some recognition in the medieval trials that a few judges knew that they were dealing with mental conditions rather than actual transformations. There is one French case where a self-confessed werewolf was judged to be "stupid and idiotic" and confined to a monastery rather than executed, as was the custom.

While some belief in werewolves probably persisted in isolated rural areas until fairly recent times, for most people the werewolf had become strictly a creature of stories to be trotted out to frighten children. In the nineteenth century a few mystics and occultists tried to retain the werewolf idea by speaking of the transformation of "astral bodies," but that never caught on.

Most people today have learned about werewolves from such films as *The Wolf Man*. The modern folklore of Hollywood has added a few innovations to the werewolf legend. The idea that a person bitten by a werewolf will turn into one is fairly new; so is the lore of the silver bullet and the full moon. The greatest innovation however, is the "wolf *man*," making the werewolf a hairy biped. Medieval and ancient werewolves looked like real wolves; the werewolf of the films does not. The probable reason is that it is much easier to make an actor look like a wolf *man* than a real wolf. However, the increased technological sophistication of such films as *An American Werewolf in London* (1981) allows the on-screen transformation from man to more realistic-looking wolf.

See also: BEAST OF LE GEVAUDAN

ZOMBIE   While the vampire has been called the undead, or the living dead, the zombie is simply the walking dead. The zombie is a corpse without soul or will, animated by secret spells and potions. It is neither good nor evil, but mechanically does the bidding of its master. It is, in short, a flesh-and-blood robot.

The zombie grew out of the voodoo beliefs of the island of Haiti. To create a zombie, the voodoo doctor or priest would steal a recently buried corpse and animate it by magic. The zombie made the perfect slave, for it needed neither food nor rest, but would toil on ceaselessly without complaint. There were rumors that crews of zombies were hired out to work in the fields. Bakers were also suspect; since they did their work at night, they were supposed to rely on zombie labor.

Because zombie beliefs grew up among slaves, they have a particular horror about them. At least the slave could look forward to release from toil in death—but if he became a zombie, he could not escape even beyond the grave.

The origin of the zombie idea is not at all clear. The word itself seems to come from the name of an African god or spirit. But there is nothing quite like the walking-dead zombie in African belief. Only in the New World was the name zombie applied to a walking-dead man.

There has been some speculation that the voodoo priests with their knowledge of drugs were really able to create zombies of a sort. These would not be animated corpses, but living men so stupified by drugs that they were unaware of their surroundings, seemed insensitive to pain, and did whatever the priest commanded them to do. Just what drugs might create such an effect we do not know, but it is possible that some narcotics, plus an intense belief in the power of the voodoo priest, might turn a living man into the image of a zombie.

There are some fairly recent "true" zombie stories. One concerns a young girl who was supposed to have died and was buried in 1935, but three years later some of her friends saw her working in a shop.

Though the girl moved stiffly and had a blank "zombie-like" look on her face, her friends were sure of her identity.

An investigation was launched, her grave was opened, and it was found that the girl's body was missing from its coffin. There were rumors that the body had been stolen by a voodoo priest and turned into a zombie. The priest had since died, but his wife confirmed that he had indeed made a zombie of the girl. The girl was taken under the protection of a Catholic priest who sent her to a convent in France. Her brother was supposed to have visited her there years later.

How much, if any, of this story is true can not be determined. However, a woman reputed to be a zombie was actually kept in a hospital in Haiti.

The woman appeared one day on a farm. She could barely speak and acted very strangely. A few people thought that they recognized her as someone who was supposed to have died years earlier. A relative of the dead woman was sent for and confirmed the identification. Rumors flew that the dead woman's husband had contrived to have a voodoo priest poison her and turn her into a zombie.

The truth of this particular tale is probably far less sensational. The "zombie" was almost certainly a woman who was mentally defective; she may have wandered away from where she had been kept, or have been turned out. She also may have borne a resemblance to the dead woman, so that when she turned up on the farm, people were frightened and confused. It is also possible that the dead woman's relatives didn't like her husband and were ready to blame him for any sort of crime.

In his book *Magic Island*, William Seabrook told an allegedly true story of a voodoo priest named Joseph who owned several zombies. One day Joseph's wife gave the zombies some salted biscuits, a big mistake, because salt is supposed to break the spell on the zombie. The salt made the zombies realize that they were really dead, and they made straight for the graveyard, where they threw themselves on their graves and tried to dig back into the earth. But their arms and hands rotted away before they could complete the task. Seabrook is considered more of a teller of tales than a purveyor of the unvarnished truth.

There is no doubt that in Haiti today voodoo is still a viable and vigorous religion. But the zombie belief is not central to voodoo and there is some doubt as to how deeply even the Haitians believe in zombies anymore. Sophisticated Haitians have, of course, always ridiculed the idea of the walking dead.

The British author Francis Huxley spent considerable time in Haiti researching a book on voodoo beliefs. He kept trying to find a real zombie. Though he met several voodoo priests who said that they would show him a zombie for a price, they always backed out of the deal at the last moment. Huxley also recorded a couple of occasions where the creation of a "zombie" had been faked for tourists. A zombie was seen to rise from the grave. But upon examination of the grave, an air hose leading down to the coffin was found. The man inside the coffin had been alive all of the time, and the air hose allowed him to breathe. When the coffin was dug up, he stepped out as a "zombie." An impressive show, but just a show.

Some Haitians do still take special precautions against grave robbers, perhaps out of fear that the stolen corpses will be turned into zombies or used for other evil magical purposes.

ANNOTATED

BIBLIOGRAPHY

It is not my intention to burden the general reader with a list of the hundreds of books and articles that I have read in compiling *The Encyclopedia of Monsters*. Much of the information came from obscure publications that would be unobtainable anyway. For the serious student of monsters help is available, or will be shortly. Garland Press soon will publish *Strange Beasts, Giant Birds, and Bigfoot: A Bibliography of Monsters*, prepared by George M. Eberhart. I have seen portions of this work in manuscript and it promises to be the most complete monster bibliography ever attempted in English.

For the less committed, I have prepared a short annotated bibliography of some of the leading and most accessible books on monsters. Many of these books contain their own extensive bibliographies.

Any list of monster books must start with Bernard Heuvelmans's two massive cryptozoological works, *On the Track of Unknown Animals* (New York: Hill & Wang, 1959) and *In the Wake of the Sea*

285

Serpents (New York: Hill & Wang, 1968). Other Heuvelmans books are not yet available in English, but hopefully will be shortly.

In *Searching for Hidden Animals* (New York: Doubleday, 1980), Dr. Roy P. Mackal, America's leading cryptozoologist, presents information and many of his own theories on unknown animals. Some of the information in my *A Modern Look at Monsters* (New York: Dodd, 1970) can be found in the present volume in an abridged and updated form.

For general information about monsters and all kinds of oddities, one must read the granddaddy of all clipping collectors, Charles Fort. *The Books of Charles Fort* (New York: Holt, 1941) is a one-volume edition of his four best-known books. These books, *The Book of the Damned, New Lands, Lo!* and *Wild Talents*, are also available in individual paperback editions.

Roy Mackal's *The Monsters of Loch Ness* (Chicago: Swallow, 1976) is the most scholarly work on that subject. But it is also pretty heavy going and the casual reader might prefer Nicholas Witchell's *The Loch Ness Story* (London: Penguin, 1975), which is a good general introduction to Nessie. An overview of lake monsters, including Loch Ness, is provided by Perter Costello in *Searching for Lake Monsters* (New York: Coward, 1974).

John Napier's *Bigfoot* (New York: Dutton, 1973) is far and away the best book on the hairy bipeds. Ivan Sanderson's *Abominable Snowmen, Legend Come to Life* (Philadelphia: Chilton, 1961) is a bigger book, but is far less reliable and not as well written.

Two of Willy Ley's books, *The Lungfish, the Dodo and the Unicorn* (New York: Viking Press, 1952) and *The Dawn of Zoology* (Englewood Cliffs, N.J.: Prentice-Hall, 1968), provide an interesting and clear picture of how some of our monster beliefs evolved. So does Richard Carrington's *Mermaids and Mastodons* (New York: Rinehart, 1957).

The best book on fake monsters is Peter Dance's *Animal Fakes & Frauds* (Maidenhead: Sampson Low, 1976). The text is informative and the pictures are marvelous.

Surprisingly, there are no good general books about human contacts with aliens. The best available is *The Humanoids* (Chicago: Henry Regnery, 1969), edited by Charles Bowen. Any book by John Keel is going to be a unique experience for the uninitiated. For the monster buff, the most interesting book by this eccentric author is *Strange Creatures from Time and Space* (Greenwich, Conn.: Fawcett, 1970).

An overview of mythical animals can be found in Peter Lum's *Fabulous Beasts* (New York: Pantheon, 1951). For medieval view of animals or just a good read), try T. H. White's *The Bestiary* (New York: Putnam, 1960), a translation of a twelfth-century bestiary, with the talented author's informative notes.

The world's undisputed expert on fairies is British folklorist Katharine M. Briggs. Her *An Encyclopedia of Fairies* (New York: Pantheon, 1977) not only provides a wealth of information on the little people, but also on giants, dragons, and a whole lot more.

While there are a lot of books on vampires and werewolves, most of them are not very good. On the general subject of shape shifting the best book is still Frank Hamel's *Human Animals* (New Hyde Park, N.Y.: University Books, 1969), a book that first appeared in 1915. Most of the basic werewolf stories are contained in *The Book of Werewolves*, written in 1865 by Sabine Baring Gould (New York: Causeway Books, 1975). Much basic vampire lore is found in *The Book of Vampires* by Dudley Wright (New York: Causeway Books, 1973), which was originally published in 1914.

Finally, the reader might want to look at the works of Montague Summers on both of these subjects. They are *The Vampire, His Kith and Kin* (New Hyde Park, N.Y.: University Books, 1960), *The Vampire in Europe* (New Hyde Park, N.Y.: University Books, 1961), and *The Werewolf* (New Hyde Park, N.Y.: University Books, 1966). All of these books first appeared in the 1920s and 1930s. Though Summers was a twentieth-century writer, his style is deliberately archaic and his outlook absolutely medieval.

Those seriously interested in the subject of modern monsters, Nessie not Dracula, would be well advised to get in touch with the International Society of Cryptozoology, P.O. Box 43070, Tucson, Arizona 85733.